**W9-BBR-949**

# MILTON'S *PARADISE LOST*

# Milton's *Paradise Lost*

## Moral Education

Margaret Olofson Thickstun

palgrave
macmillan

First published in 2007 by
PALGRAVE MACMILLAN™
175 Fifth Avenue, New York, N.Y. 10010 and
Houndmills, Basingstoke, Hampshire, England RG21 6XS
Companies and representatives throughout the world.

PALGRAVE MACMILLAN is the global academic imprint of the Palgrave Macmillan division of St. Martin's Press, LLC and of Palgrave Macmillan Ltd. Macmillan® is a registered trademark in the United States, United Kingdom and other countries. Palgrave is a registered trademark in the European Union and other countries.

ISBN-13: 978–1–4039–7757–1
ISBN-10: 1–4039–7757–7

Library of Congress Cataloging-in-Publication Data

Thickstun, Margaret Olofson, 1956–
    Milton's *Paradise lost* : moral education / Margaret Olofson Thickstun.
        p. cm.
    Includes bibliographical references.
    ISBN 1–4039–7757–7 (alk. paper)
        1. Milton, John, 1608–1674. Paradise lost—Study and teaching.
    2. Milton, John, 1608–1674—Ethics. 3. Education in literature. 4. Ethics in literature. 5. Moral education—United States. 6. Education—Philosophy.
    7. Education—Psychological aspects. I. Title

PR3562.T47 2007
821'.4—dc22                                                        2006050991

A catalogue record for this book is available from the British Library.

Design by Newgen Imaging Systems (P) Ltd., Chennai, India.

First edition: May 2007

10  9  8  7  6  5  4  3  2  1

Transferred to digital printing in 2008.

*For John and Russ —*
*"Love calls us to the things of this world."*

# CONTENTS

# PREFACE

I began this project in the winter of 1997, about ten years ago and about ten years into my life as both teacher and parent. I had been teaching *Paradise Lost* in the context of introductory "great authors" courses and in courses on Milton's works since 1985; I had been reading popular books on child-rearing, especially those of Haim Ginott, and more academic studies of intellectual development by Piaget and contemporary behavioral psychologists. I had been serving on college disciplinary committees—Honor Court, Judicial Board, Appeals Board; I had been following carefully the work of Lawrence Kohlberg and his colleagues at Harvard in their effort to define stages of moral growth, as well as the work of Carol Gilligan, also of Harvard, and her colleagues in exposing the gendered assumptions underlying Kohlberg's theories. The language that students used to excuse themselves from responsibility for their actions echoed the language that Kohlberg and Gilligan quote in their studies. It all began to resonate with the language that Milton gives to Satan, to Adam, and to Eve.

The discussions of *Paradise Lost* in this book are influenced as much by contemporary research in developmental psychology and moral development as they are by current Milton scholarship. I have found from experience that readers may resist this approach, and I ask their patience. Contemporary psychologists operate under the assumption, documented by Piaget and others, that the human mind develops structurally in predictable ways as it becomes physiologically capable of processing more and more complex concepts. Here is an example: when my son was about five years old, I tried the conservation of liquids experiment. We started with two one-cup measuring cups filled each to the one-cup line with water. I asked which had more, to which he replied that they each had the same amount of water. I poured from one measuring cup into a tall thin glass. "Now which has more?" I asked. "The tall glass," he replied. I poured that glass back into the measuring cup to show him that it was still the same amount, but I could have poured water all afternoon. He was not developmentally ready to see it. A few months later he responded to a repeat of the experiment with scorn: couldn't I see that it was the same water no matter what vessel I put it in?

Similarly, I know that I was exposed to algebra before my brain was structurally ready to understand its symbolic import: I worked very hard all year "solving for x" and performed respectably on the New York State Regents exam, but it was not until ten years later, trying to help my little sister with her homework, that I realized that "x" stood for "the thing that we don't know." No wonder it was different every time.

The psychologists, philosophers, and theologians whose work I use in this book extend this understanding of how the human mind develops from processing intellectual concepts to processing moral and ethical ones. What I value about these researchers and their studies is their attention to narratives, to the stories that young people tell about themselves and to the language with which they do so. The work of William G. Perry in *Forms of Intellectual and Ethical Development in the College Years* (1968) describes accurately the intellectual struggles of my own students. The work of James Fowler applies this perspective on human development to the structures of faith development. Each of these scholars is a person highly attentive to human nature as it is expressed in the real world.

I hope that the discussions in this book will help to illuminate Milton's own careful observation of human nature. Because John Milton read so widely and studied so intensively, we tend to forget that he lived among human beings: he had loving and supportive parents; he attended grammar school and college, where he developed and sustained friendships with Charles Diodati and other classmates. He corresponded with scholars whom he had met on his Grand Tour; he undertook the education of his nephews and select other boys. He experienced difficulties in his first marriage, but he and Mary Powell reconciled, and the couple had three children before her death. His second and third marriages appear to have been satisfactory. Although he was a scholar and a deep thinker, he was also a fiction writer, trying to represent reality in a way that would convince his readers of the accuracy of his delineation of character and scene.

This book offers a sustained reading of *Paradise Lost* as a poem that dramatizes the moral and intellectual education of young people: Adam and Eve, Satan and the rebel angels, the good angels and the Son.

I have found that this approach makes the poem both accessible and engaging to undergraduate readers. I hope that it will be useful to teachers, both those starting out and those looking to refresh their teaching. For individuals interested in Milton scholarship more than in undergraduate teaching, I believe that the discussion will offer insight as well.

# ACKNOWLEDGMENTS

A person privileged to work at a small liberal arts college understands the value of community not only in fostering personal happiness and growth, but also in providing serendipitous occasions for learning. My colleagues, past and present, both in the Hamilton College English department and beyond, inspire me daily with their enthusiasm for working with young people and their dedication to promoting their education. I am particularly grateful to Nat Strout, our Renaissance dramatist, for his willingness to talk passionately and creatively about classroom teaching, about designing assignments, and about making literature come alive for students—and for his flexibility and tolerance as I tinker endlessly with our course offerings in the Renaissance.

I owe specific and identifiable intellectual debts to Dan Chambliss, for his engaging conversation, for sharing with me his own work, and for introducing me to the work of Nell Noddings; to Jen Borton, Jan Coates, and Bev Edmondson, for patiently pointing me in the right direction as I sought appropriate developmental research and psychological studies; to Peter Rabinowitz, for always writing the right book when I needed it; and to David Paris, for his interest in education both theoretical and practical, including mine.

Dayton Haskin graciously read through this project at a very early stage and offered advice and encouragement. Ivan Marki and John O'Neill have each read drafts of individual chapters and helped me to sharpen both my argument and my prose. My former student Brian Sweeney read the entire manuscript, making helpful suggestions about clarity and elegance and assuring me that a non-expert could follow my argument. The extensive comments from my reader at Palgrave Macmillan helped me to strengthen my argument immeasurably. I should also thank the unidentified colleague who left a copy of Bert Dreyfus's essay on the office printer one winter, and Bert himself, who responded graciously to my e-mail out of the blue.

This project has benefited from other moments of serendipity. I only briefly knew Scott Elledge, whose edition of *Paradise Lost* is a model for providing footnotes and supplementary materials precisely suited for a book's intended audience. Unbeknownst to him, Elledge introduced me to William Perry's work through my friends who taught under him in Cornell's "Practical Prose Composition." Neither Elledge nor Perry had any idea of his influence on me. I deeply regret that both men died before I had the opportunity to thank them.

My indebtedness to the larger community of Milton scholars, both for ideas specific to this project and for an understanding of *Paradise Lost* more generally, will be evident in the course of this discussion. Diane McColley, Rich DuRocher, Wendy Furman-Adams, Anna Nardo, and Louis Schwartz have not only shared their expertise but have been generous to a fault in their investment of time, encouragement, and friendship. Kristin Pruitt and Charley Durham have created the environment to nourish those friendships through their biannual conferences at Murfreesboro. My debt to Mary Ann Radzinowicz is incalculable: I do not know what I would be doing if she had not arrived at Cornell as I began my graduate study.

A portion of the opening pages to this book, as well as the chapter on Raphael, first appeared as an article in *Milton Quarterly* 35 (2001). I thank Edward Jones, *Milton Quarterly*, and Blackwell for permission to reprint it here. Pieces of my discussion of Eve and the Separation scene appear as part of "Milton among Puritan Women: Affiliative Spirituality and the Conclusion of *Paradise Lost*," reprint permission granted by the University of Notre Dame, *Religion and Literature*, Issue 36.2 (Summer 2004).

Writing a book about growth through relationships, about the importance of community, about the developmental value of gratitude and love places a heavy burden on the writer of acknowledgments. I would not be who I am today and would not have been able to write this book without the support and encouragement throughout my life of my family—my parents, my sisters, my grandparents, aunts, and mother-in-law, our long-time family friend Lynne Warrin. My husband Bill is unfailingly patient and supportive—truly a meet help. But it is, after all, to my students and my children that I owe the greatest debt.

# Introduction

## Teaching *Paradise Lost* in the Twenty-First Century

### I

*Let all things be done unto edifying.*

—*1 Corinthians 14:26*

This book places moral education in *Paradise Lost* in the context of Milton's educational method, Puritan educational practice more generally, and my own experience as an educator and a parent. I have spent the past twenty years teaching Milton's poem at small liberal arts colleges: first at Mount Holyoke, then at Fordham University's Rose Hill campus, and now for eighteen years at Hamilton. The experience of teaching in these communities, and raising two sons in the process, has provoked the discovery that I work with an "age-group"—nineteen-year-olds, to be exact. That discovery has forced me to consider the way I should teach the poem to them. It has also influenced what in the poem attracts my attention. When Adam stands before the Son at the opening of Book 10, he attempts to excuse himself by the very logic that my students use: "it was her fault"; "I couldn't help myself"; "you should have stopped me." When I teach *Paradise Lost* to college sophomores I focus on the way the poem addresses directly the issues of self-determination and personal responsibility that they face in their lives: peer pressure, sexual desire, the pursuit of happiness, the choice of life work.

*Paradise Lost* is a poem peopled with educators and their students: Raphael and Michael teach Adam; Adam teaches Eve; Uriel, Abdiel, and Michael each in his own way attempts to educate the fallen angels. This is a poem about the education of its main characters and at the same time dedicated to the education of its readers. This book will explore both the pedagogical activity within the poem and the pedagogical activity that the poem facilitates, if the educator chooses to participate in its pedagogical project. Milton is an educator; I am an educator; we share the same philosophy of education: that the end of education is moral adulthood and the means to that end is the exercise of moral choice.

Most practitioners of higher education today would not articulate the mission of their institutions as "to repair the ruin of our first parents"; we no longer offer students a seminar in moral philosophy with the college president as their capstone experience. In fact, William G. Perry, a developmental psychologist and house master at Harvard whose work in some ways prompted this discussion, describes the university's role in terms that might suggest we conspire in the continuation of moral ruin:

> It was, after all, the serpent who pointed out that the Absolute (the truth about good and evil) was distinct from the Deity and might therefore be known independently—without His mediation. The Fall consisted of man's taking upon himself, at the serpent's suggestion, the knowledge of values and therefore the potential of judgment.
>
> In our records [of interviews with students], the serpent appears in the form of the university. (*Forms* 67)

But for Perry, such an understanding of "the Absolute" initiates not moral ruin but moral growth: the student must learn "how to affirm his own responsibilities" (*Forms* 68). He uses the Garden of Eden as a metaphor for illusory and undesirable innocence, interpreting "knowledge" as "the understanding of good and evil, that is, of value" that, because separable from divinity, "made possible man's escape from innocence" (Perry, *Forms* 74). That is certainly not how Milton interprets Genesis. But in Milton's version, as in Perry's vision of the modern university, Authority itself encourages students to learn about values and to exercise judgment.

Despite his apparent religious distance from Milton, Perry has developed a schema of stages in intellectual and ethical development that I have found useful and apt in my consideration of *Paradise Lost* and in my interactions with college students. This schema postulates that young adults move from Dualism—in which answers are either "right" or "wrong"—to Multiplicity—"everyone has a right to an opinion"—to a committed relativism—an understanding that facts are "true" only in a frame of reference (Perry, "Examsmanship" 550). Perry understands education as a moral activity: "the students' endeavor to orient themselves in the world through an understanding of the acts of knowing and valuing is therefore more than intellectual and philosophical. It is a moral endeavor in the most personal sense" (*Forms* 60). In order to mature, both intellectually and ethically, students must move beyond "belief," in which "morality and personal responsibility consist of simple obedience" (Perry, *Forms* 66), to "commitment," which he defines as "an affirmation made in a world perceived as relativistic, that is, after detachment, doubt, and awareness of alternatives have made the experience of personal choice a possibility" (Perry, *Forms* 151). Epistemologically, he and Milton seem quite close: *Areopagitica* articulates commitment in the face of doubt, encouraging its readers to persevere in gathering up the broken body of truth and "closing up truth to truth as we find it" (*CPW* 2.551). Perry does not equate this commitment with a theological decision, but he does recognize religious conviction as an intellectually tenable position. Without this intellectual development, he argues, there can be no faith, no personal investment, no "courage of responsibility" (Perry, *Forms* 150). The courage to choose, to exercise faith, in Perry's schema and in Milton's, marks maturity.

James Fowler, a theologian who has extended to faith development the structural developmental theory of Jean Piaget and Lawrence Kohlberg, provides a useful theoretical bridge between Milton's concerns and Perry's schema. Fowler has posited stages of faith development that describe structural rather than content-based changes in the way that a person sees the world. Fowler is careful to distinguish "faith" from "beliefs" and from "religion," following Paul Tillich and Reinhold Niebuhr in defining faith as a habit of being, "a way of seeing the world" (98). In Fowler's view, most students arrive in college at a faith stage analogous to Perry's "simple obedience" to received standards. He argues that during their college years students become more reflective about their beliefs—Perry's "relativism"— because college provides both independence from the student's faith community and exposure to other perspectives. The disequilibrium created by this encounter with conflicting truth claims provokes growth as the student struggles "to restore balance" (Fowler 100). Fowler argues that the relativism Perry identifies is "a kind of transitional moral relativism, which necessarily emerges as persons dis-embed themselves from conventional moral thinking and begin to be critical of it" (81). In Fowler's understanding of faith stages, it is only after college that most students face the next necessary developmental challenges: "the experience of sustained responsibility for the welfare of others and the experience of making and living with irreversible moral choices which are the marks of adulthood personal moral experience" (82).

Although most colleges' articulations of mission and curricular goals include ethical awareness in their lists, the implementation of this goal is vexed. We cannot provide in our classrooms any genuine sustained responsibility for the welfare of others; Honor Codes, Judicial Boards, and Student Government aside, students know full well that someone else makes and enforces the rules, just as much as someone else prepares the meals, shovels the paths, and mops out the communal bathrooms. In fact, one college president, John Strassburger, remarked to me that American higher education seems to be a national experiment in extending adolescence. Another college president invokes "Aristotle's rather sour injunction that it is no use giving lectures on moral philosophy to the young, since they have not had the requisite experience to understand what you are talking about" (O'Brien, *Half-Truths* 184). He asserts, "if there is to be any form of moral 'instruction' in the college years, it will have to be a sort of 'substitute' for the real thing, a synthetic education in morality, as opposed to the actuality of moral training and the ethical reflections raised by life experience" (171). Added to this institutional sense of helplessness, "many students see ethical concerns as separate from educational ones" (Parr 192). Given that intractable reality, how do we, as educators, facilitate our students' continued moral growth?

We can start with the humanist belief that literary study enhances empathy and cultivates the moral imagination, a belief expressed in numerous contemporary discussions of moral education and college catalogue statements about the liberal arts. In *Cultivating Humanity* the philosopher Martha Nussbaum identifies "the narrative imagination" among the three "capacities" that liberal education fosters, asserting that "the narrative imagination is an essential preparation for moral interaction" (90). As college president Bobby Fong writes, literature "allow[s] my students to rehearse their lives in their imaginations, to know themselves in versions of what they might have been in different times and circumstances and what they desire to be" (305). Another president, Susan Resneck Parr, agrees: literary study introduces students to "ethical dilemmas that their own lives have not yet occasioned" (195). Wayne Booth explains, "it is in stories, in narratives large and small rather than in coded commandments, that students absorb lessons in how to confront ethical complexity" (48). Notoriously, William Bennett published his *Children's Book of Virtues* with the conviction that reading about virtuous behavior will inspire virtuous behavior.

What justifies this belief that stories can effect ethical development? In "What Is Morality? A Phenomenological Account of the Development of Ethical Expertise," Hubert and Stuart Dreyfus argue that expertise in any field involves "an immediate intuitive response" (243) rather than a detached series of calculations. To illustrate that claim, they describe a situation with which most readers will be familiar:

> [T]he expert driver, generally without any attention, not only knows by feel and familiarity when an action such as slowing down is required; she knows how to perform the action without calculating and comparing alternatives. She shifts gears when appropriate with no awareness of her acts. On the off ramp her foot simply lifts off the accelerator. What must be done, simply is done. (Dreyfus 243)

The Dreyfuses argue that this unconscious proficiency develops out of repeated emotionally charged experiences of acquiring and practicing the skill in question, of making a deliberate choice—to release the accelerator, to step on the brake—reinforced by the rush of anxiety before, one hopes in driving, the elation of success.

Applying this understanding of expertise to ethical development, the Dreyfuses assert that "the ability to remember with involvement the original situation while emotionally experiencing one's success or failure is required if one is to learn to be an ethical expert" (10). As Thomas Lickona, a leader in the movement to return character education to public schools, argues, "moral education for reasoning, without education that develops the moral emotions and teaches the skills of effective action, will produce people who are better at talking about morality than they are at practicing it in their own lives" ("Preparing" 57). Literature, appealing to emotion as much as to reason, offers the valuable experience of learning "from the outside what a situation is like on the inside," a way of knowing that Lickona calls "the moral imagination" ("Moral Psychology" 124). It mimics the "the gripping, holistic experiences" that the Dreyfuses argue enable an individual to progress from competence to proficiency (242), in this case, the proficiency of moral response. Literary study also provides the benefit of repeated vicarious but emotionally invested experiences: as the Dreyfuses assert, "principles can never capture the know-how an expert acquires by dealing with, and seeing the outcome of, a large number of concrete situations" (17).

Unlike theoretical discussions of moral questions, literary study offers students emotional engagement in particular stories. It also offers stories about individuals who, like themselves, encounter complicated but ordinary and realistic moral choices with multiple possible outcomes. Criticizing one popular method of moral instruction—the analysis of extreme situations such as who gets seats in a lifeboat—O'Brien argues, "if students come to take lifeboat cases as typifying moral decision problems, they may (1) be blinded to the morality of the everyday moment or (2) decide that moral deliberation always ends in a hopeless, tragic dilemma where no clear right or wrong can be discerned" (*Half-Truths* 196). Although there may be no *easy* choice in the more sophisticated literary texts students encounter in a college classroom or in general adult reading, and there certainly may be the kinds of tragic situations that O'Brien finds in "lifeboat cases," there will be opportunities to consider multiple possible choices leading to varying outcomes—choices that characters make and choices that authors do or do not allow those characters to consider, outcomes that authors write into their texts as well as denied outcomes that authors nevertheless allow their readers to anticipate.

But literary study in the college classroom does not always fulfill the promise that it will challenge students ethically, or, if it does, the effect may be unanticipated, not consciously sought. In a recent discussion of the effects of the New Criticism on the literature classroom, Robert Scholes questions the prevailing wisdom that New Critical practice, by focusing on texts as isolated rather than culturally embedded objects, empower undergraduate readers. Instead, he writes, New Critics, with "their preference for subtlety and complexity," "purged the curriculum of the very poems that had once functioned to give students textual pleasure" (13, 16). In addition, they introduced a critical vocabulary that "has operated to cut poems off from their subject matter and their possible connection to the lives of their readers" (26). "By following Brooks and Warren down the New Critical path of tone and tension, we English teachers succeeded in getting life itself, with all its embarrassing features, out of our classrooms" (20–21). Although theoretical and contextual approaches to literary study have expanded the range of issues discussed in literature classrooms, I would argue that we struggle with this practical heritage: scholarly training, whether theoretical or contextual, offers the temptation to set aside the complex task of educating young people ethically in favor of an easier task, communicating one's scholarly and disciplinary expertise.

With the renewed interest in contextual discussion of literary texts, teachers are more likely to invest their energy in helping students to become what Peter Rabinowitz defines as the "authorial audience." As he explains in *Before Reading*, the "authorial audience" is not the actual audience who received and read a particular text, but the audience an author imagines—the readers she anticipates reading and understanding the text—as she writes her book, the answer to the question that we ask of students in writing classes: "who is your audience for this piece?" Becoming part of the "authorial audience" requires "the joining of a particular social/interpretive community; that is, the acceptance of the author's invitation to read in a particular socially constituted way that is shared by the author and his or her expected readers" (*Before Reading* 22). We identify the generic expectations of a piece of writing, its cultural and historical context, and undertake to educate ourselves, and our students, to join that audience.

But to educate students to become a text's authorial audience does not require that we overwhelm them with information. Not only is such a strategy discouraging, it encourages a passivity that is inimical to genuine learning. As Nussbaum argues, assigned texts, especially complex canonical ones, "are all too likely to become objects of veneration and deference, sitting in the mind without producing strength in the mind itself" (35). For literary study to stimulate the narrative imagination, books "must be permitted, and indeed invited, to disturb us" (98). The commonly expressed struggle between teaching the students and "doing justice" to an author or text poses a false conflict: we cannot "do justice" to an author or a text unless we first reach the students. They need to feel, in Milton's words, that "Books are not absolutely dead things, but doe contain a potencie of life in them" (*CPW* 2.492) and that their responsibility as readers is, in Paul's words, to "prove all things; hold fast that which is good" (Thes. 5:21). They must learn to "exercise [their] owne leading capacity" (*CPW* 2.513). How else will they develop the judgment to become their own "choosers"?

To take a work of literature seriously, to endeavor to join its authorial audience, does not require surrendering to its point of view. Rabinowitz suggests instead that "joining the authorial audience . . . is a provisional testing, not a permanent adopting, of a perspective" (Rabinowitz and Smith, *Authorizing* 14). He considers authorial reading as a potentially powerful strategy for resisting authorial authority, for only through authorial reading, through a serious attempt to understand the text as the writer expected it to be understood, can readers "come to a meaningful disagreement with a text" (26). To undertake authorial reading requires that a reader approach the text with respect, but, as Rabinowitz points out, "respect . . . is compatible with the most contentious talking back, and even with firm resistance to the text" (2). In the literature classroom, such talking back will occur only if the instructor relinquishes his or her own literary and theoretical interests in favor of encouraging the students' engaged first reading of the text.

In fact, we need to resist even the understandable desire to make the way plain before them. As Michael Smith points out, in the literature classroom "teachers have regarded their goal as teaching particular readings instead of teaching ways of reading" (Rabinowitz and Smith, *Authorizing* 82). Such a strategy not only "does the work" of organizing students' experience of the text for them, leading to passivity and detachment, it both undermines their confidence as readers and dismisses the emotions they experience as they read. As Rabinowitz explains, a first reading is necessarily disorienting: "that sense of dislocation—with its consequent surprises—is among the *fundamental* experiences of the first time through a text, especially a complex one" (*Authorizing* 100). The organized "reading" of a text acquired by "the act of holding a work up to itself—the act of looking at the formal ingenuity of its coherence rather than being carried along by the perplexing flow of the plot—stresses design at the expense of dramatic force" (98). In James Phelan's terms, this way of reading emphasizes the "total pattern" of the text rather than the "progression" of the reading experience (quoted in Rabinowitz and Smith, *Authorizing* 97). Although it is possible to read a text for coherence on a first reading, to do so requires exercising a critical sensibility that weakens emotional engagement; it "tends to stress our relationship with authors at the expense of whatever relationships we might develop with the characters" (Rabinowitz and Smith, *Authorizing* 99). Only when the intensity of students' first response to a text is acknowledged and encouraged can it produce that disequilibrium that Perry and Fowler consider essential to moral growth.

II

*"Language is but the Instrument convaying to us things usefull to be known."*

—*Of Education*

In my experience, reading *Paradise Lost* with attention to moral choice will provoke the intense engagement that requires college-age students to "talk back." No matter what their "chronological" age, the characters Milton represents in *Paradise Lost*—Adam, Eve, Satan, Sin, the angels both fallen and unfallen—enter the action in late adolescence. They are newly independent, anxious to test themselves, to discover who they are and what might be their place in the world. In Fowler's terms, they have yet to face either "the experience of sustained responsibility for the welfare of others [or] the experience of making and living with irreversible moral choices" (82): the poem charts the progress of its characters through these twin challenges into moral adulthood. The characters who succeed in navigating this transition are the ones who take responsibility for their actions, repent, and accept the consequences, even in the face of passion, emotional attachment, peer pressure, or anticipated humiliation. In light of what one critic calls "Milton's persistent emphasis on personal accountability" (Haskin 32), his epic seems peculiarly suited to contemporary educational needs.

Teaching undergraduate readers to join Milton's authorial audience is a particularly fraught enterprise given the poem's linguistic, literary, and cultural complexity. I am not the first to notice this fact or to consider the particular needs of particular students, as the table of contents to the MLA's *Approaches to Teaching Paradise Lost* attests. As teachers of Milton we know intuitively what Rabinowitz argues about the difference between the continually "foiled expectations" (Rabinowitz and Smith, *Authorizing* 100) intrinsic to "first reading" and the smoother paths of subsequent encounters. Milton scholars have worried the problem of teaching first-time readers for years, and I am indebted to their efforts. All agree, with Ellen Mankoff, that "we cannot expect to find 'fit audience'—or even a few fit readers—in our classrooms; instead we must fit our readers for Milton's text" (76), and, with Eric LeMay, that the teacher's first task is to "assess our students' initial fitness as an audience for the poem and then assist them in becoming more fit, by illuminating those matters that their prior education has left dark" (92). As representative examples of the practical pedagogical suggestions Milton teachers have offered simply for acclimatizing students to Milton's sentences, Mankoff begins with analysis of the language in his sonnets; Bonnie Melchior offers in-class exercises with "simple sentences that had been transformed in typically Miltonic ways" (77). Many teachers recommend reading aloud and the dramatic performance of brief scenes. LeMay outlines specific "rules" for reading

Milton appropriately: in a quiet location, with no distractions, during a dedicated block of time. He even hands out ear plugs (LeMay 96).

But linguistic complexity is not the only, or even the primary, barrier between our students and an appreciation of Milton's poem. As Melchior asserts, "problems of vocabulary-syntax and allusions demand our attention, but so does the more hidden problem of *nonparticipation* in the text, which stems partly but not exclusively from these initial difficulties" (76; italics mine). *Paradise Lost* is a "Great Book." Students know that their teachers think it is "good" for them: expecting it to be difficult, dry, and outdated, they are willing, in Melchior's words, "to be 'notetaking bystanders' to the reading process" (76). Its canonical forbiddingness is augmented by its being also a hyperactively learned book; it comes swaddled in introductory material, commentary, and footnotes that suggest to students not only its authoritative status but also their own ignorance and incompetence in attempting to read it. Melchior reports that her students "were so insecure that they interrupted every line with a glance at the footnotes, thus losing their train of thought" (78). I frequently have had students announce to me in despair during the first week of the Milton course that they "cannot" read his work. One of my tougher-minded students labeled Milton's style "the poetry of showing-off." As the footnotes for most teaching editions of the poem indicate, it is easy to fall into the trap of explaining.

Trying to bring students "up to speed" with Milton's learnedness turns the text into a Great Book to be feared and revered, rather than a living text with which to engage and wrestle. They will never become fit readers if they decide that the poem is too hard, too old, too alien an object for their engagement, if they believe that there is too much that they need to know before they can do anything more than "admire" it, if they persist in being "non-participants" in the text. We need to abandon our definition of fit readers as those who understand "the importance of Milton and his epic, as they summarize the great literary traditions filtering down to the Renaissance in England and as they provide the monument with which much later literature must cope" (Crump 1). Fit readers in that sense cannot be grown in a semester, or even in a college career. More importantly, students will never develop into truly "fit" readers if they believe that such knowledge constitutes fitness. We are so concerned to create in our students a "fit audience" for the great master that we prevent them from engaging in the text passionately and as if their lives depended on it, which is what Milton expected.

*Paradise Lost* is an evangelical text. As John Wooten argues, "To pretend that Milton has no intention of communicating truths for which he is asking intellectual, moral, and imaginative assent is to distort one of the most consistent features of his entire literary career" (61). The poem means to justify the ways of God; it is concerned with the education and salvation of its readers, even of twenty-first-century undergraduate ones. We cannot join the "particular social/interpretive community" (Rabinowitz, *Before Reading* 22) Milton anticipated unless we acknowledge that part of his aim. Reading *Paradise Lost* respectfully is as much an ethical and emotional commitment as it is an intellectual or aesthetic one. In fact, I would argue that it is not possible to enter the poem's authorial audience, to read it with respect, without engaging the intellect in an ethical way. We do not have to try to convert students to Milton's understanding of Christianity (even if we could agree on what that was) but we need to insist on that part of his goal. We cannot do justice to the poem or to Milton unless we can pull our students into conversation with the poem, unless we can get them to quarrel with it in class, to talk about it outside of class, and to take responsibility for their understanding of it.

In my experience, it is not hard to get students quarreling with and about *Paradise Lost*. Milton is very clear in this poem about his authorial intentions: he provokes the reader into taking his ideas seriously, into answering back. He expects his readers to know his story and the stakes involved in interpreting it. He signals his interest in the process—not *what* will happen in his story, but *how* such events could come about—by "giving away" the whole story in the invocation to the poem. Even students with no religious background feel the weight of the story's mythic status, in which Adam "stands in for" all men and Eve for all women. Students divide along gender lines in their vigorous defense of their surrogates. They try to excuse either Adam or Eve—and in desperation both—from responsibility for their choices by asserting an inevitability that the poem aggressively resists. Milton insists on each character's agency and responsibility for the choices that he or she makes.

Grappling with the moral issues the characters face promotes the disequilibrium that Perry and Fowler identify as essential to moral and spiritual growth. To discuss this unsettling quality, Stanley Fish borrowed the term "disquiet" from A. J. A. Waldock (*Surprised* 3). Like

Fish, I have observed the disquieting effects of *Paradise Lost*, but I notice them in the broader effect of the poem on students' moral awareness, rather than in the subtleties of their intra-sentence, or even inter-episode reading experience; in young adults, who can identify powerfully with the late adolescent characters Milton represents, the poem awakens not simply "a disparity between reader expectation and reading experience" (*Surprised* 3), but a disparity between reader approval and moral message. Some of them may be "surprised by sin," but they are more likely to resist the whole economy in which "sin" operates. For such readers, *Paradise Lost* is challenging emotionally because it makes a claim that they don't want to hear: to become adults, individuals must take responsibility for their choices and for the consequences of those choices. In Lickona's words, they must accept that "their first moral responsibility is *to use their intelligence to see when a situation requires moral judgment*—and then to think carefully about what the right course of action is" (*Educating* 54). It is also their first responsibility as readers.

To read *Paradise Lost* responsibly, students need to take seriously Milton's claim that he intends "to justify the ways of God to men" and then read the poem assuming that he means to show that the Fall was *not* inevitable. As they watch Satan organize and enact his revenge, they need to acknowledge the tensions within him, his regrets about his past, his impulses toward good. As they watch Adam and Eve stumble in their response to events, students need to look for ways in which they might have acted differently. Such authorial reading does not necessarily lead them to assent to Milton's agenda. As Rabinowitz argues, to read respectfully requires the "provisional testing" of a point of view. They need to test their reading of scenes against God's claim that he created beings "sufficient to have stood, though free to fall" (3.99)[1] and that his "foreknowledge had no influence on their fault" (3.118). Students need to decide for themselves whether Milton dramatizes the action convincingly; their decision-making complements the choices the characters make in the poem.

Each character who falls in *Paradise Lost* tries to argue that his or her choice is fatally constrained, but the choices they face are neither insoluble nor extreme: they are not "lifeboat cases," even though the fate of the human race hangs on them. Working with students' emotional investment in these characters' choices, the teacher can help them to identify the alternative scripts that Milton plants within each character's faulty reasoning. Using the first three chapters of Genesis to define the parameters within which Milton worked, the teacher can lead students to a clearer sense of the liberties he chose to take with the received text, liberties that address key issues in the poem and suggest further alternative outcomes to the story Milton must tell.

Because the characters who fall in *Paradise Lost* are disobeying God's express commands, the authorially sanctioned right choices are clear. On the other hand, each of these characters experiences pressures against obedience that resonate with college-age readers: Satan desires to be independent, to define himself, to determine his own future; the fallen angels want to belong and fear looking like fools; Sin longs to escape her suffering and to pass responsibility for that escape onto an authority figure; Eve desires wisdom; Adam fears being left alone. Whatever choices the characters face, Milton allows them plenty of room to elaborate the reasoning behind their decisions. Listening in on these characters' thought processes, students experience vicariously the movement of mind that leads to sin, the emotional experience of being sinful, the effect of sinful self-centeredness on intimate relationships, the mental anguish of remorse. They experience, to go back to the Dreyfuses' analogy, the horror of the crash without actually wrecking the car.

Most importantly, Adam and Eve recover from their crash. Our students have been trained to imagine their lives as stories; they read them as they have been trained to read stories—for narrative coherence. Every year I face an entering class of students who expect that they should have their lives all planned out, who are panicked if, at eighteen, they haven't completely charted their futures. Although they seem young to us, they are already powerfully invested in particular stories about themselves. These young people need to be reminded that their lives' stories are only beginning and that they themselves will write, revise, and emend those narratives through their individual choices. They need to be shown that people who make mistakes can move beyond them: a single disastrous choice, even one that was made consciously, does not define a person now and for always, as Adam's and Eve's recovery demonstrates. Allowing such a choice to do so, and to determine future choices, as Satan's example warns, leads to increasing stasis and despair.

As teachers of *Paradise Lost* to first-time readers, we certainly must help students to become confident in their ability to read the poem, to find their bearings: doing so may require study guides, illustrations, language games, and map-making exercises. But the activities we choose need to direct our students toward engagement with the central moral questions of the poem. To join Milton in his pedagogical project, we must invite our students to occupy the inner lives of the characters and to experience imaginatively and vicariously the moral development, or the moral degeneration, of individuals like themselves "sufficient to have stood" (3.99). Then we need to push them about their responses, to get them to react to the poem's own pressure to take a stand in relation to it. Their first reading of *Paradise Lost* will be, of necessity, difficult and confusing. Fortunately, the foiled expectations and experiences of dislocation intrinsic to first reading are essential to the engagement in the poem that Milton intends.

## III

*"Such discourse bring on / As may advise him of his happie state."*

—*Paradise Lost* 5.233–34

Recently critics have raised again concerns about the success of *Paradise Lost* as a theodicy that I must address before continuing with this discussion. Those concerns arise from the false assumptions that *Paradise Lost* must conform to Calvinist theology and that Milton ascribes to the theory of the Fortunate Fall. First, *Paradise Lost* is an Arminian document, not a Calvinist one.[2] The confusion develops out of misunderstandings about the term "prevenient grace" (11.3) and about the nature of theological positions in the seventeenth century. During the Council in Heaven, God promises to extend grace to all of humankind preveniently: "Man shall not all be lost, but sav'd who will, / Yet not of will in him, but grace in me / Freely vouchsaft" (3.173–75). As Dennis Danielson points out, "prevenient grace" is a term seventeenth-century Arminians shared with Calvinists, but Arminians understood such grace to be "granted universally and sufficiently, so that one's salvation depends on what one does with it once it has been granted. Grace is not, as it is in orthodox Calvinist theology, irresistible; rather its efficacy depends, strictly speaking, on one's freely deciding not to resist it" (*Milton's Good God* 86). In other words, Arminians believe that God "predestines" that individuals shall be saved if they will it and that they will have the grace to support them in their choice should they so will. By the 1660s in England, even the English "Calvinists" had developed a theological position—covenantal theology—holding that, despite his absolute sovereignty, God condescended to bind himself into a contract with his creatures.[3] In order to help students become part of Milton's authorial audience, we need to be sure that they recognize that the God of *Paradise Lost* voices the Arminian position—"Man shall not all be lost, but *savd who will*" (italics mine)—and covenants himself to provide the grace "freely" to support such a choice. The call to salvation in *Paradise Lost* is an open call.

Given his Arminian position, and his subsequent pedagogical desire "to produce good and righteous people, as well as make theology conform to the view that there is a good and righteous God" (Danielson, *Milton's Good God* 75), Milton insists upon creaturely freedom and responsibility: the grace God offers freely must be offered only, rather than imposed. To make a meaningful choice about their salvation, creatures must be free to refuse it, as Satan persistently does. They must also be vulnerable to temptation: "man's 'happy state' in one sense *must* be left 'imperfect by the maker wise'; man's happiness *must* be frail; and, given the requirements for 'the constituting of human vertue,' Eden were no Eden *unless* 'thus exposed' " (199). Readers who approach *Paradise Lost* as a Calvinist document will be unable to recognize and acknowledge the creaturely agency, and God's concomitant self-restraint in circumscribing his sovereignty, so crucial to Milton's justification of God's ways and to the moral education of his reader.

In addition, students need to be disabused of the persistent idea that Milton believes in and represents "the Fortunate Fall." This will be especially important for students raised in faith traditions, who have a difficult time reading *Paradise Lost* without the interference of their catechetical training. The first obstacle to their understanding is the unfortunate label, the Tree of Knowledge, a name that Milton inherits from Genesis. Many students assume that Adam and Eve before the Fall are ignorant, meaning that they do not know or understand anything worth knowing. But in *Paradise Lost*, the Tree of Knowledge does not contain "knowledge." If it did, all Satan would have to do would be to slip some cut-up pieces into Adam and Eve's fruit salad. He must, instead, persuade them to eat so that they know what they are doing as they do it.

Undergraduates need to distinguish the kind of knowledge Adam and Eve "gain" from disobedience from the learning and wisdom that they acquire through conversation, inquiry, and analysis. As my book will emphasize, a lot of education takes place in *Paradise Lost* long before anyone reaches for that fruit. The prelapsarian Adam and Eve lead busy and interesting lives, gardening, making love, eating the magnificent variety of other fruits in the garden, visiting with an angel, learning from God, from Raphael, and from each other. In fact, Eve's decision to believe the serpent when he tells her that the fruit will make her wise may in some sense represent a regression. She suddenly decides that ingesting something, rather than exercising her intelligence, will make her "wise," that the forbidden fruit does contain "knowledge." As Milton writes this scene, she bows down before the Tree. It is just this idolatry of "facts" that characterizes the most intellectually immature individuals in Perry's schema, the ones who believe that "truth" exists in little ingestible nuggets that someone else has and can hand over to you: the correct spelling of words, important dates, "math facts." The poem does raise constantly the question of why a person wants to know something and what that person will do with the information provided. But this poem does not represent Eden as a sterile and boring place occupied by ignorant children who are relieved to break out of it into the exciting world of knowledge.

Consonant with this claim, the Tree of Knowledge in *Paradise Lost* is not "a provoking object" (*CPW* 2.527), even if it is singular in being forbidden (Campbell 241). Adam mentions it casually in his conversation with Eve in Book 4, but he does so in the context of expressing his gratitude to God for the lavish gift of Creation. He understands the prohibition as a slight request that God makes—"this easy charge" (4.421)—rather than as some deprivation. As I will discuss further in chapter 7, Adam sees the tree as simply a sign, "the only sign of our obedience left / Among so many signs of power and rule" (4.428–29). Raphael mentions the prohibition as he recounts Creation, and Adam reports God pronouncing it when he discusses his birth day, but other than that, no one in the poem (except Satan) expresses much interest in the Tree, and Satan is interested only in how he can use the idea of the prohibited fruit to his advantage: he does not so much as nibble at the fruit, let alone gorge "without restraint" (9.791).

Although Milton does in *Areopagitica* wonder whether "perhaps this is that doom which Adam fell into of knowing good and evill, that is to say of knowing good by evill" (*CPW* 2.514), he presents the prelapsarian Adam and Eve in *Paradise Lost* as "knowing good": they appreciate each other and the world that God has given them and express gratitude to God for it. The loyal angels rejoice in their lives even before they are exposed to evil by witnessing and withstanding Satan's rebellion. It is Satan and the rebel forces who, like fallen humans, know good by knowing that they have lost it. None of them are happier at the end of this poem; this fall is not "fortunate," even though God has figured out a way to undo most of the damage.

But Michael does tell Adam that, having accepted Christ as his savior, he will attain "a paradise within thee, happier farr" (12.587) than the one he has lost. If human beings can achieve the most perfect happiness the poem imagines—intimate union with God in Heaven—only through their sin and Christ's redemptive sacrifice, then the Fall must be fortunate. If God's plan for human history requires the Fall in order to effect human translation to Heaven, then assuredly God is responsible for human sin. As Danielson has laid out the argument against this misreading so clearly, I will summarize it briefly here: for Milton, the Fall is *un*fortunate because humans could have reached heaven without sin, once "improved by tract of time" (5.498). Additionally, although the absence of a Fall would preclude the necessity of Redemption, and hence the necessity of the Crucifixion and Resurrection, it would not preclude the possibility of the Incarnation. In fact, Milton has the Son proclaimed Messiah in Heaven (5.663–64) before the Fall, before even the creation of humans, and without reference to the need for future sacrifice or redemption (Danielson, *Milton's Good God* 222). He is at that moment Incarnate among angels, "uniting all things under him as their Head, the 'epiphany' that the creatures can experience by no other means— the Son being *the* divine similitude . . . all of these benefits are in *Paradise Lost* conferred on a wholly sinless universe" (*Milton's Good God* 219). Milton has constructed his narrative to demonstrate that the God's plan for human elevation—the Son's Incarnation among humans—does not require that humans sin, just as his Incarnation among angels preceded angelic sin. It is this declaration, the Primal Decree, to which Satan refuses assent. The role of Incarnation is to unite all creatures, and only incidentally to redeem them from the catastrophe of disobedience.

To make such an argument requires understanding the "relationship" between heavenly and earthly experience in *Paradise Lost*. It is true that Milton asks for inspiration "to tell / Of things invisible to mortal sight" (3.54–55) and that Raphael wonders how to explain "to human sense th'invisible exploits / Of warring spirits" (5.565–66), but Raphael, in determining to "[liken] spiritual to corporal forms" also asks "though what if Earth / Be but the shaddow of Heaven [?]" (5.574–75). As John Reichert remarks, "the very fact that he twice in this part of the narrative takes the trouble to make distinctions between heaven and earth, distinctions of a very minor sort, points in another direction. So numerous are the rough equivalences between heaven and earth that it seems more likely that Milton here, as elsewhere, is blurring the borders" (125). Yes, angels can fly, whereas humans cannot; they can eat more rarified food than humans and experience more intense and complete intimacy in their personal relationships. But in terms of moral agency, certainly, the angels and humans in *Paradise Lost* are not very different creatures. The poem and its God insist that these creatures are morally equal, "sufficient to have stood, though free to fall" (3.99). They also share the task of witnessing to God's goodness in order to educate others.

In order to further his creatures' moral and spiritual growth, the God in *Paradise Lost* has organized Creation in a system of relationships arranged in layers of what the feminist psychologist Jean Baker Miller defines as "temporary inequality": "the lesser party is *socially* defined as unequal" (4). As Raphael explains to Adam and Eve, God has expressed a universe of "one first matter all" (5.472) "from which all things proceed, and up to him return, / If not depraved from good" (5.469–71). Although beings differ in "their several active spheres" (5.477) and "degree" (5.490), those spheres and degrees are not permanent. All things should develop toward God. Tellingly, Milton has Raphael describe this emanation as a tree, rather than as a chain. As Danielson argues, Milton presents a universe created not to express divine plenitude but to provide scope for creaturely development, "how the world, given the requisites of meaningful human existence, *ought* to be created" (*Milton's Good God* 168). Like a tree, the universe grows toward perfection; like a tree, the individual develops toward its full flowering. As Mary Ann Radzinowicz argues, Milton champions, in his political tracts and in his epic, "a class structure with unfixed status for every individual and plenty of room to rise 'improved by tract of time' " ("Politics" 136). Within relationships of temporary inequality, such as those between parents and children, teachers and students, "the superior person is supposed to engage with the lesser in such a way as to bring the lesser member up to full parity; that is, the child is to be helped to become the adult" ( J. Miller 4). In *Paradise Lost*, each being is charged with the responsibility for educating and elevating any "lesser" being toward that final moment when "God shall be all in all" (3.341). By conferring on them this responsibility, God extends his parenting through his creatures and provides each of them the opportunity to mature through helping others develop.

The responsibility for obedience that angels and humans share is complicated by God's omnipotent omniscient omnipresence, but not in the way that the Calvinist camp imagines. In the sonnet "When I Consider," Patience asserts that "God doth not need / Either man's works or his own gifts"; certainly the tasks of the good angels in *Paradise Lost* bear out that philosophy: Uriel, the sharp-sighted, who cannot see what God foresees, Gabriel and his troops guarding the gates while Satan leaps the wall, Abdiel rushing back to warn God of what he foreknew, the good angels holding, but not gaining, ground during the three-day war—none of these angels acts for God in a capacity that God could not fulfill himself; in fact, not one of these angels accomplishes the task God apparently sets before him. But neither do any of these angels suffer a rebuke; many, in fact, receive explicit reassurance and praise. What God rewards, as many critics have pointed out, is intention, not accomplishment. "God doth not need / Either man's works or his own gifts," any more than a parent needs a three-year-old's help setting the table, but the child needs the responsibility in order to grow. As Adam explains, with responsibility comes dignity:

> Man hath his daily work of body or mind
> Appointed, which declares his dignity,
> And the regard of Heav'n on all his ways. (4.618–20)

Or, as God explains, in the discharge of responsibility individuals express their qualities and convictions:

> Not free, what proof could they have giv'n sincere
> Of true allegiance, constant Faith or Love,
> Where only what they needs must do, appear'd
> Not what they would? What praise could they receive? (3.103–06)

Diane McColley writes, "obedience is not a following of a set of instructions but a response to a divine calling made in one's own distinctive way" (56). God gives his creatures tasks that challenge them according to their abilities in order to foster in each personal growth. He requires that his creatures respond to those challenges not simply with obedience, but also with trust and imagination.

It is in this spirit that I offer this book. Although I have been discussing undergraduate readers, their moral development and their responses to the poem, my arguments are addressed to educators, scholars, and teachers interested in extending and complementing the pedagogical project that Milton has begun. Much of what I address can be incorporated into classroom discussion in order to guide student responses to the poem; some material anticipates a more mature audience, one that has some experience, through teaching or parenting, of sustained responsibility for the welfare of others. Chapter 6, in particular, addresses educators wishing to reflect on their own pedagogical practice.

My reading of *Paradise Lost* opens with a chapter that explores the metaphor of God as Father, considering the interactions of Milton's God with his creatures in the light of covenantal theology, contemporary Puritan attitudes toward fatherhood, and Milton's own writings about fathers and about God as Father in his prose tracts and commonplace book. The chapters that follow address the moral development of individual characters in the poem, beginning with the children who offer the greatest challenge to God's parenting: Satan and the rebel angels. In the context of the rebellion, I also consider Abdiel as a model for withstanding peer pressure. I then address what the poem reveals about the moral education of the loyal angels and of the Son.

Chapter 6 on Raphael brings the discussion back down to earth, placing his teaching and ministry in Eden in the context of Puritan educational practice and of Milton's own educational method. I conclude my discussion by tracing the moral development of Adam and then of Eve in the poem, especially in the context of relationships, both that between parent and child and between husband and wife. It is in relationships, I argue, between God and his creatures and among those creatures, that Milton locates the ethical life.

# CHAPTER I

# GOD AS FATHER IN *PARADISE LOST*

I

*And call no man your father upon the earth: for one is your Father, which is in heaven.*

*—Matthew 23:9*

Milton works in the tradition of a Scripture that he believes his poem extends. He takes seriously the way that he represents the God whom he worships and whom he wishes to justify to other humans. Operating on these assumptions, I would like to read that God "authorially" as carefully as possible. To do so requires acknowledging the metaphor that Milton emphasizes: God *the Father*. Because *Paradise Lost* is a poem about education, about young people and their moral development, it is a poem about the parent who fathers them, nurtures them, educates and disciplines them.

Parenthood provides a more useful metaphor than kingship or military precedence for considering God's role in *Paradise Lost* because it highlights issues of interiority and intimacy that the other two roles do not. First, the metaphor God as Father raises the question of creation itself that Milton places at the center of the poem—"what cause / Mov'd the Creator in his holy Rest / Through all Eternity so late to build [?]" (7.90–92)—and pushes that question backward from the creation of Earth and humans to the very beginning: why does God *create* in the first place? Then, it forces our consideration of the motives behind that choice—of God's affective life—but directs that attention away from ontology toward relationships: it makes us ask not "what is the nature of God" or "what are the attributes of God," but "what is the creaturely experience of God in this poem" and "how does Milton's God want to be in relation to his creatures"?

These different questions will yield strikingly different answers. An infant learns of its caregiver's "nature" through interaction: this other is gentle, responsive, physically warm, and relieves the discomfort of wet diapers or a gnawing stomach. Learning that the human body is ninety-eight percent water and created by a genetic code that determines sex, hair color, and the likelihood of developing heart disease does not improve a young person's understanding of who her parents are. We know others through relationship, and that "knowledge" evolves over time. In order to develop his readers' conception of God, Milton represents him in relationships.

A strong thread in Milton criticism still argues that in representing God as a passible being Milton risks, or creates, aesthetic and theological catastrophe. As Michael Lieb outlines in "Reading God: Milton and the Anthropopathetic Tradition," orthodox theologians, from Augustine to Calvin, have argued for the unknowability of the divine and dismissed representations of God expressing human feelings as theological pablum for the ignorant, the equivalent to the milk Paul offers his readers before they can digest the true meat of faith. Georgia Christopher, working in this tradition, argues that, in *Paradise Lost*, God the Father's "words do not imply a familiar psychic life as do those of Satan and Adam. Milton is adamant that the human metaphors by which God presents himself in Scripture cannot be construed as a key to God's experience (CD, pp. 133–134)" (Christopher 112).

But Milton is also adamant in his prose writings that Scripture, not theological abstraction, is the only accurate source of information about God, and Milton works with a Scripture that insists on a God who experiences and expresses an intense emotional life. According to Lieb, Milton's exegetical practice constituted a version of what I have been calling "authorial reading," searching Scripture that he believed to have been "written" by God as he believed God intended his audience to read it: "reading the Scriptures becomes for Milton an exercise in the discovery of God's intentions, of forming a mental image of him corresponding to that which he, in bringing himself within the limits of our understanding, desires us to form" ("Reading God" 224). Milton reads Scripture as God's self-revelation; what Scripture provides is not systematic theology, not a theological discourse on "the nature of God," but a series of stories about God's intervention in human history, about God's interaction with human beings.

Although any representation of the divine must necessarily accommodate the truth of the divine life to human understanding, a theory of accommodation does not require that we jettison metaphors in favor of abstraction. Milton has written a narrative that communicates the "immediate" events of the divine through "process of speech" and time so that humans can understand it, but he also claims that his text has unusual authority. Asserting that his muse "from the first / Wast present" (1.19–20), Milton claims that he offers an authorized account of God's creation of the physical world and his first interactions with human beings. As Lieb writes, "*Paradise Lost* is not the Bible, and Milton's God does not possess the same authorized presence as he does in the Bible. As far as Milton is concerned, however, his poem is the most authoritative reenactment of what happens in the Bible as one can possibly imagine" ("Reading God" 237). Milton writes in *De Doctrina Christiana*, "we ought not to imagine that God would have said anything or caused anything to be written about himself unless he intended that it should be a part of our conception of him" (Milton, *CPW* 6.134, in Lieb, "Reading God" 225). *Paradise Lost* extends God's self-revelation through narratives of interaction and relationship.

What God says in Scripture, and repeats in *Paradise Lost*, is that he is a loving, jealous, occasionally angry, feeling father. Where the Hebrew Scripture develops the range of those emotions, the New Testament focuses on the loving aspects of God, a God who "so loved the world that he gave his only begotten son" (John 3:16), a God who sent that son "to redeem them that were under the law, that we might receive the adoption of sons" (Gal. 4:5), a God who is the Father of a God who is the Son and who is the Father of other children through the agency of that Son. Milton's retelling of the Genesis story amplifies this loving interaction between God and the individuals created in his image. Milton's God is not "his epic's one major aesthetic mistake" (Bloom 93) or a literary fiction drawn to stoop to frail human intellects. His "accommodation" does not veil but rather expresses divine reality.

William Flesch presses the argument against the representability of God to the point where it tips over into my own position: "*Paradise Lost* dramatizes a series of more or less mistaken interpretations of God in order to claim a terrific prerogative for poetry as the only human endeavor pitched high enough to be adequate to the God the poem imagines" (234–35). I agree with Flesch that no individual's "interpretation" of God in the poem represents God "adequately"; but those interpretations are not "mistaken," only limited, a limitation that is the very nature of contingent experience. As Flesch argues,

Milton crafts these partial representations "in order to claim a terrific prerogative for poetry": through attending to others' narratives of their experience with the divine, individuals can deepen and enrich their own understanding.

According to *Paradise Lost*, God wants to parent, to engage with others in relationships of responsibility and love. As Lieb argues, rather than committing the fallacy of *anthropopatheia* by attributing to the divine human emotions, "Milton divinizes the emotional life by viewing it as an essential attribute of God.... For Milton, the emotional life of God is real and indeed holy" ("Reading God" 231). Human beings have affective lives because they are made in the image of an affective God. In *Paradise Lost*, Milton divinizes freedom of agency as well: human beings have free will because they are made in God's image. The central and original action that his poem represents is the divine choice to create. For human beings, of course, the decision to become parents is not entirely free, complicated as it is by biological and social influences. Because Milton's God transcends these influences, his action entirely unconstrained, he makes a true choice. As Regina Schwartz points out, for the God of *Paradise Lost* "Chaos offers an awful temptation: not to create; to let darkness reign. And so, in Milton's scheme, creation, like all acts, becomes a choice—a choice, of course, that is freely made" (37). The free choice to father must be central to our understanding of how Milton imagines God, even as it seems to lie outside our experience.

Even for human beings, parenting, as opposed simply to reproducing, requires a genuine choice. As feminist philosopher Nell Noddings explains, a caring relationship develops out of the decision on the part of the one-caring to respond to the needs of the cared-for: it fulfils the caregiver's sense of how he or she wants to be. It also challenges the one-caring to discover and nurture not only the other but also the self. The psychologist Jean Baker Miller points out that "relationships can lead to more, rather than less, authenticity" (98) for both participants: "as these two people, with very different states of psychological organization and desires, interact, the outcome will be the creation of a new state in each person" (128). Joan Webber puts it this way: "the God [Milton] justifies is a God in process, whose very justification lies in his capacity to encourage change," and to change himself, a God "both in process and perfectly realized" (519, 520). From the interaction with a child, the parent derives satisfaction and joy; the child rewards the parent with "spontaneous delight and happy growth" (Noddings 181). God's decision to father provides him with just these opportunities for intimacy and for joy and delight as he interacts with his children and witnesses their happy growth. Time and again, Milton emphasizes the spontaneity of gratitude and praise in Heaven and in prelapsarian Eden.

In depicting life in Heaven and in prelapsarian Eden, Milton dramatizes extensive emotional and physical intimacy radiating from God toward his children, an intimacy that we tend to associate with mothering and that, in distinguishing God as Son from God as Father, we unwisely dissociate from its original source. As Anthony Low argues, "although Milton embodies divine love in the Son, he is careful not to speak of it without clearly indicating that the source of the Son's love and mercy is the Father" (29–30). Although Milton's God dwells in "unapproached Light" (3.4) unembodied, his children in the poem experience him as physically demonstrative in his nurturing. The narrator describes God embodied as Spirit "brooding on the vast abyss" (1.21), an intimate verb that Raphael repeats in his recounting of the same moment. This intimate God takes the newborn Adam by the hand (8.300) and rears him up when Adam falls "in adoration at his feet" (8.315); he forms Eve with his hands. In Heaven, where God can interact with his children without mediation, the Son floats "in bliss embosomed" (5.597) like a nursing infant, while the good angels bask in "beatitude past utterance" (3.62), each sensation an even more intense experience of love than the angelic "Union of pure with pure" (8.627) that far surpasses human sexual expressions of love.

Disregarding this evidence, as Augustine and Calvin disregard the narrative evidence of Scripture, Flesch uses the argument for God's radical otherness to make an unorthodox argument for the Fortunate Fall: "I suggest that the fall of man turns out to be fortunate (to argue that it's not, as Danielson does, is inevitably to prefer God's poetry in book 3 to Milton's) because it enables a much deeper understanding of God" (251). The facetious parenthesis suggests that he recognizes the outrageousness of his claim. To argue that it is good to have "a much deeper understanding of God" through sin is like arguing that it is good to commit adultery because it leads to a much deeper understanding of your spouse's loyalty when you confess it or that the loss of a child is good because it provokes a much deeper understanding of how you loved the child. It is true that "for Milton (and for Satan) loss of Eden or heaven gives rise to a deeper sense of what God's inaccessibility entails than the angels had" (Flesch 257). But such a change ought not to be confused with a blessing, nor such a discovery with insight. In the postlapsarian world, Adam and Eve, Satan, Milton, and fallen humans have a deeper "understanding" of God's inaccessibility because God is more deeply inaccessible to them—not because of God's "essence," but because of a change in the nature of God's relationship to humans as a consequence of sin.

## II

*"Wherefore thou art no more a servant, but a son; and if a son, then an heir of God through Christ."*

—*Galatians* 4:7

Milton's God seeks fulfillment through expansion, interaction, and nurturance, through intimacy; this intimacy benefits all parties. But to achieve such intimacy, God must enter into relationship with his creatures. In "The Marrow of Puritan Divinity," Perry Miller identifies a qualitative difference between a pure Calvinist belief in God's sovereignty and the more humanly acceptable position of English covenantal theology. In the covenant of grace as articulated by Ames, Perkins, and their intellectual descendents, God condescends to bind himself to perform a set of terms that circumscribe his agency: despite his utter autonomy, God engages to act within restraint. As Danielson explains, human prelapsarian freedom "requires of God a kind of self-limitation. He must not bombard man with knowledge of the truth, but allow him to discover and judge things for himself" (*Milton's Good God* 123), just as parents must allow their children to discover, to judge, to accomplish on their own.

Having chosen to create independent children, God the parent faces the same challenges that human parents do; his parenthood complicates issues of autonomy and control that his kingship or military authority flatten, even when attending carefully to the model of feudal kingship that Stevie Davies develops. A king or commander expects loyalty and obedience from his subordinates, to be expressed in action; a parent desires attachment and development. Where vassals and soldiers enter into a relationship of mutual responsibility as full-grown adults, children cannot choose their parents or to be parented, nor do they enter the relationship with responsibilities. The parent initiates a one-sided relationship of love and care, trusting that love offered will elicit love in return; that love cannot be coerced but only encouraged. Neither can a parent script intellectual and ethical development. The parent must create occasions for growth and offer opportunities for development. The child remains free to respond: not free, "what praise could they receive? / What pleasure [give] from such obedience paid?" (3.106–07), what proof of maturation? A king exercises power equally over the course of his lifetime, but a parent must adapt as the child grows, relinquishing power, increasing freedom.

In the context of his argument, Perry Miller points out that "a bargain between two persons with duties on both sides is an arrangement between equals" ("Marrow" 61). In choosing to enter a covenant with his creatures, the Reformation God enables individuals who are not ontologically his "equal" to become "equal" by virtue of the covenant into which they have entered. In fact, as I argue in the introduction, in *Paradise Lost* God's creatures exist in relation to him and to each other in a fabric of relationships of "temporary inequality" ( J. Miller 4). Parenting, like teaching, is a process leading toward its own obsolescence, toward the child taking his or her place in the community of fully grown persons. In *Paradise Lost*, being God is like being a parent: it requires emotional investment and selflessness, but also, and most importantly, self-restraint.

The God in *Paradise Lost* is affectionate and effective: he nurtures his children, develops their intelligence, their judgment, and their confidence, challenges them in ways appropriate to their individual developmental levels, and leads them toward autonomous adulthood. Milton's portrait of this Godly parent develops out of contemporary Puritan ideas of fathering, once we disabuse ourselves of preconceptions about that institution. The Puritan father has been characterized in popular and academic consciousness as a distant, forbidding parent who never spared the rod to spoil the child. But, as John Morgan argues, "resort to the rod was to be seen not as the best method of discipline, but rather as the failure of other methods. Correction, in this Christian age, was preferably to be by the encouraging lesson of the pulpit, and the proximity of the printed Word, the guide to eternal life" (149). In *Albion's Seed*, David Hackett Fischer reports of Samuel Sewall and Ralph Josselin that "both subscribed to the Puritan epigram, 'better whipped than damned,' but they disliked corporal punishment and used it only in extreme circumstances (commonly when a child threatened danger to itself or others), and much preferred to lead their children by precept, example, reward and exhortation" (101). He reports that these "fathers took an active and even a leading part" in their children's lives and their diaries express love, affection, and tenderness. David Leverenz, in fact, suggests that advice books recommend discipline because parents "were so loving they could not bear to administer any discipline at all" (71). To support his claim, he quotes from John Dod and Robert Cleaver, *A Godlye Form of Household Government* (London, 1621, 1st ed. 1614): "there is more need in these dayes, to teach and admonish them, not to love them too much, than to persuade them to love them" (in Leverenz 71).

Yet, as Leverenz points out, Cleaver himself champions nurturing rather than authoritarian parenting. In *A Brief Explanation of the Whole Book of Proverbs of Salomon* (London, 1615), published only one year after the first edition of *A Godlye Form of Household Government*, Cleaver places Proverbs 13.24—"He that spareth his rod hateth his son: but he that loveth him chasteneth him betime"—in the context of the opening verse: "a wise son heareth his father's instruction." In this manner, he reinterprets "chastening" as exhortation rather than corporal punishment and verbal, rather than physical, intervention (Leverenz 80). Leverenz asserts that, "in an age accustomed to violence, both domestic and social, Puritans were adamant about the necessity for love as the shaping motive for all acts of authority" (70). In Milton's own words, "persuasion certainly is a more winning, and more manlike way to keepe men in obedience then fear" (*CPW* 1.746).

Puritan parents and educators desired their students' engagement and personal commitment. As N. Ray Hiner argues, "the Puritans viewed enculturation, the process by which the central values of a culture are internalized by the child, as more critical than socialization, the process by which a child learns the ways of a society so that he can function within it" (7). But I would qualify this assertion: if the end of socialization is individuals who behave well in public out of self-interest and the end of enculturation is individuals who ascribe to the values of society out of desire for praise and fear of shame, then the culture of dissent or nonconformity must be seeking a next step. The whole point of withdrawing from mixed multitudes, of emphasizing spiritual testimonies as a prerequisite to church membership, of shifting from infant to adult baptism, is to move beyond conformity (the thing they despised) to a commitment that requires genuinely independent judgment. As Milton argues, "Nor can he fear so much the offence and reproach of others, as he dreads and would blush at the reflection of his own severe and modest eye upon himselfe" (*CPW* 1.842).

Within the Puritan community, as Hiner documents, "the father had the primary responsibility for instructing and guiding his children in the way to salvation" (13), although "everyone in such a community was a potential 'teacher,' if only by the force of his example" (10). Hiner's masculine possessive pronoun here is not simply a function of grammatical rather than political correctness. As Leverenz confirms, "the father is clearly in charge of what religious instruction goes on" (74). Puritan mothers assisted Puritan fathers in the spiritual education of their children, but the father was considered the senior teacher, not simply because of his spiritual or educational superiority over his wife, but because of his loving relationship to his children; Puritan fathers were encouraged to nurture affectionate, intimate relationships with their children in order to increase their potential influence.

Milton, in his theoretical writings, emphasizes this paternal intimacy. In *The Reason of Church Government*, he grounds his championing of presbytery order on affectionate fatherly intervention: "if God be the father of his family the Church, wherein could he express that name more then in training it up under his owne allwise and dear Oeconomy" (*CPW* 1.755). Under the Gospel, God encourages his adopted sons "to have fellowship with him" and ministers to them in "a more familiar and effectual method than ever before": he is now "a most indulgent father governing his Church as a family of sons in their discreet age"; the minister, God's "spiritual deputy," serves as a surrogate father, set over his children "in the sweetest and mildest manner of paternal discipline" (*CPW* 1.837).

Milton suggests in his commonplace book that fathers and educators should know their children intimately so that they can nurture them effectively and individually: "the nature of each person should be especially observed and not bent in another direction; for God does not intend all people for one thing, but for each his own work" (*CPW* 1.405). In *Paradise Lost*, God reveals this intimate understanding of his children, challenging and then praising the Son during the dialogue in Heaven, explaining reflection to Eve and then gently leading her from the pool to Adam, questioning and encouraging Adam as they discuss his new life in Eden. He tailors his response to each creature to that person's particular abilities and needs; as Irene Samuel argues, God knows his children well and encourages each individual's "distinctive tones" (470). He also provides responsibilities that encourage imaginative engagement and then rewards that response: the good angels, for example, are all set tasks that appear to be straightforward, but that actually challenge them to summon all in their efforts to fulfill them.

Ultimately, the relationship that Milton's God desires, the intimate interaction of free beings, exposes him to the serious risk that every parent faces, that your child might reject your love. To ensure creatures who stand freely, God argues, he must allow them the freedom to fall; he has chosen, as Danielson explains, to be self-limiting, to relinquish control of the child's life to the child. Every parent faces this challenge, the daily debate about how much independence and responsibility is appropriate for the child at this stage—first playing in the yard unsupervised, then walking to school alone, riding a bike to a friend's house, taking the car. Eventually, every parent must say something equivalent to "we are going away for the weekend; do not have a party." It is very likely that the teenager will have a party, but, at some point, the parent has to go anyway, trusting to the accrued effect of past instruction, to the reinforcement of earlier experiences of independence well-exercised or the lesson of independence abused. And we trust that, should our children stumble, we have laid the foundations for their ability "to repair the ruin" and move forward.

In order to lay that foundation, Milton's God extends his parenting through his establishment of natural law: sinful actions have natural and reasonable, rather than arbitrary and punitive, consequences. In this respect, Milton and his God seem to have anticipated the principles of positive discipline developed by Alfred Adler and Rudolf Dreikurs in the 1930s and 1940s. This method aims precisely to avoid "punishment" because punishment—an arbitrary, authoritarian response to behavior—provokes the retrenchment of conflict. Instead, the parent allows nature to take its course: if the child refuses to wear a raincoat, she will be wet; if the teenager misses the bus, he must walk to school. Or the parent extends the natural consequences in a logical manner: if the teenager fails to return at an established curfew of ten o'clock, the teenager loses that privilege and must now be home by nine. Having created the universe to work naturally, the God of *Paradise Lost* has set in motion a series of consequences that are at once "natural" consequences and divine "interventions."

When necessary, God also intervenes explicitly. He explains to Adam and then to Eve how their world has been organized and what their responsibilities are in it. He sends Raphael, and later Michael, to further their education. He congratulates the good angels on their fortitude during the War in Heaven: "Faithful hath been your warfare, and of God / Accepted, fearless in his righteous cause" (6.803–04). Later he reassures the angelic guard on their return from fallen Eden: "be not dismaid, / Nor troubl'd at these tidings from the

Earth, / Which your sincerest care could not prevent" (10.35–37). Significantly, in these direct addresses, Milton's God describes behavior rather than evaluates individuals: their actions have been "faithful," "fearless," "sincere." Milton's God seems to understand that "the long-range effect of encouragement is self-confidence. The long-range effect of praise is dependence on others" (Nelson 103). He says to Abdiel not "you have been good," but "you have done well in this action": "Servant of God, well done, well hast thou fought / The better fight" (6.29–30), just as later Adam will reinforce Eve's behavior by saying, "Well hast thou motion'd, well thy thoughts imploy'd" (9.229), rather than "you are a good girl." He sets up a world in which individuals can develop responsibility for their own actions and for others and so come to understand themselves as responsible, caring individuals. He provides them the space to experience "satisfaction at a job well done" (Lickona, *Educating* 213).

In Satan, God meets any parent's worst nightmare, yet Satan's capacity to resist grace should not blind readers to God's efforts to extend it: the poem documents continuous loving outreach through which God attempts to provoke repentance. Probing his memory through "my Umpire *Conscience*" (3.195), exposing him to the sharp disparity between his spiritual desolation and the glorious plenitude of creation, provoking the insight that "my self am Hell" (4.75), God urges Satan toward spiritual growth. Every environment he enters, every person he encounters, challenges Satan's perception of reality and threatens to "convict" him of responsibility for his actions and his situation, a conviction he evades with ingenuity but with difficulty. Time and again, as chapter 2 will demonstrate, God confronts Satan with the consequences of his actions, the recognition of which could provoke change.

When Adam and Eve reject him, Milton's God again responds firmly but lovingly. Milton dramatizes this response through the flow of prevenient grace, through the Son's delighted intercession, and the Father's calm response, "without Cloud, serene" (11.45), a serenity that purposely excludes vengeance and anger. The Father grants his forgiveness and his consequences equally dispassionately: Adam and Eve and their seed shall not die immediately, shall find eternal life in heaven, but also must leave the Garden. In his instructions to Michael, God presents this expulsion not as a punishment, but as a natural consequence of their corruption, for "longer in that Paradise to dwell, / The Law I gave to Nature him forbids" (11.48–49). The Garden expels the sinners, as a healthy body fights off infection: "those pure

Immortal elements that know / No gross, no unharmoneous mixture foule / Eject him now" (10.50–52). In fact, by the time Adam and Eve leave the Garden, it too has been despoiled. Michael, therefore, explains their expulsion as a logical, rather than simply a natural, consequence: they must leave physically lest the physical Garden mislead them to idolatry as they seek to memorialize their former happiness. As Michael assures them, they will find God "still following thee, still compassing thee round / With goodness and paternal love" (11.352–53) as they move out into the postlapsarian world.

The God in Paradise Lost fathers abundantly in all senses of the word. He creates because he desires what the speaker of Frost's "The Most of It" describes as "not [his] own love back in copy speech, / But counter love, original response" (lines 7–8), rewarding the Son in Book 3 not for passing a test or fulfilling a duty, but "because in thee, / Love hath abounded more than glory abounds" (3.311–12). The "intense, emotionally connected cooperation and creativity necessary for human life and growth" ( J. Miller 25) may not be necessary for Milton's God, but appear to be exactly what he chooses.

# Chapter 2

# Satan, Interpretive Choices, and the Danger of Fixed Stories

I

*What man of you, having a hundred sheep, if he lose one of them, does not leave the ninety and nine in the wilderness, and go after that which is lost, until he find it?*

—*Luke 15:3*

Having chosen to create free beings, Milton's God exposes himself to the risk of rejection. In Satan, he meets any parent's worst nightmare. As Nell Noddings explains, a person choosing to enter a caring relationship makes a commitment to the cared-for that may not be reciprocated but nevertheless becomes a fundamental part of the caregiver's ethical being (18). God as caregiver ministers to those in his care, understanding that it is in relationships that contingent beings flourish. Noddings argues that "it is our longing for caring—to be in that special relation—that provides the motivation for us to be moral" (5). I would like to explore Satan's own longing to be in "special relation" to God through the psychological portrait Milton draws of Satan's response to perceived rejection—the elevation of another, the Son, rather than himself—and through his subsequent desperate struggle to resist God's continued efforts to reestablish relationship. I would like to reread God's interactions with Satan in the poem as a long and painful story of loving outreach, the tireless overtures of a caring parent, rather than as the efforts of a rigid God to "render him inexcusable." As Anna Nardo asserts in her discussion of the good angels, "human beings are not God's only beloved creations, and the drama of their fall and redemption is not God's only care" ("Education" 27); the good angels' trial and perseverance complements the trial and regeneration of Adam and Eve. The drama of Satan's fall and non-redemption constitutes a third, tragic plot within the poem.

Georgia Christopher, representing a line of critics steeped in Reformation theology, reads this plot as a predestined script for Satan's damnation: "having once rejected the Primal Decree of God (5.600–615), he is utterly reprobate" (64).[1] Further divine overtures simply confirm an inevitable trajectory: "with subsequent hearing, one's heart was hardened more or one grew in grace and understanding" (108–09). Regina Schwartz, from a more theoretical orientation, reads the same plot as compulsive repetition born out of hopelessness:

> It is a desperate assertion of mastery where there can be none that drives Satan to choose that hell of a bound will rather than suffer it. Satan's resolve of an unchanging mind and his appropriation of hell can now be seen as analogous efforts: to convert defeat into a choice. (96)

Both Schwartz's reading and Christopher's suggest, however, that Satan truly has "no choice." Certainly that is how Satan persists in choosing to perceive his plight. As Keith Stavely writes, "it is but a short step from assuming that Satan will remain Satan, the very source and spring of evil, to assuming that Satan *must* remain Satan. And this is a step that Milton, ruthlessly consistent in his Arminianism as in all else, refuses to take" ("Satan" 125). *Paradise Lost* insists that its characters, even Satan, have choices, genuine choices. As Mary Ann Radzinowicz asserts, "every fall is accompanied by the proposal of one coercive fixed meaning and concludes with the falsity of that claim made clear in the illumination of alternative meaning" ("Politics" 138). Just as Chaos offers God the awful temptation not to create, each fall offers the creature the awful temptation to stasis. But in *Paradise Lost*, God continually reaches out to his creatures to provoke them toward growth.

As I have argued in the introduction, the call to salvation in *Paradise Lost* is an open call. During the Council in Heaven, God promises to extend grace to all of humankind preveniently: "Man shall not all be lost, but *sav'd who will*" (3.173; italics mine). This promise follows a conversation in which God first asserts the moral equivalence of humans and angels, who are all created "sufficient to have stood, though free to fall" (3.99), and then distinguishes between the sin of Adam and Eve and the rebellion of Satan and the fallen angels:

> The first sort by thir own suggestion fell,
> Self-tempted, self-deprav'd: Man falls deceiv'd
> By the other first: Man therefore shall *find* grace.
> Th'other none. (3.129–32; italics mine)

I would like to suggest that Milton has chosen the verb "find" consciously and carefully: the assurance that those who seek God shall find him reverberates throughout Scripture (see Deut. 4:29; 1 Chron. 28:9; 2 Chron. 15:2; among others), coupled frequently with the warning that those who forsake him will also be forsaken. Milton's God participates in this tradition, declaring,

> This my long sufferance and my day of grace
> They who neglect and scorn, shall never taste
> But hard be hard'nd, blind be blinded more,
> That they may stumble on, and deeper fall:
> And none but such from mercy I exclude. (3.198–202)

Those who seek God's grace shall find it; those who harden their hearts will have hearts that harden more.

But the biblical record shows a tension over the efficient cause of such "hardening." When the text records the stubbornness of Israel's enemies, it reports that God has hardened their hearts so that he might punish them, as in the confrontation between Moses and the Pharoah in Exodus chapters 4–14 or in Israelite encounters with the King of Hesbon in Deuteronomy chapter 2 or with the Hivites in Joshua chapter 11. But the text also records situations in which individuals "hardened their necks, and hearkened not to thy commandments" (Neh. 9:16). In those instances, the writer asserts that God persevered in extending grace: "for thou art a God ready to pardon, gracious and merciful, slow to anger, and of great kindness, and forsookest them not" (Neh. 9:16). Most significantly, whenever a prophet, psalmist, or apostle addresses the reader of Scripture, he locates responsibility for and control over that hardening squarely in the reader: "Wherefore then do ye harden your hearts, as the Egyptians and Pharaoh hardened their hearts? when he had wrought wonderfully among them, did they not let the people go, and they departed?"

(1 Sam. 6:6); "Harden not your heart, as in the provocation, and as in the day of temptation in the wilderness" (Ps. 95:8; Heb. 3:8); "He, that being often reproved hardeneth his neck, shall suddenly be destroyed, and that without remedy" (Prov. 29:1). In each of these passages, God extends his grace—offering wonders and reprovings—that individuals are exhorted to accept.

Milton uses the word "find" in a spiritual sense frequently during the Council in Heaven. The Son expresses relief at the Father's assertion "that man should find grace" (3.145) and then, in offering to sacrifice himself for humankind, asserts,

> Father, thy word is past, man shall *find* grace;
> And shall grace not *find* means, that *finds* her way,
> The speediest of thy winged messengers,
> To visit all thy creatures, and to all
> Comes unprevented, unimplor'd, unsought. (3. 327–31; italics mine)

Grace visits *all* of God's creatures and to *all* of them comes "unprevented, unimplor'd, unsought." In this sense "grace" in the poem is like "hope," which the narrator asserts "comes to all" (2.67) even as he denies its presence in Hell. Unless we choose to disbelieve what the Son and the narrator say, the poem seems clear and consistent on this point: God extends grace to all; with grace comes hope, equally offered and equally unsought. Any individual may through hope seek grace. And God promises to respond:

> To Prayer, repentance, and obedience due,
> Though but endeavored with sincere intent,
> Mine ear shall not be slow, mine eye not shut. (3.191–93)

Earlier, in the Invocation to this book, the narrator complains,

> but thou
> Revisit'st not these eyes, that rowle in vain
> To *find* thy piercing ray, and *find* no dawn. (3.23–24; italics mine)

But the light his eyes cannot find is the physical light of day; the spiritual light that he truly seeks is there to be found. That light will "shine inward, and the mind through all her powers / Irradiate" (3.52–53) because he endeavors with sincere intent. When God asks the heavenly host, "where shall we *find* such love" (3.313; italics mine), the love manifests itself.

The God of *Paradise Lost* is "a God ready to pardon," a God who offers grace to all his self-knowing creatures. It would not be merciful, it would not be justifiable, for God to condemn Satan and his co-conspirators out of hand and eternally for a single bad choice. If he did that, then Satan would be right in asserting God's tyranny and in arguing that he persists in his rebellion out of necessity. God explains that he created both angels and humans "sufficient"; he promises that he will place within fallen humanity "as a guide / My Umpire *Conscience*" (3.194–95). In fact, that umpire conscience appears to predate any fall and to have been handed out without discrimination to human and angel alike: the poem demonstrates that Satan, in particular, still possesses that umpire conscience. If Satan *cannot* find grace, then God's interventions in provoking Satan through his conscience, which the narrator states explicitly happens when Satan reaches Mount Niphates, would become a gratuitous bit of torture. Milton's poem is not a Calvinist paean to divine sovereignty but a theodicy: it means "to justifie the wayes of God to men" (1.26). As the Son declares, God is the "Judg / Of all things made, and judgest onely right" (3.153–55). Satan and the fallen angels shall not *find* grace not because God withholds it but because they continuously refuse it. God's statement about the future is a painful piece of foreknowledge, not a judgment or decree.

From this passage, it appears that what distinguishes Satan and the fallen angels from Adam and Eve in God's eyes is not penitence *per se* but intention: "The first sort by thir own suggestion fell, / Self-tempted, self-depraved: man falls deceived / By the other first" (3.129–31). Oddly, God then sends Raphael to inform Adam and Eve of danger, to prepare them, apparently, against deception, all the while asserting that they will still be deceived. Deception, therefore, must mean something other than what we have always believed. As Milton dramatizes the Fall, Adam and Eve are "deceived" by Satan but "not deceived" by the meaning of their actions, and they are "deceived" in different ways. Eve has allowed herself to be led to believe that God is withholding the fruit for some purpose—perhaps out of greed, perhaps as a test. Adam knows that he must not eat this fruit and that God has imposed this test as a sign of his obedience only; he is not fooled about what he is being asked to do. But Adam believes, as does Eve, that the serpent did eat it—"foretasted fruit? Profan'd first by the serpent" (9.929–30), which is one way he rationalizes why it may be all right for him to eat as well: "Nor yet on him found deadly" (9.932). So both Eve and Adam are deceived about the serpent's eating habits and the apparent consequences: it appears to have acquired the gift of language by eating the forbidden fruit and it appears to have survived the experience. Adam and Eve are no less responsible for their actions because of these faulty premises, but their decision to eat the fruit does not arise out of anger at God. Satan's rebellion does. Because Eve and then Adam are "tricked" into sin, they do not have an emotional investment in refusing forgiveness; Satan does.

Satan is "self-tempted"—and so not "deceived" in a way that warrants forgiveness—because he is and persists in being "deceived"—self-deceived—in his understanding of what has happened to him and who is responsible for it. Having made a disastrous choice in an effort to preserve his sense of himself and his world, Satan feels he must continuously reaffirm that choice in order to reaffirm his "self." In his discussion of Milton's sonnet "When I Consider," Dayton Haskin explains the seventeenth-century practice of identifying personal biblical "places," passages that a person comes to believe define the self. He argues that the sonnet's speaker has latched onto the fate of the undeserving servant in the Parable of the Talents as the story of his own life: although the speaker admits that he has lived only "half my days," he anticipates being judged at his death on his accomplishments to this point. Although he whines at the injustice, the speaker seems ready to join that community of predestinarians who found the uncertainty about their salvation so insupportable that they committed suicide or drowned their own children to "fix" their fate. In her rebuke, Patience "offers the reader an interpretive option [to fixed places], the implications of which are a matter of eternal life and death" (Haskin 106). Like these people, Satan wants to fix his life story, to know "who he is" even at the price of damnation. Satan fixes on a definition of himself that he asserts will not change—"what matter where, if I be still the same" (1.256)—out of a mistaken understanding of "integrity" as stasis.

The Satan of *Paradise Lost* has "read," has interpreted, the Primal Decree as a judgment on himself, in the way that Milton's contemporaries "read" Biblical passages as defining their spiritual stories: God has chosen to elevate someone else over me, so God has rejected me, not just now, but forever. Refusing to pursue alternate interpretations to his own gut reaction, Satan responds precisely as Haskin warns that a person believing in predestination and reading the parable of the talents might:

> If you choose to see yourself as a victim, and to assign responsibility
> for the injustice of your situation to a despot, you cannot move

towards a comic ending. Living in a world where everything has been predetermined, there would be no possibility of receiving, or of responding decisively to, a free gift. (106)

That predetermined universe is where Satan wants to believe he is living, and where Christopher thinks he is living, and where Schwartz suggests he is living, but where he is not. *Paradise Lost* documents time and time again God's efforts to intervene, as Patience does, to undo his "murmur," while Satan continually struggles to reaffirm his rebellious stance. Satan suffers pain and defeat during the War in Heaven, endures the physical misery of Hell, and experiences the beauty of Eden.[2] He confronts Abdiel, then other good angels both in Heaven and in Eden, his own offspring—Sin and Death—and then Adam and Eve. Each of these moments challenges Satan's perception of reality and threatens to "convict" him of responsibility for his actions and his situation, a conviction that he evades with ingenuity but with difficulty. Each instance that renders Satan "inexcusable" is potentially prevenient; even as Satan resolves to harden his heart, God offers repeated opportunities for relenting.

The process of hardening one's heart involves the exercise of individual will as much as the process of renovation does, and the portrait of Satan that Milton paints in *Paradise Lost* offers a remarkable psychological study of that process. As William Perry documented in his interviews with students at Harvard during the mid-twentieth century, the educational process repeatedly challenges adolescents' understanding of the world and their sense of themselves, their identity. As I have explained in the introduction, out of those interviews Perry identified "stages" in normal intellectual development, as a young person moves from dualism to multiplicity to informed commitment. In the world of dualism, answers are either right or wrong, as a person in a position of authority will certify; the student's responsibility, then, is to listen to and learn from that authority: at this stage, "morality and personal responsibility consist of simple obedience. Even 'learning to be independent,' as Authority asks one to do, consists of learning self-controlled obedience" (Perry, *Forms* 66). A young person at this stage expects the person in authority to be consistent and clear: the suggestion that there may be multiple answers to a question, that some answers may be better and some worse, can cause severe psychic distress. For the most part students cooperate, "accord[ing] pluralism of thought and judgment the status of a mere procedural impediment intervening between the taking up of a problem and finding *the* answer" (87). Their willingness to do so, their willingness to trust "that Authority knows its business and is presenting all these complexities as mere exercises for the students' own good" (81), enables them to move forward.

But not every young person is willing to trust Authority, because to do so requires students to relinquish, or at least to suspend belief in, whatever truths or absolutes had governed their lives and organized their sense of themselves up to this point. Satan is one such student: the world in which he lived has become unsettled by a change in the way Authority operates. God has made an unexpected and, to Satan, surprising decree—the anointing of the Son as Messiah—that provokes interpretive choices: why has God chosen this being? What does this elevation mean to me and about me, now and in the future? To respond positively to change requires moral courage, a courage that Satan refuses to exercise. Instead, he reacts "conservatively." Because he does not understand the terms through which the Son has been elevated, Satan concludes that Authority is being arbitrary and unjust. God has "impos'd" new laws, and, as Satan tells Beelzebub, "New laws from him who reigns, new minds may raise / In us who serve" (5.680–81). But Satan's "new mind" is not really new. He feels that he has been "impair'd" (5.665) and "eclipst" (5.776) by this external change and so clings stubbornly to internal stability. Even if God doesn't acknowledge it, Satan knows his own value: defensively, he prizes "that fixt mind" (1.97) "not to be chang'd by Place or Time" (1.253). In Perry's terms, he acts from "the apprehension that one change might lead to another in a rapidity which might result in catastrophic disorganization" (*Forms* 58). As Regina Schwartz argues, in different terms, "Satan is not willing to give anything up with the expectation of a return, and, unwilling to invest in his future, he denies himself one" (68). In the Primal Decree God offers the angels the challenge of interpretive independence, of growth, and Satan rejects it.

Satan's anxious reaction to the Primal Decree is not typical—the rest of the angelic host spends that evening celebrating the event with song and dance and feasting—nor is it unchallenged. During the conspiratorial meeting in Heaven, Abdiel, "knowing" no more than Satan, responding creatively to God's challenge, offers an alternative interpretation: that through the elevation of the Son, God is "bent rather to exalt, / Our happy state under one head more near / United" (5.829–31). Although Abdiel's explicit assertions—Satan is now "alienate from God" (5.877); he should expect swift and violent response—may serve to absolve God of "responsibility" for the angels' rebellion and to harden Satan's heart, they are also potentially convicting and converting. Any listening angel, including Satan, could at this moment repent and return. In this encounter, Abdiel functions as mediator of prevenient grace toward Satan in the way that Raphael will function toward Adam and Eve. From now on, Satan will have these words to remember, to ponder; he will confront other potential openings as well.

Milton expresses God's parental concern and intervention in the physical conditions of Hell and their potential effect on Satan's self-awareness. In the apparent poetic justice of Satan's circumstances in Hell, God has created a natural and logical consequence for Satan's rebellion, rather than a "punishment": rejection of God as Creator and sustainer leads to spiritual alienation expressed as physical distance. In this creation, Milton and his God seem to implement the principles of positive discipline that I discussed in chapter 1 on God's parenthood. Rather than enact an arbitrary "punishment," God fulfils the trajectory of Satan's behavior. Having rejected God, he finds himself "as far removed from God and light of heav'n / As from the center thrice to th'utmost pole" (1.73–74). Being unwilling to "see," he finds himself in "utter darkness" (1.72). This hell is an expression of Satan's rigidity and refusal to advance emotionally. What he can "see," "a dismal situation waste and wild" (1.60), confronts him with stasis, with alienation, with an outward and visible sign of his inward and spiritual reprobation.

As Stanley Fish remarks of the fallen angels as a whole, Satan is "blind to the moral meaning of their situation, that is to their evil plight" (*Surprised* 99). He sees, but he does not see. Still, what he sees is there for him *to see*, is a potentially awakening vision and mirror: first, the physical conditions of Hell, then the deformed face of his beloved Beelzebub—"how fall'n! how changed" (1.84)—and later, his prostrate followers. The situation in Hell fills Satan, as the narrator comments intrusively, with "deep despair" (1.126), with "remorse and passion" (1.605). As John Reichert demonstrates, from the opening moments of the poem, Satan is "a man reeling under the devastating impact of what he sees, and overcome by spiritual insight he has never had before . . . 'knowledge of good bought dear by knowing ill' (4.222)" (87). Read in terms of developing the main plot, Satan's anguish is, as John Carey argues about his later wonder at Eve's beauty, "a gratuitous piece of 'characterization' " (139). The despair and grief he expresses may underline for the reader the distinction between Satan's rhetoric and his inner state, but his feelings about his situation, since he doesn't act upon them, seem from a narrative perspective beside the point. Nor does his distress contribute to the poem's theological argument about God's omnipotence: if Milton only wished to undermine the claims to power that Satan makes, he could rely on the lines about divine providence that follow the leviathan simile, because what would matter in that case is whether Satan can fulfill his vaunts, not how he feels about them. Instead, Milton repeatedly pauses in his narrative to emphasize Satan's interiority.

Critics who attempt to dismiss this interiority resort to the tyrant's plea necessity. In "The Salvation of Satan," C. A. Patrides identifies Satan's soliloquy in Book 4 as the moment "where the dramatic context demanded that Satan's redemption should at least be entertained as a possibility" (472). But his article places Milton among Protestant thinkers who reject the idea of "apocastasis," the argument formulated by Saint Clement and then Origen that denying Satan's redemption restricts God's love; Patrides suggests that Milton has Satan himself articulate and then reject the possibility of his repentance in order to satisfy a dramatic necessity without compromising his theological principles. Carey agrees that by putting these words in Satan's mouth, Milton makes "Satan's irredeemability his own fault" (135).

Surprisingly, support for reading apocastatic potential in Satan's story comes from another extremely orthodox reader of *Paradise Lost*: C. S. Lewis. Responding to a Romantic tradition that sympathizes with a Satan whom they claim Milton made "more glorious than he intended" (100), Lewis argues against valorizing Satan precisely by emphasizing his interiority. He reminds readers "that the terrible soliloquy in Book IV (32–113) was conceived and in part composed before the first two books. It was from this conception that Milton started" (Lewis 100). Lewis means to enlist this fact to support recognition of Satan's consistency as a character, but it also underscores Milton's theological perspective: Milton conceived Satan, from the start, as a troubled creature with an intense inner life. If Satan is presented in anguish as a warning to sinners not to be like him, if he retains an inner life and personal responsibility, as the poem insists he does, then Satan must still be like humans, capable of ontological change and growth (Robertson 63).[3]

Satan is both a "consistent" character and a person capable of change: his consistency lies in his anguished refusal to risk repentance.

As Reichert argues, the tormented Satan of the soliloquy in Book 4 develops seamlessly out of the defiant Satan of the first books. What critics have traditionally first noticed in that soliloquy—"the movement from wonder to envy to self-redefinition"—Reichert identifies in the Satan "in hell, as he struggles to control what Dr. Johnson might have called 'the perplexity of contending passions,' and Milton 'the refluxes of mans thoughts from within'" (85). The "magnificence" of the Satan Milton first represents "lies as much in his agony, his despair, his remorse, his keen sense of the happiness he lost, as in any qualities of leadership he may from time to time exhibit" (97). His tragic stature resides in his stubborn resistance to God's freely offered grace.

Satan's capacity to resist grace should not blind readers to God's efforts to extend it. Both the soliloquy on Mount Niphates and the material prefacing it point toward this moment as a divine intervention. The narrative voice informs us that this anguished monologue of suppressed insight and rationalization is provoked by "conscience," God's voice within; the Argument states that Satan "falls into many doubts with himself, and many passions, fear, envy, and despair; but at length confirms himself in evil." The soliloquy begins with a remembrance, not simply of former glory, but of love:

> Ah, wherefore! he deserved no such return
> From me, whom he created what I was
> In that bright eminence, and with his good
> Upbraided none; nor was his service hard. (4.42–45)

That this passage follows Satan's naming God as Heaven's "king" distracts readers from the familial nature of the relationship Satan remembers. Before Satan asserts the burden of a grateful mind, he expresses a memory of intense gratefulness:

> What could be less than to afford him praise,
> The easiest recompense, and pay him thanks. (4.46–47)

Immediately after claiming "the debt immense of endless gratitude" (4.52), he acknowledges a new insight,

> that a grateful mind
> By owing, owes not, but still pays, at once,
> Indebted and discharged. (4.55–57)

This is not simply *notional* knowledge. Satan feels this truth *experimentally*: it issues in twenty-three lines of lament and finger-pointing that lead to conviction of sin—"since against his thy will / Chose freely" (4.71–72)—a sharp moment of self-recognition, and the precipice of repentance. Probing his memory through "my Umpire *Conscience*" (3.195), exposing him to the sharp disparity between his spiritual desolation and the glorious plenitude of creation, provoking the insight that "myself am hell" (4.75), God urges Satan toward spiritual growth. Unfortunately, as Nell Noddings points out, "one cannot be rescued from evil as from a burning house; one must choose its opposite" (115–16).

Through Satan, Milton models for his readers how not to think, how not to respond to proffered grace. In his analysis of interviews with students, Perry remarks that "the very pain of personal guilt, as one who is failing of his own life, is perhaps the most hopeful awareness in alienation" (221). Milton has Satan express that pain, that acute sense of alienation, obligation, and responsibility. He comes close to reaching the insight that Haskin identifies both in the parable of the talents and in "When I Consider": "if you can free yourself from an intense consciousness of the demands inherent in having 'talents,' there is space within which to risk a creative response to what has been given" (106). Repentance would be just such a creative, and courageous, response, but Satan refuses to risk it. He chooses the alternative Haskin outlines—"to see yourself as a victim, and to assign responsibility for the injustice of your situation to a despot" (106)—and resists renovation. Milton documents in Satan's degeneration the natural consequences and immense psychic cost of that resistance. As Perry observed in his interviews, students resisting intellectual growth "seemed to be actively denying or fighting off within themselves awareness of their urge to progress. In short, they maintained their position at the cost of the integrity they were attempting to conserve" (*Forms* 59). Their resistance required "an emotional fortification of near-violent energy, a mustering of a sense of inner strength and categorical righteousness best experienced in resentment, hate, and moral rage against otherness" (Perry, *Forms* 119). It is costly and violent and destructive because it is a position that must be freely chosen and vigilantly maintained; at any moment, should he let down his guard, Satan might be surprised by faith.

# II

*But if any provide not for his own, and specially those of his own house,
he hath denied the faith, and is worse than an infidel.*

—*1 Timothy 5:8*

Satan's experience in *Paradise Lost* provides repeated evidence of God's intervention in his willful descent into damnation: the correction from Abdiel, the hopelessness of the war in Heaven, the physical lesson of Hell, the suffering of his compatriots, the conscience-probing rays of the sun, the lushness of Eden, the beauty and innocence of Adam and Eve. But the most startling intervention is God's placement of Sin and Death at the Gates of Hell: God makes Satan encounter his family. Critical response to the allegory of Sin and Death provides a useful comment on our desire for interpretive clarity, for the easy reading of fixed stories. Whether they consider the allegory successful or embarrassing, parodic or sublime, readers prefer to read Sin as an allegorical counter, as a satiric idea rather than as a disturbingly human avatar of sinfulness. Victoria Kahn identifies in this episode "an allegorical critique of allegory" that provokes reader engagement: Milton attempts "to educate the reader to view rhetorical structures as indeterminate and thus finally less as things than as activities of discrimination and choice" (188). The theoretical nature of her discussion, however, tends to distance readers emotionally from the allegory, rather than to provoke affective as well as intellectual engagement with it. More recently, Louis Schwartz, responding to the complexity of Sin's narrative, suggests that "Milton seems to be inviting us to some extent to respond to Sin as a subject" (65), although he stops short of claiming for her ontological potentiality. But, as I have argued before, the terms of Sin's situation in the poem belie her allegorical fixity: God places her at the Gates of Hell with a clear set of responsibilities, responsibilities that she recognizes, offering her the opportunity to choose not to sin, to free herself from allegorical fixity by exercising personal agency (Thickstun, *Fictions* 65).

When readers choose to read Sin as a fixed allegorical counter, they fail a test of compassion: this is a daughter used sexually by her father and raped by her son. Her physical and psychological sufferings are enormous, irrespective of her moral complicity. During their confrontation in Hell, Satan does his best not to acknowledge her, not to recognize who she is and what her situation means about him. Readers of the poem see those things clearly. But our response should not be horror at her, followed by an intellectual analysis of what her image means about him. If we are simply disgusted by Sin, we hate the sinner as well as the sin. If we intellectualize her situation, we join Satan in reducing her to a thing and denying her independent identity. We should instead allow ourselves to respond fully and affectively to her story. To read Sin as a subjective being, however, involves risk: it exposes the reader to a visceral recognition of personal sinfulness.

As Schwartz's essay compellingly demonstrates, the parodic inversion of the Holy Trinity that is Satan, Sin, and Death "names something dark and urgently real for men and women in seventeenth-century London" (81): the pain and suffering in childbearing that "manifest[s] the nature and consequences of sin" (85). *Paradise Lost* was written at a time of unmedicated childbirth, when complications led to traumatic deliveries and often death, when vaginal tears healed naturally, if at all, when even women who did not suffer extreme trauma during deliveries might be rendered incontinent by the experience of repeated births.[4] By placing Sin's physical suffering in the context of seventeenth-century obstetrics and the effects of birth trauma, Schwartz highlights the unsettling resonances of her "allegorical self-consciousness" (L. Schwartz 79). She is "a suffering mother" (79), and all human mothers participate in her sinful suffering. He pushes readers to see the personal implications of Sin's condition, to open themselves to what Puritans would call "experimental" rather than "notional" knowledge of her meaning.

But I do not believe that this iconography of suffering targets simply readers of the poem. Satan is the first "reader" of Sin—the first interpreter. In Heaven, Satan chooses to "read" Sin as himself, "his perfect image," failing to recognize difference; in Hell, Satan chooses to read Sin as a "fixed story" because it enables him both to distance himself from her (he never honestly acknowledges their relationship) and to evade responsibility for her present and her future. He is repulsed, but not at what about himself Sin represents. He expresses revulsion at her sinfulness without acknowledging his complicity in it. He doesn't go far enough in rejecting her, and he doesn't go far enough in claiming responsibility for her. But in this confrontation with his first victim, in a scene in which Satan is forced to interrupt his journey in order to listen to her sufferings, God offers Satan the possibility of *experimental*, of saving, self-knowledge. Just as Sin's godly responsibility—to follow God's direct command by keeping the Gates of Hell locked—underscores her ontological potentialities and offers her the choice of choosing to be other than she is, Satan's fatherhood presents him with an extreme challenge to put the welfare of others ahead of his own, even though this is a challenge that he chooses to ignore and evade.

Satan's fatherhood, like Sin's motherhood, is a condition that critics consider abstractly, rather than viscerally. In his psychological self-representation, Satan vigilantly restricts his attention to his isolation and his "integrity": by continuing to privilege this perspective, critics participate in the continuation of his misreading of reality, whether they sympathize with him or condemn him. In reading Satan, as in reading God, focusing on fatherhood and parenting highlights aspects of the narrative that conventional readings overlook. The divine perspective requires a radical wrenching of point of view.

By providing Satan with a family, Milton underscores, for Satan as well as for the reader, the undeniable fact of his continued moral agency.[5] As James Fowler argues, a genuinely adult moral life involves "the experience of sustained responsibility for the welfare of others and the experience of making and living with irreversible moral choices" (82). Sin's presence in the poem signals Satan's moral adulthood and offers him two moments of potential awakening far more disturbing than his encounters with any other beings. As Noddings writes, "to be touched, to have aroused in me something that will disturb my own ethical reality, I must see the other's reality as a possibility for my own" (14). Like a human child, Sin is both "flesh of his flesh," capable of touching him more profoundly than even his most intimate angelic associates, and a contingent being whose utter dependence upon his actions calls upon his selflessness more powerfully than the dismay of his fallen legions. Sin's initial appearance and her subsequent degradation challenge Satan's narcissism; her visible suffering should profoundly challenge his compassion.

Certainly, in Heaven and then in Hell, Satan recognizes Sin only partially. If he were to recognize her in the fullest sense of the word, he would have to acknowledge the truth about himself: he would have, in the first instance, to retain a sense of her startling unfamiliarity and, in the second, to see her present deformity as still his "perfect image" (2.764) (Thickstun, *Fictions* 64). At each encounter, Satan the individual should recognize, shun, and reject Sin.

But as both Sin's parent and the author of her distress, Satan should take responsibility for her condition by acting on her behalf, as Adam should do when Eve presents herself with the fruit and as Adam eventually does when Eve flings herself, distraught, at his feet. Because Satan does not accept such responsibility for the welfare of his offspring, the "irreversible moral choices" that he has made are played out in the poem through their bodies. Milton figures the horror of Satan's rejection of God and glorification of himself in his incestuous disregard for Sin's welfare in Heaven. The terribleness of what he has done receives repeated embodiment: first, in the act of incest itself; then in the product of that incest, Death, and its violent recapitulation in Death's rape of his mother; finally, in the physical suffering and repulsive circumstances of Sin, with her nether parts ripped open and her festering body gnawed by hounds. By placing Sin at the Gates of Hell and so creating the occasion for Satan's re-encounter with her, God orchestrates a version of victim-identification therapy: Sin tells her story directly to the person who harmed her, a story with the potential to provoke a moral awakening in response to her suffering.

Satan's parenthood is, potentially, the most hopeful relationship he enters. Simply the fact of Sin, irrespective of her physical deformity, threatens to disrupt the fixed narrative about himself that Satan has created. Her presence challenges him to see himself as the agent rather than the victim of his story, because he sees before him a genuine victim of his actions. Her suffering calls into question the "integrity" of his self-image and embodies the destructiveness of his desperate attempts to fix his identity: in Sin, Satan should be able to see that, far from preserving "self," the conservative impulse initiates the catastrophic disorganization he so fears. To put the point biblically, in order to find himself, Satan must lose himself, which is the one thing of which he is terrified. Instead, Satan loses himself first by seeing himself, not an other, in Sin: he fails what Kahn calls a necessary recognition of difference. Then he fails another test by refusing, in this second encounter, to recognize identity. Noddings argues that "when one intentionally rejects the impulse to care and deliberately turns her back on the ethical, she is evil, and this evil cannot be redeemed" (115). Following Noddings's philosophy, if there were to be a point at which Satan has moved past forgiveness, this moment ought to be it. But Milton's God is not a God of vengeance and punishment, and his response is not constrained by the actions of his creatures. He will not turn his back on the ethical, the impulse to care. As Stavely asserts, "God never withdraws the possibility of such reconciliation, such repentance, such an emergence" ("Satan" 137) from isolation and despair to communion and joy.

Throughout the poem, God attempts to intervene in Satan's spiritual crisis although, because Satan has rejected him, he must do so through mediators or mediating events and environments. In some encounters, God's orchestration is explicit: he sends the good angels into battle; he places Sin and Death at the Gates of Hell; he posts Uriel on the sun; he orders Gabriel and his troops to guard Eden. Other encounters seem more accidental: Abdiel, quite unaccountably, journeys north with the heavenly conspirators, apparently completely unaware of the expedition's true purpose. He almost seems to be a plant, except that his intensity, provoked by the startling challenge that Satan's rebellion presents him, argues against his foreknowledge. In each case, however, Satan is brought up short by an interpretation of reality that differs starkly from his reading, by an alternative meaning that challenges the fixity of his own. In Sin and Death, Satan could see, if he chose, his own spiritual deformity and the consequences of his actions; in Adam and Eve, Satan could see, if he chose, creatures to love and to pity (4.363, 374). Time and again God confronts Satan with the consequences of his actions, the recognition of which could provoke change.

Shortly after the encounter with Sin and Death, God provides Satan with an inverse experience: if Sin is one mirror in which to see his degraded self, Ithuriel and Zephon present Satan with the "mirror" of their unrecognition. Having refused to "recognize" Sin, Satan finds himself confronted with others' inability to recognize him. If in viewing Sin, Satan failed to acknowledge her deformed self as his new and degenerate "perfect image," Satan is forced to hear two angels of whom he takes no account assert that he "resemble'st now / Thy sin and place of doom obscure and foule" (4.839–40) and to experience through their response how "his lustre [is] visibly impaired" (4.850). They deduce that he must be one "of those rebell Spirits adjudg'd to Hell" (4.823), but not which one. As a logical, one might even call it natural, consequence of not "knowing" God to be God, Satan finds himself "unknown." In his retort to their "halt; who goes there?" he ironically convicts himself from his own mouth: "not to know mee argues your selves unknown" (4.830). He does not acknowledge himself as a created being, so he has put himself outside the communion of Heaven. Because he will not "recognize" God, God's creatures are unable to recognize him: he is no longer who he thinks he is.

In his discussion of Satan's radical iconoclasm, Flesch argues that "by giving up a title that invests him with God's image, Satan seems to attempt to rival God's invisibility and inaccessibility" (242). At this moment, Satan feels the full force of such rivalry: the erasure of that "self" which he struggles so intensely to preserve. Flesch concedes that "Satan is not able to maintain his impossible namelessness" (243); in Book 10 "he wholly accepts the adversarial name that heaven had given him and revels in its meaning" (244). As Flesch explains, "if there is no power but of God, then a rebellion against God is not a rebellion against a temporary vessel of power but against the source of power itself. Satan's error is, first, in not understanding the difference between normative iconoclasm, which has the worship of God as its end, and one without teleology" (239). But I do not see Satan embracing namelessness at any point in *Paradise Lost*. He is, instead, determined to "name" himself, a frantic and futile effort. Because Satan's effort at self-definition is, like his iconoclasm, without teleology, he can sustain neither his original name, which located him within the created universe, nor his "namelessness," which asserts his separation from the only "real world" there is.

The remainder of the poem documents Satan's further catastrophic disintegration as he struggles masterfully to preserve his "integrity." In clinging steadfastly to his unchanging self, his "fixed mind," Satan begins to ossify: he becomes more and more like an allegorical representation of resistance and rebellion than like an individual acting in those ways. But even in his resistance, Satan demonstrates moments of potentiality as he responds instinctively to the continuous embodiments of God's goodness, both in the universe God has created and in the individuals with whom it is peopled. Eden itself, of course, provokes the intense soliloquy of anguish and grief at the opening of Book 4; his first sight of Adam and Eve elicits another bout of grief and self-doubt, followed by retrenchment and a further casting of the blame onto God: this is a couple he admits his "thoughts pursue / with wonder, and could love" (4.362), "whom I could pittie thus forlorne / Though I unpittied" (4.374–75).

Satan resists his good impulses and the divine love that prompts them only by distancing himself from responsibility for his actions: it is not Satan himself, but God "who puts me loath to this revenge" (4.386). Standing before Zephon and Ithuriel, Satan is "abasht"

> And felt how awful goodness is, and saw
> Virtue in her shape how lovely, saw, and pined
> His loss. (4.847–50)

He will experience a similar moment of confusion upon discovering Eve unaccompanied in Book 9. There her innocence will "overaw[e] / His malice" and "bereav[e] / His fierceness" so that he will stand "abstracted[ ] / From his own evil, and for a time remain[ ] / Stupidly good" (9.460–64). It will require the recollection of his loss, his alienation, and the determination to continue in it, reinforced by a fierce rejection of those pleasanter feelings as his own, to recover his fixed purpose. Refusing to accept responsibility for his will, Satan addresses his good impulses as a "sweet / Compulsion" thrust upon him by unruly, and personified, "Thoughts" (9.473–74). Having just felt awe, rapture, perhaps even "hope / of Paradise" (9.475–76), Satan asserts that he cannot feel these things, that all pleasure for him lies now in "destroying." He interprets the repeated reminders that God offers of his Goodness, Plenitude, and Love as lessons in humiliation. As Perry remarks of a student who resented general education courses because they sought to expand his range of interests, to change "him" as he defined himself: "this is a bold lonely renunciation of Eden in loyalty to self" (*Forms* 83).

One of the acknowledged challenges of *Paradise Lost* is to read the plot of Adam and Eve as if it were open-ended: as if, at the moment that she reached for the apple, Eve might choose not to reach; as if, at the moment that Adam decides to eat, he might decide to refrain. A further, not yet acknowledged challenge, I argue, is to resist reading Satan's story as fixed: like the rest of the poem, it is presented as open-ended, even though the alternative scripts may be harder and harder for Satan to discern or the reader to entertain. To read his fate as fixed is a failure of interpretive response. Significantly, even the metamorphoses of Satan and the fallen angels into serpents is not permanent: "thir lost shape, permitted, they resume" (10.574), although it may be an "annual humbling" (10.576), but this the narrator will only present as hearsay. Satan and the fallen host remain "themselves," though fallen: individuals created "sufficient to have stood" and possessing the same intellectual powers and moral responsibilities in their postlapsarian state as before.

In her discussion of Satan's encounter with Sin, Victoria Kahn argues that Satan "reads" Sin incorrectly; in her words, he "dismisses the sign (surface) for the psychological origin (genealogy) and so substitutes both structurally and thematically determinism for freedom, fate for faith and free will" (191). When we try to read Satan as a fixed sign incapable of change, when C. S. Lewis refers to Satan as "a personified self-contradiction" (97), when Georgia Christopher describes him as "*peccatum cum voce*" (61), we commit that same interpretive substitution. We run the risk of reading a narrative of alternatives and possibilities as a "fixed" story. Satan, like all of God's creatures, both in his original perfection and in his degeneration, remains a creature with responsibilities and choices.

If *Paradise Lost* is to have any evangelical effect, if it is to offer, as does "When I Consider," a warning and a promise that are neither too severe nor overly consoling, then Satan's example must be educational not in the manner of Lot's Wife in *The Pilgrim's Progress*, but in the manner of Ignorance and the Man in the Iron Cage. The pilgrims encounter Lot's Wife after her story is finished and her meaning fixed. She is a sign of covetousness, no longer a person, not even the physical remains of a person: she has been transformed into a pillar of salt. Ignorance and the Man in the Iron Cage, on the other hand, are still human beings even as they are allegorical agents; Bunyan represents in them extreme and precise psycho-spiritual states in which humans may find themselves and out of which they may and, especially with spiritual counsel and the help of books like *The Pilgrim's Progress*, often do emerge. Similarly, Milton has Satan frequently express an inner life that is rich, complex, and extremely troubled. Christian's encounters with the Man in the Iron Cage and with Ignorance are horrifying because of his inability to persuade them to see God's grace, because they might escape damnation; Satan's story is agonizing because he, too, has and persistently rejects that choice.

# CHAPTER 3

# ABDIEL, PEER PRESSURE, AND THE REBEL ANGELS

I

*Take heed, therefore, how ye hear.*

*–Luke 8:18*

Satan is not the only rebel in Heaven. When Abdiel stands up to protest Satan's blasphemous speech, he faces "the third part of Heav'ns Host" (5.710). How have these other angels come to be here? Why, learning "the suggested cause," do all obey "their wonted signal"? And why does not one of them follow Abdiel's lead and hightail it back to God? How, given that they are upright, unfallen beings, does one third of Heaven's host screw up so badly?

One critical tradition, bracketed by the work of William Empson and Seiwoong Oh, reads the War in Heaven as the culmination of a conspiracy in progress long before the opening action of the poem, rather than a sudden plan initiated by Satan alone. Empson seems to base his belief in this preexisting conspiracy on a misreading of the birth of Sin, which he assumes must have taken place before God elevates the Son. He also assumes a high level of resentment and paranoia on the part of all angels—those who remain loyal and those who rebel—over God's plan to create humans. Similarly, Oh posits a Heaven rife with resentment and corruption, with angels "ready to accept the invitation of Satan, who more or less speaks their minds" (56). He dismisses out of hand Michael's assertion that the rebel angels were "once upright and faithful," stating that Michael simply has failed to discern hypocrisy (Oh 59). This critical tradition simply pushes the questions that I have raised back beyond the opening of the poem, and beyond the possibility of analysis. Why do Adam and Eve find grace, the rebel angels none? What does Milton's God mean when he calls the rebel angels "self-tempted, self-deprav'd" (3.130). In attempting to explain, these critics evade the problem.

In order to address these questions, we need to consider further the nature of Milton's angelic beings. As Robert West asserts, "Milton was telling a story that required angels not merely as 'machinery' but as characters" (112). As I argue in the introduction, the angels in *Paradise Lost* are essentially humans with special powers. True, they are able to fly, to change shape, and to heal back up when split in half, but, as Raphael relates, they do share physical character-istics with other created beings, eating and sleeping, even if "for change delectable not need" (5.629).[1] Milton's angels do not appear to reproduce, but they do have intimate relationships (and this Raphael reveals only when pressed, so his explanation cannot be dismissed as simply "accommodation"). His angels may be immortal, but they do grow and develop, both physically and morally: there are, after all, "stripling Cherubs" for whom Uriel can mistake the disguised Satan. Uriel's interest in guiding and praising this apparent Cherub's enthu-siasm suggests that not all angelic knowledge is innate or intuitive nor are all angels equally "mature." They do not know the future (Nardo, "Education" 200); they can and do make mistakes. For angels are, like humans, "free to fall," and only "sufficient," not perfect (3.99).[2] Most of the time they must muddle forward just as humans do.

Like humans, Milton's angels are social creatures, made to func-tion as a group, to work with the group, to look to the group. They are certainly more social than fallen humans, for we see little evidence of the concept of "privacy" in Heaven (until Satan whispers his dissent to his "dear companion"). Satan may have a "Royal Seat" (5.756), but when the angels congregate near God they dwell in temporary "pavilions" and "tabernacles," which are "sudden reard" (5.653) when needed. These shelters seem to be open-sided, for they do not prevent cool winds from fanning the angels as they sleep (5.655). The angels make these encampments in "Bands and Files." Every angel is related to every other angel through a complex hierarchy of rank, which all seem instinctively to identify and understand, and this complex organization orbits in ring upon ring around God at its center.

The Heaven that the angels experience before the Rebellion is a place of spontaneous unanimity. As one body, the angels sing, dance, praise God, and feast with their friends, without any apparent discus-sions about what to do. No angel suggests singing when others want to eat or eating when others want to sing. At no point in the repre-sentation of angels in *Paradise Lost* does Milton show them so much as deciding whether to dance in a circle or in a line. The angels seem to function more as social insects do, with each of the angels instinctively conforming to the desire of the group. This congruity of will and desire emanates from the angels' unfallen nature and expresses the harmony of their "communion sweet" (5.637), just as their singing and praising express the harmony of their gratitude to God. Heaven, after all, operates according to divine law, which "legislates" the well-being of all creatures, and every creature in heaven, being unfallen, responds to the promptings of his healthy, well-regulated will. It is only the fallen who experience, like Saint Paul, the disordered will that leads to confused desire and wrong choice: "for the good that I would, I do not: but the evil which I would not, that I do" (Rom. 7:19).

As a result of this spontaneous harmony, the angels who follow Satan are, at the moment in their departure, unused to making any choices at all, let alone moral ones. They are completely unaccustomed even to minor disagreement. Like Adam, who will ask (or has in the poem just asked) in complete perplexity, *"if ye be found / Obedient?* can we want obedience then / To him, or possibly his love desert" (5.513–15), they have never confronted such an outrageous idea as Satan will propose. I do not argue that their inexperience, any more than Adam's and Eve's inexperience, excuses their actions or shifts the responsibility for their choices onto God. Others as inexperienced as they will stand fast by God in the War in Heaven. The rebel angels themselves will recognize instinctively the evil of what Satan proposes, as Sin's account of her birth reveals. But I would like to look at the psychological dynamics that Milton writes into the moral fall of the rebel angels: their initial turning from God and the process of poor but still sinless decision-making that leads to that moment. He has constructed this process carefully with attention not only to how charismatic leaders may manipulate their followers but also to how individuals function in groups. He would expect his readers to study this incident for instruction and warning. A careful reading of these scenes will illuminate the distinction between being seduced and being "self-tempted."

Satan initiates his conspiracy by presenting his troops with a plausible and apparently innocuous order: they are to march north immediately, "there to prepare / Fit entertainment to receive our King" (5.689–90). Social psychologists have documented that authority, or even "the appearance of authority," affects an individual's willingness to comply with a request or order (Aronson 27). Satan, of course, has actual authority over the angels at his command, "for great indeed / His name, and high was his degree in Heav'n" (5.706–07). He also, by virtue of his rank and social status, possesses the ability to influence their behavior, both through his own actions and through their identification with him. His name is known; his degree is high; he is "great in Power, / In favor, and praeeminence" (5.660–61); and he is beautiful. As one of God's select few, "of the first, / If not the first archangel" (5.659–60), he is a powerful role model for his subordinates. Individuals look to others for guidance as to their own behavior, especially to those in positions of authority and influence. What Satan and his commanding officers appear to model in this move north is swift and unquestioning obedience to a divine command. Satan claims, after all, that *he* has been commanded to move his troops north: he himself is only "following orders."

Satan insures that his troops are susceptible to following this order. In her discussion of the conspiracy in Heaven, Revard notes that, like the conspirators in poems about the Gunpowder plot, Satan "moves quietly, unseen by all but God" (96). Connecting this strategy for concealment with Satan's penchant for seducing his victims while they are asleep (Eve) or newly waking (Beelzebub), she points out how he arranges that the angels under his command are "dislodged at night" (98). Both their sleepiness and the disruptive and unusual nature of this event would cause the angels to experience disorientation and, hence, uncertainty. The communication itself adds to their confusion. As Raphael explains, no one states baldly, "let's start a rebellion." Beelzebub's message to the soon to be rebel host is highly ambiguous. Raphael describes their response in a way that leaves entirely uncertain what those angels actually "hear." As Beelzebub circulates "the suggested cause," he

> casts between
> Ambiguous words and jealousies, to sound
> Or taint integritie; but all obey'd
> Thir wonted signal. (5.702–05)

That "but" suggests that these angels both "get it" and yet don't quite "get it," as later, in Hell, they will perceive only imperfectly the extent of "thir evil plight" (1.335). Here in Heaven, as Revard points out, they are " 'allur'd' by the superior voice, the name and countenance of their great potentate, and so they follow him, 'heretic' as it were, in their accustomed obedience" (161). These falling angels may be in the process of giving over control of their own wills in deference to hierarchies and duties. But this process is not inevitable or uncorrectable.

In fact, as Abdiel's participation in this march north demonstrates, it is also possible that these angels do not yet perceive their error: awakened from sleep, presented with an unusual command and purposely obscure intimations, they may mistrust their understanding and respond to authority as they are accustomed, thus resolving the disorientation of an unusual experience by responding to it as an accustomed one. They themselves have been part of the spontaneous celebration following the Son's begetting. Although Raphael's "All seemd well pleas'd, all seem'd, but were not all" (5.617) might suggest that more than one individual is not well pleased, it is only Satan who stays awake for a reason other than hymning his Creator and only Satan who expresses discontent—to a Beelzebub who has managed to drift off to sleep despite his dear companion's restlessness. The other soon-to-be-fallen angels dance, feast, and disperse to their pavilions for rest along with and indistinguishable from their brethren who will remain faithful. Their participation in the celebration lends weight to the argument that their decision to depart with Satan is "only following orders," and not yet even a "heretic obedience." Under normal circumstances, their response to Satan's words might well echo Eve's response to Adam's: "What thou bidst / Unargu'd I obey; God is thy law, / Thou mine" (4.635–37). These circumstances are not entirely "normal," but Satan has not yet revealed his hand.

Only when Satan does speak openly of conspiracy do the gathered angels face their moment of decision. As Revard argues, once Abdiel has said his say, the other angels "change from the dupes of Satan's policy to its willing converts, adhering in their 'faith' to him" (161) over their faith to God. Satan offers a complex interpretation of the meaning and effect of God's Primal Decree. In Revard's words, his manipulation "undermines the angels' confidence in God's kingdom and leads them to believe they have before them no alternative but to revolt" (220). But these angels are still unfallen. How compelling or interesting Satan's arguments may be ought not to signify. Charles Durham is right to assert that " 'To stand approv'd in sight of God' is the single requirement for any being endowed with reason and choice in *Paradise Lost*" (17). The real question is, why don't they also burst forth in spontaneous defense of God's goodness? How are they manipulated when Abdiel isn't?

Satan and Milton have crafted this scene very carefully. It begins with Satan still "Pretending so commanded to consult / About the great reception of their king" (5.768–69). As far as the falling angels know, the Son is, in fact, planning such an event. To them the opening parts of the speech seem true: they have undertaken "All this haste / Of midnight march, and hurried meeting here" (5.777–78) to plan for that reception, as Empson notes (72). Only after laying out again this apparent command does Satan express an attitude toward it. It is an attitude that some of the host may have suspected from hearing Beelzebub's "ambiguous words and jealousies" (5.703), but not an attitude that anyone has yet expressed or perhaps even thought explicitly. Through the intensity and distress of Abdiel's response to Satan's attitude, Milton indicates that at least one of these angels sincerely believed the cover story to be true—and finds nothing offensive about the Son's undertaking a royal progress nor about the prospect of participating in a ceremony of fealty. Since "neither Man nor Angel can discern / Hypocrisy" (3.682–83), Abdiel and the falling angels never see through the initial deception, as Eve never sees through the serpent's claim about how it learned to speak. They must, instead, decide how to interpret the Primal Decree and the Son's purported royal progress. Confronted with Satan's speech, they need to make that decision now.

Unlike Eve, the falling angels have a potential role model in their midst to help with this decision, and we learn elsewhere in the poem that they do respond appropriately at first. In her conversation with Satan, Sin reports of the angelic host that "back they recoild affraid / At first, and called me *Sin*, and for a Sign / Portentous held me" (2.759–61). It is only when Sin becomes "familiar" that she pleases and wins the falling angels.[3] In order to determine how sin, which is frightening and repugnant, can become comfortable and attractive, we have to read these two poetic moments in light of one another: what is it about the dynamics of the conspiracy in Heaven that allows sin to become "familiar"?

First, the falling angels are off-balance. It is natural that individuals look to others for information about how to behave, especially in ambiguous situations, and also that they may misread others' responses. Social psychologists call this process "informational social influence" (Aronson 458). Until Abdiel stands up, no angel objects to or attempts to interrupt Satan's speech: "his bold discourse without controule / Had audience" (5.803–4). Readers tend to interpret this lack of interruption as signifying assent. But anyone who has spent time in a large classroom knows how unlikely individuals are to break into someone else's monologue, especially when that person is in a position of authority. An audience's silence does not always signal its agreement. In fact, it is possible to receive no overt response even to the most outrageous statements. The falling angels are part of an enormous group—one-third the Heavenly host. If angels behave like humans, as Milton's angels do, then each falling angel looks to the angels around him for cues about how to behave, and what he sees is no response at all.

Then Abdiel stands up. Significantly, Milton has altered the conventional representation of this confrontation. In most other Renaissance treatments of the War in Heaven, it is the Archangel Michael who denounces Satan (Revard 165). One poem replaces Michael with another archangel, Raphael. Those poems pit two powerful archangels against one another in verbal battle. In *Paradise Lost*, Milton substitutes a lowly seraph as God's champion. Though this choice highlights the theme of the One Just Man and provides an inspiring role model for both Adam and Eve and Milton's larger audience, it also puts the falling angels at a disadvantage. In making judgments, individuals weigh both the attractiveness and credibility of the persons supplying information (Aronson 38–39). Satan is powerful and attractive, the sort of angel a person looks up to and desires both to please and to emulate; Abdiel has neither authority nor status. He is just one of the crowd. It is only natural that the falling angels, who trust and admire their leader, will look to him first for guidance. After that, they will look, as I have said, to the group.

At the close of Abdiel's speech, Raphael reports a continued silence: "None seconded" (5.850). Because of the large group, and the attendant diffusion of responsibility (Aronson 49), each falling angel expects some other angel to speak. As Revard demonstrates, Milton has depicted his rebel angels as less active and participatory, less "equal" to Satan in their rebelliousness, than the rebel angels of other Renaissance poems (162–64). No angel stands to second Abdiel, but neither does any angel stand to support Satan. It is possible that, as the debate continues uninterrupted, each falling angel resonates to Abdiel's critique but assumes his own reaction to be inappropriate: perhaps Abdiel's objections are incorrect; perhaps Satan's assertions are more reasonable than they appear. As they contemplate Satan's position, sin becomes less startling, more familiar.

Milton has Raphael offer three possible reasons for this angelic silence: that the falling angels may have found Abdiel's zeal "out of season," "singular," or "rash" (5.850–51). Notice that these evaluations do not involve moral judgment. Instead, each of these adjectives applies to how behavior may be perceived by a group, and each adjective implies that to respond in kind would make the responder also appear "out of season," "singular," or "rash." Given their ultimate response, each falling angel—like most readers of this scene—seems to interpret the silence of the group as assent to Satan's position. This process is called "pluralistic ignorance," in which everyone thinks that everybody else holds a particular position and so each individual yields to the supposed consensus of the group (Katz and Schanck 174). Considering how Milton has represented angelic experience in Heaven, this yielding appears to be partly the result of habit. It also reveals a kind of humility: "we conform because we believe that others' interpretation of an ambiguous situation is more correct than ours" (Aronson 458).

But Abdiel has been able to resist this apparent consensus. What distinguishes Abdiel from his peers? He is certainly not smarter. Abdiel clearly did not "get" the "ambiguous words and jealousies" that framed Beelzebub's order to march north. He is a dunce reader who accepted the cover story at face value. He is, as Revard says of all the falling angels at this point, Satan's dupe (Revard 161). He is not even more informed about the nature of God: his rushing back to warn God about what is going to happen reveals that he doesn't "see" any more perfectly than the angels around him who choose to side with Satan. But Abdiel possesses humility of a different order from that of the other angels. Raphael's initial presentation of Abdiel emphasizes his devotion to God—"none with more zeal ador'd / The Deitie" (5.805–06). Coupled with that devotion, or perhaps caused by it, is the willingness to risk embarrassment. In his violent reaction to Satan's speech, he admits publicly his fallibility; to second Abdiel would require each falling angel to acknowledge and reveal his own.

Individuals don't like to look silly. Satan, the wily manipulator, offers in place of Abdiel's model humility an even grander vision of angelic nature than he did in his first speech. Now angels are not only "Natives and Sons of Heaven" (5.790) but also "self-begot, self-rais'd" (5.860). In following the command to march north despite possible suspicions about its sincerity, in listening passively to Satan's initial speech, in failing to rally to Abdiel's defense, the falling angels have inched their way toward joining Satan's rebellion. As social psychologists argue, "once a small commitment is made, it sets the stage for ever-increasing commitments" (Aronson 197); we call this in common speech "the slippery slope." The pressure to stand by a decision is especially strong if the initial "commitment" was hesitant, or not commitment at all: "Suppose you bowed to group pressure even though you remained certain that your initial judgment was correct. This might be embarrassing for you to admit because it would make you appear weak and wishy-washy" (Aronson 23). Abdiel is willing to risk just that. His courage underscores their weakness.

Revard makes the same point about Satan's behavior in this scene that I am making about the rebel angels. In Satan's case, provisional commitment to a position, coupled with the threat of embarrass-ment in front of others, pushes him into a face-saving gesture that commits him further to rebellion:

> But ultimately, I think, we must see Satan's act in terms of his having been brought, unwillingly, to the persuasion that God may not be sepa-rated from Messiah, as Satan had originally asserted. God has decreed that he and Messiah are one in government as in act of creation. Satan belatedly must face the truth of that connection. He is subject to the rule of God through Messiah because he is the creature of God through Messiah. Therefore he must bow to Messiah as to God or deny God with the denial of Messiah. There are no alternatives. But, of course, to assent to Messiah's rule would mean to abandon those angelic preroga-tives (to govern, not to serve) he has only now promulgated. Satan is trapped. His leap of logic from denying the Son as agent of creation to pronouncing himself self-begot illustrates as much. (Revard 65)

To put this in psychological terms, "if people are committed to an atti-tude, the information the communicator presents arouses dissonance; frequently, the best way to reduce the dissonance is to reject or distort the evidence" (Aronson 188). Satan cannot accept Abdiel's claim that the Son merits elevation and worship while at the same time retaining his sense of his own self-worth and injured merit. He faces this dilemma in front of an enormous audience that looks up to him as their leader. How can he admit his error and maintain his dignity? It is easier at this moment, as it will be again and again in the poem, for Satan to reassert his own righteousness than for him to admit his sin.

If peer pressure weren't a powerful thing, then Abdiel's resistance and exit would not be admirable. He cannot, after all, be harmed by the rebel host. What Milton has him praised for here, by Raphael, and in the opening to Book 6, by the divine voice, is that "Nor num-ber, nor example with him wrought / To swerve from truth, or change his constant mind / Though single" (5.901–03), and that he has borne "Universal reproach, far worse to beare / Than violence" (5.34–35). All he does is to admit he was fooled; all he endures is "hostile scorn" (5.904). To do each of those things, however, is more than the other angels can bear.

## II

> *For godly sorrow leadeth to repentance that is not to be repented of, but worldly sorrow leadeth to death.*
>
> —*2 Corinthians 7:10*

As I argued in chapter 2, Abdiel functions in this scene as a vessel for God's prevenient grace: if laying out the truth of the situation helps to render the rebels "inexcusable," it also offers them the opportunity to reconsider their choice and provides a proof-text against which to test their future experiences of God's nature. The War in Heaven continues God's ministry toward his rebellious children even as it offers the faithful angels the opportunity both to demonstrate their loyalty and to discover for themselves its depth. The physical experience of their fall and the Hell that receives them should reinforce, for even the densest rebel, the stupidity of what they have done. Like prelapsarian humans, the rebel angels were sufficient to have stood; like fallen humans, they are capable of repentance and regaining to know God aright. To show why they do not repent, Milton develops a series of scenes in which the social circumstances of the rebellion militate against the rebels making a right choice but do not excuse their failure. As Dustin Griffin argues, in the fallen angels Milton offers "our first glimpse of fallen human experience" (244). In doing so, he presents his readers with a cautionary tale of the seductive appeal and moral danger of yielding to the will of the group.

In introducing the fallen host in Hell, Milton emphasizes their communal response, as well as their awareness of themselves as members of a particular community. But whereas in Heaven that awareness issued in harmony and fellowship, in Hell the fallen angels have become self-conscious about how they fit into the group and how they appear to others. Community becomes conformity. The narrator explains that, on hearing Satan's warning, "Awake, arise, or be forever fall'n,"

> They heard, and were abasht, and up they sprung
> Upon the wing, as when men wont to watch
> On duty, sleeping found by whom they dread,
> Rouse and bestir themselves ere well awake. (1.330–34)

Satan has again caught his victims unawares; the rebels scramble up, too startled and groggy to be alert to the unconscious irony of his call. They are also "abasht," meaning ashamed or embarrassed, which are social emotions that appear, on first reading, to result from having disappointed their great leader by their inaction. But having described how the prostrate and stunned fallen angels leap to their feet at Satan's voice and compared them to individuals for whom such sudden standing to attention would be natural, the narrator comments, "Yet to their Generals Voyce they soon obeyed" (1.337). The turn—the "yet"—suggests that an analogy that seems to be leading toward just such swift obedience may, in fact, have pointed toward a different outcome: toward repentance.

The shame the fallen angels feel at this moment may derive not only from being caught off-guard but also from having failed God. The narrator intensifies this potential alternative narrative by interpolating two lines between the simile and the fallen angels' rising:

> Nor did they not perceave the evil plight
> In which they were, or the fierce pains not feel. (1.335–36)

I have always found this moment a useful crux for discussion about the grammatical "rule" that "two negatives make a positive," for these lines clearly disprove that maxim. Hell is a wretched place: darkness, smoke, fire and brimstone, intense heat. But the angels' evil plight encompasses as well their alienation from God, their spiritual fallenness. As Fish writes, "they do perceive the fire, the pain, the gloom, but they are blind to the moral meaning of their situation, that is to their evil plight" (*Surprised* 99). This physical manifestation of their spiritual condition partially penetrates the fallen angels' consciousness and provokes another sort of abashedness: the fallen angels are ashamed and embarrassed to be found lying inert on the burning lake, but they may also be abashed, or "disconcerted," in a hopeful way. They are trying to understand how they have landed in such a situation and ashamed, not simply to have been caught there by Satan, but also to have gotten there through defying God. If they truly did perceive their evil plight, the fallen angels would repent of their rebellion and seek forgiveness. Through the physical environment that he has created for them, God provokes a cognitive dissonance, a state of disequilibrium that ought to push the fallen angels toward that repentance.

But Satan's ringing cry sets them all in motion toward further damnation, because moral discomfort seems easier to ignore than social shame. They arrive at the rendezvous "with looks / Down cast and damp" (1.522–23), a posture denoting not only dejection but also shame and embarrassment. No fallen angel wants to catch the eye of any other fallen angel, just as the fallen Adam and Eve become self-conscious, unable to look each other in the face and unwilling to be seen by God. But here are thousands of other rebels, equally guilty, equally embarrassed, a crowd within which to lose oneself, and a leader who seems "Not in despair" (2.525). The narrator reports universal relief among the host "to have found themselves not lost / In loss itself" (1.525–26).

Satan reinforces this momentum and relief with "high words" (1.528), martial music, and military display. These strategies provoke the rebel angels out of themselves as they take their places within their ranks and hierarchies, reclaiming the gratifying social roles to which they are accustomed. They are quick to reaffirm their membership in the group and, in doing so, their commitment to the group's decision to rebel, because that membership buffers them from the discomfort of self-assessment and the loneliness of moral growth.

In his rallying speech, Satan continues to offer the fallen angels a heroic vision of themselves and their rebellion as an alternative to any self-awareness that their current situation might foster. They are "Powers / Matchless, but with the Almighty" (1.622–23) and the battle in Heaven "not inglorious" (1.624). Their discomfiture was not only unforeseeable and unlikely, so remediable, but effected by deception and pettiness on God's part, for he "his strength conceal'd, / which tempted our attempt, and wrought our fall" (1.641–42). The rebel host need not feel embarrassed about their initial defeat; they are now better prepared to face this enemy who is, after all, the one really at fault.

In his study of catastrophic political decision-making, the social psychologist Irving Janis coined the term "groupthink" to describe a pattern of decision-making behaviors among groups in crisis, where the pressure for conformity "tends to override realistic appraisal of alternative courses of action" (Aronson 18). His list of the qualities characterizing such groups reads uncannily like a description of the fallen angels and their Council. Like the groups Janis studied, Satan and the fallen angels express "an illusion of invulnerability . . . which creates excessive optimism and encourages taking extreme risks," coupled with "an unquestioned belief in the group's inherent morality, inclining the members to ignore the ethical or moral consequences of their decisions." Both Satan's first speech to the general host and the Council debate demonstrate "collective efforts to rationalize in order to discount warnings or other information that might lead the members to reconsider their assumptions before they recommit themselves to their past policy decisions." They express "stereotyped views of enemy leaders as too evil to warrant genuine attempts to negotiate, or as too weak and stupid to counter whatever risky attempts are made to defeat their purposes" (Janis 174).

Janis found, coupled with this almost giddy hubris, strong "pressures toward uniformity," pressures that are clearly visible in the rebel host's response to Satan's initial proposal of rebellion. Their rejection of Abdiel exhibits the "direct pressure on any member who expresses strong arguments against any of the group's stereotypes, illusions, or commitments, making clear that this type of dissent is contrary to what is expected of all loyal members." Within the Council in Hell, the debaters practice a "self-censorship of deviations from the apparent group consensus, reflecting each member's inclination to minimize to himself the importance of his doubts and counterarguments," and demonstrate "a shared illusion of unanimity concerning judgments conforming to the majority view (partly resulting from self-censorship of deviations, augmented by the false assumption that silence means consent)." Finally Beelzebub's intervention at the end of the Council reveals "the emergence of self-appointed mindguards—members who protect the group from adverse information that might shatter their shared complacency about the effectiveness and morality of their decisions" (Janis 175).

Social pressures as much as strategic thinking determine the shape of the debate during the Council in Hell. Moloch opens his speech by sneering at the activity of debate itself: the leadership wastes time talking, while the rest of the fallen host, he claims, stands ready to resume the assault on Heaven without hesitation. He then emphasizes the ignominy of being stuck in Hell, a "dark opprobrious Den of shame" (2.58), and hints at his hearers' cowardice, for to them "perhaps / The way seems difficult" (2.70) that he and the lesser rebels outside the council chamber are itching to attempt. In responding to Moloch's speech, Belial must first flatter and fawn—and pretend enthusiasm for battle—before exposing the flaws in Moloch's plan to exact revenge through "open Warr." In fact, he attempts a kind of one-upmanship, insinuating that Moloch's eagerness for battle, and possible annihilation, is itself a form of cowardice:

> I laugh, when those who at the Spear are bold
> And vent'rous, if that fail them, shrink and fear
> What yet they know must follow. (2.204–06)

His reasons for voting to remain in Hell never admit to any physical fear of storming Heaven.

Belial's attempted intervention in this debate reveals that he is more aware than Moloch of both the literal and moral situation in which the rebel host finds itself. In light of experience, he accepts God's omnipotence and their own impotence before him (2.137–41), as well as God's omniscience:

> for what can force or guile
> With him, or who deceive his mind, whose eye
> Views all things at one view? (2.188–90)

He seems to recognize God's ontological difference from angels, a concession indicating that he has internalized some part of Abdiel's message. Belial even acknowledges the rebels' own responsibility for their predicament: actions have consequences, "nor [is] the Law unjust / That so ordains" (2.199–201). But he represents these consequences as "chosen," giving the fallen host a kind of negative power: "this was at first resolv'd / If we were wise, against so great a foe / Contending" (2.201–03). They anticipated such an outcome—at least the "wiser" ones did—and chose to risk it. He offers the rebel host a way to maintain its sense of its own integrity, while conveniently not requiring them to *do* anything at all. Accepting their defeat becomes, perversely, the means to enacting their agency.

As in Satan's case, intellectual dexterity does not make Belial "wise." The narrator comments that Belial "could make the worse appear / The better reason" (2.113–14). But toward the end of this speech, Belial introduces the possibility that the conflict between God and the rebel angels is not inevitable and insurmountable. He posits that "our Supream Foe in time may much remit / His anger" (2.210–11). He wonders whether changes in their behavior might not affect God's attitude: God may "not mind us not offending, satisfi'd / With what is punish't" (2.212–13). Although his description of the circumstances that might provoke such a change does not name repentance explicitly, his final proposal expresses an inclination toward it.

Mammon, certainly not the swiftest fallen angel, catches the hint and moves quickly to name and reject it. "Suppose he should relent / And publish grace to all" (2.237–38), Mammon asks his audience, only to emphasize the shamefulness and humiliation of an imagined return to Heaven, for "with what eyes could we / Stand in his presence humble [?]" (2.239–40). Unwilling to risk that social embarrassment,

Mammon will not imagine the possibility that God might accept repentance without exacting "new Subjection" (2.238–39) and imposing "strict laws" (2.241). Like Moloch, Mammon casts his proposal as the courageous and manly option, daring the others to prefer "the easie yoke / Of servile Pomp" to the "Hard Liberty" of Hell (2.256–57). His characterization signals to any fallen angel considering repentance that such an action would meet with the derision that Abdiel's earlier objections provoked. Who would dare suggest a return to "splendid vassalage" (2.252) or any other action that might lead toward such a goal?

In forwarding his proposal, each speaker exploits his understanding of his co-conspirators' insecurities and misgivings about their enterprise, even as he tries to conceal his own. In bringing the discussion back to Satan's initial plan, Beelzebub appeals to these anxieties without stating them explicitly; he also attempts to silence those misgivings, especially the ones that might lead the group toward a more careful appraisal of their evil plight and a more productive response to it.

Like Belial, Beelzebub has a fairly clear perception of reality: God "will Reign / Sole King, and of his Kingdom loose no part" (2.324–25). Covert action and self-serving "good behavior" are equally futile, "for what peace will be giv'n / To us enslav'd, but custody severe, / And stripes, and arbitrary punishment / Inflicted" (2.332–34). To counter Belial's concession that their suffering follows as the just consequence of their actions, Beelzebub hypothesizes about such torments or tasks as God may inflict upon them in the future; in doing so he implies that their current situation—being in Hell—is itself "an arbitrary punishment." Echoing Mammon and anticipating Satan's reasoning in his soliloquy in Eden, Beelzebub rejects the possibility of genuine good behavior: they cannot change their attitude toward God, because he will not change his attitude toward them. In doing so, he forestalls any possibility of imagining the divine response to genuine repentance.

Having dismissed the competing proposals, Beelzebub crafts his presentation of Satan's plan not only to appeal to his co-conspirators' desire to avoid a repeat of the battle in Heaven, but also to tap into their newly discovered social self-consciousness. His proposed mission to Earth receives instant approval: an "easier enterprize" against "punie inhabitants." But suddenly this easy enterprise becomes a solo journey fraught with peril and burdened with responsibility for the one who undertakes it. Beelzebub begins by asking, "whom shall we find / Sufficient" (2.403–04)—not "willing" or "capable," but merely "sufficient," as if in all the rebel host there may be no one even barely adequate to the task. In fact, he describes the journey in such a way as to insure that it is unimaginable: this angel must traverse "the palpable obscure" (2.406) and pass "the vast abrupt" (2.409). Here I must part company with critics who believe Milton has used adjectives as nouns: Beelzebub is using adjectives as adjectives so that his auditors will be unable to visualize the journey. Who would volunteer to find his way through an obscure? It is bad enough to imagine tempting "with wandering feet / The dark unbottom'd infinite Abyss" (2.405), which, although equally unvisualizable, at least bears some relationship to actual geographical features. This description is intentionally unnerving. It is meant to induce intellectual paralysis.

Beelzebub intensifies the anxiety he has provoked by posing three rhetorical questions that pile up on each other and seem to cancel out the possibility of success: "what strength, what art can then / Suffice, or what evasion bear him safe / Through the strict Sentries and Stations thick / Of angels watching round?" (2.410–13). Clearly strength will fail, and art be found inadequate; evasion seems the only hope. And to cap it off, there will be no further chances: "on whom we send / The weight of all and our last hope relies" (2.415–16). It is a "dreadful voyage" (2.426), filled with peril, but most dreadful of all is the prospect of being the one upon whom all depend, the most potent threat the final humiliation of failing the group. Beelzebub has hardly suggested that this mission might succeed.

As he and Satan have planned it, Beelzebub's speech leaves the fallen angels stunned and terrified. Again, the fallen angels look to others in the group to determine how to interpret the situation and how to respond. This time, "each / In others count'nance read his own dismay / Astonisht" (2.421–23). Satan soothes their pride even as he rises to solidify his claim, assuring them that "with reason hath deep silence and demurr / Seis'd us, though undismaid" (2.431–32); he suggests activities to fill their time while he is gone, projects that may be beneficial to the group, or even necessary: they are to "intermit no watch / Against a wakeful Foe" (2.462–63). But he understands the fragility of his triumph and the nature of group psychology, declaring "This enterprize / None shall partake with me" (2.465–66). As the narrator comments, now that Satan has volunteered, "Others among the chief might offer now / (Certain to be refus'd) . . . / And so refus'd might in opinion stand / His Rivals" (2.469–72). Everything now depends upon public opinion, upon rhetorical skill, upon managing and performing before the group.

The rebel angels have managed to convince themselves that their situation is both irreversible and chosen, and they work hard to maintain that belief. After Satan departs, one group composes songs that celebrate their epic exploits and "complain that Fate / Free Vertue should enthrall to Force or Chance" (2.550–51). In a footnote to the Riverside edition of Milton's works, Roy Flannagan writes, "the fallen angels are attempting to celebrate what is philosophically impossible for them: the freedom of the will" (397). But the story that Milton has told insists that the angels retain responsibility for their choices, and with that responsibility the power to choose differently from the way that they have chosen and continue to choose. These songs of nostalgia for the heroism of battle, rather than for the loss of Heaven, focus the group's emotional energy in a safe direction—toward worldly sorrow, toward blaming some force other than themselves.

The members of a second group cultivate intellectual detachment as their means to evade responsibility for what has happened to them. Their conversation ranges over

> Providence, Foreknowledge, Will and Fate,
> Fixt Fate, free will, foreknowledg absolute,
> And found no end, in wandring mazes lost. (2.558–61)

As Perry writes of adolescent development, "the capacity to think about thought offers a position of detachment which can be exploited, as the sophists learned to exploit it, to evade responsibility" (119). These fallen angels use philosophy as a means to avoid any emotional investment in their conversation. These angels are not true philosophers: they practice inquiry and debate not as a means to the end of wisdom but as ends in themselves. Milton's contemporaries would call their determinations *"notional"* rather than *"experimental"* knowledge, the intellectual, or worldly, sorrow that leads to death, rather than the heartfelt, godly sorrow that leads to repentance.

Significantly, among the topics debated at this infernal philosophical institute are "glory and shame" (2.564). The fallen angels who are not singing and debating use glory to distract themselves from the external discomforts of Hell and the internal discomforts of a guilty conscience. They exercise themselves in feats of arms or set out "On bold adventure" (2.571). All of these activities are designed, the narrator tells us, to provide "Truce to [their] restless thought[s]" (2.526). The fallen angels are more like Adam than like Eve: although they are fed disinformation as Eve was (the Son's proposed progress in their case, the effect of the fruit in hers), they clearly understand what choice they are making, and understand that choice repeatedly: in choosing to rebel, in fighting the war, in continuing to follow Satan once in Hell. They no longer believe—or no longer are willing to risk believing—that God can forgive them or that they could survive being forgiven. It would be too humiliating. The values of "glory and shame" are antithetical to moral growth, as they focus the individual toward the approval of the community rather than inward on self-appraisal and self-knowledge. As long as the fallen angels avoid a frank appraisal of their "evil plight," as long as they frame their responses to their situation in terms of how possible actions might appear to others, they will choose to continue on their course of rebellion. "Self-tempted, self-deprav'd" (3.130), they will endlessly enthrall themselves.

# CHAPTER 4

# GOOD ANGELS, GRATITUDE, AND GROWING IN COMMUNION

I

*For ye yourselves are taught of God to love one another.*

—*1 Thessalonians 4:9*

If a person were to approach *Paradise Lost* using the metaphor of God as king, she might reasonably suppose that Milton has included most of the good angels for comic relief. A king expects obedience from his subjects expressed in action and success; God sets tasks for the good angels, and they fail. They appear on the surface to be extraordinarily incompetent: Uriel gives Satan directions to Earth; Gabriel and the angelic guard twice fail to keep him out of Eden; Abdiel cannot out-argue him in Heaven, nor can Raphael provide instruction compelling enough to inoculate Adam and Eve against his seduction. Their failures do not even "advance" the plot: for example, Satan already has traversed most of the ground between Hell and Eden before he approaches Uriel; he is in the correct solar system; if Uriel had not been there to ask, Satan needed only to investigate the available planets in order to find the one he seeks. Uriel might have recognized and tried to stop Satan, but, as the subsequent intervention of Uriel, Gabriel, and the angelic guard demonstrates, such an action might have delayed but would not have prevented Satan from getting at the human pair. The "story" of angelic obedience appears to be that "they also perform the duties of a servant who only remain erect on their feet in a specified place" (Barton 109). By focusing on the good angels as young adults in relation to a divine parent, however, we can read their story as one of challenge, response, and growth.

From a human perspective, the good angels in the poem exist to guide and protect Adam and Eve, just as the good angels after the fall exist to intervene on behalf of humanity. This perspective is not incorrect, only partial. As Nardo explains, the good angels learn discursively about God's plans for humankind: the poem "records their continued growth in understanding God's ways with humankind as well as their own angelic role in the history of salvation" ("Education" 194). Her discussion focuses mainly on what the angels learn intellectually, but she also points out that the good angels "enter the drama" (194) at God's command, fighting the rebel angels, guarding Eden, instructing Adam and Eve: "the more the angels learn about man and woman—their vulnerability, mutual love, and sorrows—the better they will be able to teach God's ways with compassion, love, and respect" (193). I would like to extend her discussion by arguing that such empathy and compassion cannot be taught discursively or *notionally*; in order to feel such empathy and to respond compassionately, the angels must first experience love, respect, and vulnerability themselves. Through the interaction of angel with angel, Milton dramatizes their moral growth.

Compared with other Renaissance retellings of the Fall, *Paradise Lost* devotes a disproportionate amount of space to describing life in Eden: Adam and Eve eat, serve God through their gardening, make love, converse with each other and with an angel, give a dinner party, learn about Earth and about Heaven, praise God and interact with him. Milton seems determined to create for them a life that resembles contemporary human lives as closely as its prelapsarian happiness will allow, a life that is engaging, vibrant, challenging, and complex, with an interesting past and the prospect of a stimulating future into which they will grow. Adam and Eve anticipate becoming parents; Raphael suggests a way that they may partake of more frequent meals with angels and "find / No inconvenient Diet" (5.494–95). He outlines a future in which they may in fact not only host the angels but also visit them in Heaven:

> Your bodies may at last turn all to Spirit
> Improv'd by tract of time, and winged ascend
> Ethereal, as wee, or may at choice
> Here or in Heav'nly Paradises dwell. (5.498–500)

This passage suggests that, as far as Raphael is concerned, humans and angels are not significantly different creatures and do not live significantly different kinds of lives: although the angels can already experience God through beatific vision, and, as I have conceded before, they can fly and change shape, in this conversation Raphael imagines a future in which humans may be able to do those things as well. Like Adam and Eve, the good angels eat, serve God, converse with each other and with humans, experience intense emotional intimacy, learn about Earth and about Heaven, praise God and interact with him. They also dance and sing together and practice martial arts, both for exercise and in earnest.

Milton represents the good angels as individuals with names, activities, and inner lives because they are, like humans and like the fallen angels, "sufficient to have stood, though free to fall" (3.99). As Nardo argues, "this heretical and eccentric doctrine of angelic freedom gives Milton's good angels the potential for conflict, failure, and growth" ("Education" 193). Because this angelic activity is completely biblically extra-textual, the "story" of the good angels allows Milton an artistic freedom unavailable to him in recounting the story of Adam's and Eve's fall: he is not hedged in by the events in a received text, but can spin plot and imagine interactions completely as it suits him. In telling their stories, Milton can present readers with counterexamples to those of his main story lines: Adam and Eve, Satan, and the rebel angels are supposed to be sufficient, yet they fail. With the good angels Milton is able to represent sufficient creatures who are successful in demonstrating "true allegiance, constant Faith or Love" (3.104). Just as he fully develops Adam and Eve's prelapsarian life in Eden so that his regenerate readers may learn from their example how to conduct their godly lives, Milton fully develops the lives of the good angels so that readers can learn from them what exactly it takes to be "sufficient."

Paradoxically, "sufficiency" requires accepting one's place in a web of relationships; it requires that one accept that he is not "self-sufficient." As I have argued, God offers his creatures—angel and human—responsibilities that encourage growth, rather than tasks that require successful completion. He presents those responsibilities in ways that encourage imaginative engagement and then rewards that engagement. He expects both the angels and humans to fulfill those tasks because they recognize that he loves them and has their best interests at heart. That "best interest" involves not only their perseverance in his good graces but their moral development: for the good angels, as for humans, growth occurs within relationships. The good angels in *Paradise Lost* fulfill the commandment "that ye love one another as I have loved you" (John 15.12). As Raphael explains to Adam, "freely we serve because we freely love" (5.538–39).

The story of the good angels reveals that this love naturally extends from loving God to loving his Creation and his creatures.

Angels are, as I have discussed in the introduction and demonstrated in the chapter about the rebel angels, intensely social creatures. Milton never represents a good angel as being alone unless that angel has been charged by God to fulfill a specific task: Uriel standing on the Sun to guard Eden, Raphael visiting Adam and Eve, Michael instructing Adam. For the most part, the good angels appear in the poem as a heavenly host: as God draws attention to Satan's escape from Hell, "about him all the Sanctities of Heaven / Stood thick as Starrs" (3.60–61); when God approves the Son's offer of sacrifice and promises his future exaltation, the host responds with "a shout / Loud as from numbers without number" (3.345–46). At the summons to witness the elevation of the Son, Raphael reports that the crowd appeared "innumerable" (5.585), with "ten thousand thousand Ensignes high advanc'd" (5.87), surrounding the Father "in Orbes / Of circuit inexpressible . . . / Orb within orb" (5.596–98). When the Son goes forth to create Earth, he is attended by a crowd that is enthusiastic and "numberless" (7.197). He returns "followd with acclamation and the sound / Symphonious of ten thousand Harpes" (7.558–59). To Nardo's rhetorical question, "could a hymning angel among the heavenly host ever feel alone?" ("Education" 203), I must answer, of course not, because he would not *be* alone.

"Singing their great Creator" is not a solitary task for angels, or for the prelapsarian Adam and Eve; they all join their voices to a cosmic choir. Milton frequently associates angelic music with complex harmony; Raphael reports that the ten thousand Harps responding to Creation created a symphony that "tun'd / angelic harmonies" (7.559–60); at the exaltation of the Son, the angels also produce another "charming symphonie . . . , / No voice exempt, no voice but well could joine / Melodious part, such concord is in Heaven" (3.368–71). It is true that Adam reports hearing "Celestial voices to the midnight air, / Sole or responsive each to other's note" (4.682–83), but he explains that this occurs "while they keep watch, or nightly rounding walk" (4.685). As Fish points out in *How Milton Works* (*HMW*), "the song is always *corporately* sung even when the singer is apparently single" (285). It does not follow, however, that this corporate celebration is "sung *to* no one" simply because "there isn't anyone not already singing it" (*HMW* 285): anyone who has sung in a large choir can understand the intense joy of singing and listening simultaneously. The occasional solo voice offers its praise while pursuing some responsibility that requires temporary isolation, fully aware of its participation in the larger choir.

As Matthew Jordan points out, in *Paradise Lost*, "the act of soliloquizing is often apprehended primarily as an experience of exclusion from one's surroundings. This exclusion, the burden of an interiority produced by the consciousness of a radical difference between the self and what is exterior, is one of Satan's constant themes" (Jordan 122). For the good angels, as for the unfallen Adam and Eve, one's surroundings manifest God's goodness and love and thereby embody a sense of inclusion; their song and praise are a natural response to and a vocalization of their feeling of belonging and community. Satan soliloquizes repeatedly; Adam and Eve each soliloquize at the moment of sin and after. But unfallen creatures praise God together, in the spoken praise of Adam and Eve's mutual spontaneous prayers before bed and upon rising and in the musical praise of the angelic host's mutual spontaneous song, or they converse with one another about their happiness, gratitude, and joy at God's creation. Jordan asserts that for Adam and Eve in Eden praise and work are "for the most part an activity of self-fulfilment keeping with and completing the rest of creation" (135). Praise and work contribute primarily to the self-fulfillment of the good angels as well.

In her discussion of ethical development, Nell Noddings argues that "the celebration of everyday life contributes to the maintenance of the ethical ideal" because such celebration "requires and is likely to enhance receptivity" (126). The good angels celebrate their lives continuously, expressing through their song and dance, through their readiness to fulfill God's commands, through their concern that others do so as well, their gratitude for God's love and care. Through Satan, Milton expresses his understanding "that a grateful mind / By owing owes not, but still pays, at once / Indebted and dischargd" (4.55–57), that gratitude is the natural and healthy response to goodness and love. Psychologists are just catching up with him. Recent studies by Robert Emmons and Michael McCullough define gratitude as "an attribution-dependent emotion that results from attributing one's favorable circumstances to the actions or effort of another person" (McCullough et al., "Affect?" 251). It "typically results from and stimulates moral behavior, that is, behavior that is motivated out of concern for another person" (251). Grateful individuals are empathic and so "more likely to attempt to render aid" to persons in distress and "more willing to forgive individuals who have committed transgressions against them" (252). An individual with a "grateful disposition" exhibits "a generalized tendency to recognize and respond with grateful emotions to the roles of other people's benevolence in the positive experiences and outcomes that one obtains" (McCullough et al., "Grateful" 112). Far from diminishing a person's sense of self, "seeing oneself as the beneficiary of other people's generosity may lead one to feel affirmed, esteemed, and valued" ("Grateful" 113–14). Gratitude is, then, "a form of love, a consequence of an already formed attachment as well as a precipitating condition for the formation of new affectional bonds" (Emmons and McCullough 388). In order to achieve moral adulthood, to undertake the "sustained responsibility for the welfare of another" (Fowler 82), an individual begins by recognizing and appreciating the responsibility of another for herself. Angelic gratitude contributes to their growth as moral beings.

The good angels express gratefulness themselves and encourage others in their worship and understanding of God. Their witness to God's love, goodness, magnificence, and creative power issues most frequently in song. On earth, as Adam attests, that harmony "lift[s] our thoughts to Heaven" (4.688); in Heaven, it serves to unite their community in even closer bonds of love. But the good angels also interact with others discursively, encouraging conversation that leads to recognition of one's blessings and appreciation of the Creator, reproving conversations that tend toward ingratitude. To share one's experience of God's goodness and blessings—to encourage a grateful mind—is itself to confer a blessing on another. Milton's contemporaries would call these activities "witnessing"; social psychologists would point out that such expressions of gratitude stimulate a sense of self-worth and the disposition to act with love and concern for others, both in the benefactor and in the beneficiary.

## II

*But speaking the truth in love, may grow up into him in all things.*

—*Ephesians 4:15*

From his vantage point on the Sun, Uriel is well-positioned to appreciate God's creative power. He "saw when at his Word the formless Mass, / This world's material mould, came to a heap" (3.708–09); he appears to spend the time he has alone—a rare experience for an angel—in earnest contemplation both of the Creation before him and of the agency through which he watched it come about. Having experienced himself the awe that accompanies witnessing God's creativity and beneficence, Uriel responds enthusiastically to the stripling cherub's apparent zeal in seeking out first-hand knowledge himself: here is an angel, a young one at that, who has undertaken a long journey "To witness with thine eyes what some perhaps / Contented with report hear onely in heav'n" (3.700–01). While conceding that "Uriel's joy and wonder at the creation are proper angelic work," Nardo criticizes him for a "rapt attention to God's overflowing goodness [that] renders him blind to evil" and leads him to "discourse[] at length on the wonder and delight of God's work of creation" ("Education," 198–99). Her discussion of this episode suggests that Uriel not only errs, innocently, in failing to discern hypocrisy, but that he errs in allowing witnessing to God's creative goodness to distract him from more important work.

But in the economy of *Paradise Lost* Uriel's decision to respond fully to this solitary cherub's request is important work, just as Raphael's thoughtful response to Adam's questions is important work and Adam's loving response to Eve's questions is important work. In responding with attention and care to one of God's creatures, Uriel fulfills the command to love one another. Uriel is an arch-angel, "one of the seav'n / Who in God's presence, nearest to his Throne / Stand ready to command" (3.648–50); clearly adolescent angels are not his usual associates in undertaking God's behests. Satan approaches Uriel as a "stripling Cherube . . . / Not of the prime, yet such as in his face / Youth smil'd Celestial" (3.636–38). The cherub demonstrates an unusual and commendable investment in worship: he expresses "Unspeakable desire to see, and know / All these his wondrous works" (3.662–63). That understanding, especially in light of the recent rebellion, merits reinforcement. He also understands that God's beneficence to one embodies his beneficent care for all: he desires to behold the one

> On whom the great Creator has bestowd
> Worlds, and on him hath all these graces powrd;
> That both in him and all things, as is meet,
> The Universal Maker we may praise. (3.673–76)

Here Satan ironically expresses the true economy of divine goodness: that all creatures benefit from generosity extended toward any one creature.

In accepting his responsibility toward this less-experienced angel, Uriel demonstrates his moral maturity: to fulfill God's will, individuals should promote gratitude and love for God's creation in others.

Uriel shares his own experience of God's glory, praising and encouraging what he mistakenly assumes is similar enthusiasm in another of God's creatures. But Uriel not only affirms the cherub's desire to witness God's creative goodness first hand; he also asserts, in a rather torturous manner, that his investment of time, energy, and emotion are praiseworthy:

> thy desire which tends to know
> The works of God thereby to glorifie
> The great Work-Maister, leads to no excess
> That reaches blame, but rather merits praise
> The more it seems excess. (3.694–98)

What might make Uriel imagine that this cherub fears that his behavior is "excessive" and so requires reassurance? First, the cherub is alone, a fact that the "cherub" himself addresses in his opening remarks: his desire to worship "Hath brought me from the Quires of Cherubim / Alone thus wandring" (3.666–67). Satan may raise this point because he knows that solitude is not a normative angelic condition, or he may feel he needs to explain the presence of a mere adolescent out among the new creation, where God appears to send only his more mature angels. No matter what Satan's motives are, Uriel picks up on this detail, acknowledging the intensity of an emotion "that led thee hither / From thy Empyrean Mansion thus alone" (3.698–99) and involved the sacrifice not of time and energy only, but of companionship. He even praises the cherub in a manner that seems to work at the expense of those angels who "Contented with report hear onely in heav'n" (3.701) what the cherub has journeyed "To witness with thine eyes" (3.700).

Just as Adam and Eve's conversations in Book 4 stand in for their interaction throughout their prelapsarian lives, this encounter represents all angelic catechetical encounters. In offering reassurance and instruction, Uriel participates in a pattern of educational activity within the poem in which an individual in a higher social position praises an individual in his care for seeking information about God through his creation. When Adam asks Raphael his question about how the solar system works, Raphael validates his desire to learn more about God's ways:

> To ask or search I blame thee not, for Heav'n
> Is as the Book of God before thee set

To read his wondrous Works, and learne
His Seasons, Hours, or Dayes." (8.66–69)

But he then reframes Adam's inquiry in a way that will produce a more appropriate affect: God's secrets are not "to be scann'd by them who ought / Rather admire" (8.74–75). Uriel, too, seems to find some points of concern in this cherub's otherwise praiseworthy motives. Adam opens his question to Raphael by explaining that "reasoning [he] oft admire[s]" (8.25), in a critical sense, the apparent profligacy of God's creative energy. Adam appears to have been considering some tweaking of celestial organization toward greater efficiency. Like Adam, this cherub seems to imagine that he can "comprehend" God and his ways through study; his enthusiasm might be considered, as Uriel acknowledges, "excessive." Uriel corrects his charge by asserting that "wonderful are *all* his works, / Pleasant to know, and worthiest to be *all* / Had in remembrance alwayes with delight" (3.702–05; italics mine). Perhaps the angels who remain in Heaven are not slackers, after all. They are learning about God's goodness in their appropriate place.

Uriel reinforces this idea by witnessing to his own experience, an experience at once of wonder and of astonishment:

> But what created mind can comprehend
> Thir number, or the wisdom infinite
> That brought them forth, but hid thir causes deep. (3.705–07)

He saw, he marveled, he witnessed God's power as "order from disorder sprung" (3.713) at his mere word, but what does he understand of God, after all? No more than he has always known: that God wants the best for his creatures and provides for them abundantly. What new thing does this cherub, traveling all this way, imagine that he will "learn"? It is a small point, and the cherub apparently a toward pupil; his desire to see and know, to experience first-hand, God's generosity toward individuals wholly unconnected to himself may be unusual for one his age but will not go unpraised. Uriel affirms the cherub's enthusiasm and directs him toward an appropriate object of study.

Significantly, although Uriel dismisses the cherub, he does not dismiss him from his attention. He only realizes that the stripling cherub is not what he seemed because his "eye pursu'd him down / The way he went" (4.125–26). The narrative is not explicit about why he continues to monitor the cherub's actions; in fact, Uriel had sent the younger angel along with the assurance that "thy way thou canst not miss" (3.735) and the implication that his own attention was required elsewhere. In some sense, noticing the movements of the traveling cherub is part of his responsibility as God's eyes keeping watch over the new creation, but it seems equally likely that he observed his progress out of interest and affection, as one watches the progress of any young person who has been, however briefly, under one's tutelage. As Noddings argues, "to teach involves a giving of self and a receiving of other" (113). The investment of self that comes from engaging in the instruction of another issues in genuine care.

It is because of his continued interest in the progress, both physical and spiritual, of this younger angel, that Uriel is in a position to recognize his mistake. Once apprised of it, he acts swiftly to atone for his error. Because the good angels are motivated by love for God and for his creation, they are willing to take responsibility for their failures and to risk embarrassment in order to do what's right—in this case, to protect Adam and Eve from danger. Being loving and understanding themselves, they trust others to be loving and understanding toward them. Uriel not only informs Gabriel that he recognized "one of the banisht crew" (4.573) because of "his looks / Alien from Heav'n, with passions foul obscur'd" (4.570–71), but that he had conversed with this spirit and been duped: "a Spirit, zealous, as he seem'd, to know / More of th'Almighties works" (4.565–66). In this instance, Uriel's trust is not misplaced: Gabriel does not criticize Uriel's naiveté, but promises immediate action with a comparable humility: expressing his certainty that no one could have gotten past his guard, he nevertheless declares that his troops will search the Garden. Like Abdiel among the rebel troops, these angels value loyalty and service to God above saving face: they are willing to admit to one another the possibility that they have been wrong.

As they make and learn from their mistakes, the good angels grow as moral adults. Uriel belatedly recognizes Satan for what he is, but not before Satan has slipped past him. Gabriel's troops will find and evict him, but not before he has inflicted what he mistakenly believes to be spiritual damage on Eve; they will also fail to prevent his next incursion. But the loyal angels are not judged for their failures; they are praised for their effort and for their perseverance. They persevere and prosper because they believe that God has their best interests at heart. As is the case with the gardening Adam and Eve do, the work God assigns the good angels exists to benefit those doing the labor, not because God "needs" their service. As Nardo has argued, the "commission of guardianship . . . serves the angels themselves, not their charges; it is the gift of an opportunity to serve and learn" ("Education," 197). The mistakes they make, recognize, and correct provide those "gripping, holistic experiences" (Dreyfus and Dreyfus 242) of near failure that reinforce physiologically the danger of the wrong choice and the success of the right one. In the Dreyfuses' words, "the ability to remember with involvement the original situation while emotionally experiencing one's success or failure is required if one is to learn to be an ethical expert" (246). Ethical expertise develops through emotional engagement, not intellectual exercise, because moral behavior has at its root an emotion—love for one's fellow creatures—that finds its expression in care. Expert moral behavior is embodied in "an immediate intuitive response to each situation" (243).

Abdiel's behavior during the rebellion demonstrates just such an immediate intuitive response. When Abdiel stands up against the rebel host in Heaven, Raphael claims that he does so out of "zeal." Clearly Abdiel feels zeal for God: he is the one "then whom none with more zeale ador'd / The Deitie, and divine commands obei'd" (5.805–06). But Abdiel's initial speech is prompted as much out of zeal toward Satan and concern for the rebel host as it is out of love for God and outrage at Satan's blasphemy. Abdiel is astonished, but also hurt that Satan has uttered such words, "words which no eare ever to hear in Heav'n / Expected, least of all from thee" (5.810–11). Abdiel is a lowly seraph; Satan is his superior, his commander, the kind of angel, as I have said, that one looks up to, admires, and takes as a model: how could such an angel speak such thoughts? The urgency of Abdiel's rebuttal indicates his investment not only in expressing his loyalty to God, but also in persuading his fellow angels to see the truth, for these are Abdiel's *fellow angels*, his comrades. Scant hours ago, he and these same angels, Satan included, participated in the celebration following the Son's elevation, singing and dancing in "mazes intricate" (5.622), producing complex harmonies, "and in communion sweet / Quaff[ing] immortalitie and joy" (5.637–38). He is not here among strangers, but among those angels with whom God has grouped him in the heavenly hierarchy, the closest thing that any angel has to a family.

Significantly, as he reasons with Satan, Abdiel returns constantly to the theme of gratitude. Satan's unexpected blasphemy is particularly striking coming "from thee, *ingrate* / In place thy self so high above thy Peeres" (5.811–12; italics mine). Abdiel, who is not nearly so highly favored, has been "by experience taught [ ] how good, / And of our good, and of our dignitie / How provident [God] is" (6.826–28). How can Satan, upon whom so much more beneficence has been showered, not see that goodness? God has never acted and is not acting in a way that would "make us less" (5.829). The elevation of the Son promises to intensify their happiness, "to exalt / Our happie state under one Head more neer / United" (5.829–31), a heightening of communion that Abdiel considers a blessing. Far from provoking envy and rebellion, this action should prompt increased gratitude and joy.

Abdiel attempts to encourage gratitude in Satan by reminding him that God "made / Thee what thou art, and formd the Pow'rs of Heav'n / Such as he pleasd, and circumscrib'd thir being" (5.823–25). Although he concedes that it might be unjust should "equal over equals Monarch Reigne" (5.832), the Son is not Satan's "equal," or, more properly, Satan is not the Son's. Although it is God who has created the angels "in thir bright degrees, / Crownd them with Glory, and to thir Glory nam'd / Thrones, Dominations, Princedoms, Vertues, Powers" (5.838–40), he created them through the Son: the angels should feel gratitude toward the Son as well as toward the Father, especially now that the Son, their benefactor, has "reduc't" (5.843) himself to join more intimately with the angelic host. In the economy of gratitude, "all honour to him done / Returns our own" (5.844–45). Abdiel might easily have asked, as Satan will on Mount Niphates, "what could be less then to afford him praise, / The easiest recompense, and pay him thanks [?]" (4.46–47); surely Satan's soliloquy indicates that he has heard Abdiel's instruction, although he continuously resists accepting it. As he closes his speech, Abdiel advises Satan to "cease then this impious rage / And tempt not these" (5.845–46). In his experience, God is forgiving as well as generous: "Pardon may be found in time besought" (5.848). Satan and the angels with him should heed his counsel.

Abdiel's perseverance is impressive not only because he resists peer pressure, standing up to Satan, his superior and commander, and to an "infinite host" (5.874), but also because he extracts himself from what has been his community: he is not standing up against "enemies" but against his closest companions, his friends, his family. It is hard not to think of the rebel host as Abdiel's "enemies." Certainly the narrator encourages us to do so: Abdiel is "encompass'd round with foes" (5.876); he is "faithful found, / Among the faithless, faithful only hee" (5.896–97). As he leaves, he passes "long way through hostile scorn" (5.904). But these enemies are only newly enemies, and the painfulness of their scorn and abuse is intensified, coming from those whom Abdiel loves and from whom he expects love. By extricating himself from this conspiracy, Abdiel demonstrates that he understands that individual relationships exist within a larger context of relationship: his love for his fellow angels exists within the framework of his love for God, his creator, who expects his creatures to demonstrate their love for him through their loving concern for their fellow creatures. Abdiel can only demonstrate his true love and concern for his fellow angels by acting upon his understanding of what is right, rather than by assenting to what they want. In order to do that, he must abandon them to their choice.

But Abdiel has not abandoned them without a fight. When Abdiel returns to the center of Heaven, he receives a hero's welcome, both from the rest of the loyal angels and from God himself. He merits this recognition not because he has resisted rebellion himself, but because he "hath maintaind / Against revolted multitudes, the Cause of Truth" (6.30–32). He easily could have snuck quietly out of the crowd of conspirators once he realized what his fellow angels were plotting. Instead he speaks up for what he believes to be right. But what has possessed him to do so? Who benefits from this defense? Not God, whose understanding of his own righteousness has not been shaken by Satan's defiance; not the loyal angels, who are not there to hear. The potential beneficiaries of Abdiel's testimony are the rebel angels themselves. According to the *OED*, which uses this moment in *Paradise Lost* to illustrate definition number five, a testimony is an "open attestation or acknowledgement; confession, profession. Obs. or arch. except in Evangelical circles." It can also mean, as a qualification of this usage, "an expression or declaration of disapproval or condemnation of error; a protestation." In giving his "Testimonie of Truth" to the rebel angels, Abdiel both confesses his faith and condemns their error. It is for his willingness to suffer "universal reproach" (6.34) in order to speak the truth to his fellow angels that Abdiel receives praise. He demonstrates his love and concern for Satan and for the rebel host by risking, and bearing, their "hostile scorn" and "reproach."

Although in subsequent encounters with the rebel angels Abdiel and the other loyal angels are stern and judgmental, they also express concern and remorse. During the War in Heaven, Michael expresses outrage not only that Satan has created "evil, unknown till thy revolt, / Unnam'd in Heav'n" (6.262–63), but also that he has "brought / Miserie, uncreated till the crime / Of thy Rebellion" (6.267–68) and "instill'd / Thy malice into thousands, once upright / And faithful, now prov'd false" (6.269–71). Since, through their loyalty and perseverance, neither Michael nor the good angels can experience misery, his anger at Satan's having produced it must derive from his compassion toward the rebel angels, the only fallen creatures at this point, the only creatures subject to pain and suffering. Gabriel mostly expresses disdain and scorn when he confronts Satan in the Garden, but he also attempts to bring him to his senses, not only calling attention to his contradictions and lies, but also calling into question Satan's "moral code":

> O sacred name of faithfulness profan'd!
> Faithful to whom? to thy rebellious crew?
> Armie of Fiends, fit body to fit head;
> Was this your discipline and faith ingag'd,
> Your military obedience, to dissolve
> Allegeance to th' acknowledg'd Power supream? (4.951–56)

When asked by Adam to explain about the angels who forgot "to love / Our maker, and obey him" (5.550–51), Raphael indicates that his anxiety about the task derives in part from personal anguish: how, he asks rhetorically, can he relate "without remorse / The ruin of so many glorious once / And perfet while they stood" (5.566–68). The good angels may persevere in their loyalty and stand up against God's enemies, but they do not take pleasure in their superiority or in the fallen angels' sufferings.

In the midst of her discussion about Raphael's interaction with Adam, Nardo argues that "to carry out their future tasks of guarding and guiding humankind, angels must feel love and pity for their charges" ("Education" 202). She develops persuasively the interactions between Raphael and Adam that lead the sociable spirit to appreciate the human being. But the angelic guard has far less interaction with Adam and Eve, who express some awareness that these beings exist, but only because they hear "Cherubic Songs by night from neighbouring Hills" (5.547). That the angelic guard do develop such feelings the narrator attests as he describes their departure after the Fall:

> Up into Heav'n from Paradise in haste
> Th' Angelic Guards ascended, mute and sad
> For Man, for of his state by this they knew. (10.17–19)

These angels learn to care about Adam and Eve because they have, in Fowler's words, been given "sustained responsibility for the welfare of another" (82). But even the loyal angels who have not ventured to Earth express this loving concern:

> Soon as th' unwelcome news
> From Earth arriv'd at Heaven Gate, displeas'd
> All were who heard, dim sadness did not spare
> That time Celestial visages, yet mixt
> With *pitie*, violated not thir bliss. (10.21–25; italics mine)

What affection, understanding, and compassion these loyal angels feel toward the human pair must develop in part out of their experiencing affection, understanding, and love for one another, sorrowing over the loss of the rebel angels and commiserating with the angelic guard over their sense of failure. The other person from whom they have learned about love—about compassion for vulnerability, about mercy—is, of course, the Son.

# CHAPTER 5

# THE EDUCATION OF THE SON

## I

*Thou art my beloved Son, in whom I am well pleased.*

—*Mark 1:11*

Milton first introduces the Son in the narrative of the poem at the moment of his most heroic and morally mature action: when he is confronted with what will happen to humanity, he objects, discovers his Father's alternate plan, and offers himself as the one to fulfill it. At the close of that scene, the Father declares that the Son is

> By Merit more then Birthright Son of God,
> Found worthiest to be so by being Good,
> Farr more then Great or High; because in thee
> Love hath abounded more then Glory abounds. (3.309–12)

This statement invites readers to ask, why is the Son "the Son"?

As dramatized in the poem, God the Father and God the Son are separate individuals, even though the Son acts in Creation as the agent for the Father.[1] As the effectual might of the Father, the Son creates "all things, . . . and all the Spirits of Heav'n" (5.837; see also 3.390–91), orders, and names them (5.838–40). He is "begotten" as Messiah, an event that provokes Satan's rebellion. On the Father's behalf, the Son then casts the rebel angels out of Heaven, creates the Earth and all things in it, including Adam, takes Adam to Eden, and explains to him his role and responsibilities. He watches Adam name the animals, converses with him about needing a partner, creates Eve, and returns to Heaven. Shortly after his return, he learns that Satan is on the loose, intends to corrupt humans, and will succeed. At this point, he certainly has experienced ethical engagement: he has decided, in Noddings's terms, to become "one-caring" and, in Fowler's, to undertake "sustained responsibility for the welfare of others" (Noddings 24; Fowler 82). He empathizes with soon-to-be-fallen humanity and acts courageously and spontaneously on their behalf, first by challenging his Father's apparent plan and then by fulfilling the actual one. In this act, he becomes the perfect embodiment of moral maturity: love incarnate. Since God knows the future, he foreknows how the Son will behave in each circumstance and so anticipates that behavior with recognition and reward: in other words, the Son *is* Son by merit more than by birthright; he has earned the role to which he appears to have been born.

Even the first chronological glimpse of the Son, "in bliss imbosom'd" (Book 5:597) at his "begetting," complicates the nature of his Sonship. The Father's speech mixes language of begetting, acknowledging, naming, and ceremonial elevation in a tight passage that echoes the second Psalm:

> This day I have begot whom I declare
> My onely Son, and on this holy Hill
> Him have anointed, whom ye now behold
> At my right hand; your Head I him appoint. (3.603–06)

The Son is begotten, declared "onely Son," anointed, and appointed. In his discussion of Psalm 2, Luxon places the word 'begotten' in the context of ancient Yahwist theology: "the generally accepted interpretation of this verse understands the king as reporting the Lord God's metaphorical use of the word "begotten" to imply his adoption as a son of God, and thus as a legitimate King of Israel" (*Literal Figures* 68). Surrounded by a pagan population that believes their kings to be divine offspring in a literal sense, the Hebrew poet blends the language of generation with the language of adoption in the ceremonial anointing of the Hebrew king and thereby "finesses the crucial distinction between a king who is a son of God by decree and a king who is son of God more literally" (68).

This complicated relationship between generation and adoption characterizes Judaism from the beginning, when Abraham, called out of Ur to become the father of a great nation but long childless becomes the father of Ishmael by Hagar only to discover himself the father of Isaac by Sarah. Ishmael, although a biological child, is cast out; Isaac, also a biological child, is accepted. Treating this story in Galatians, Paul distinguishes between children "after the flesh" and children "by promise" (Gal. 4:22–31), and he has strong scriptural justification for doing so: in Genesis, God charges Abraham to circumcise every male child entering his household, regardless of biological origin: "he that is born in the house, or bought with money of any stranger, which is not of thy seed" (Gen. 17:12). Through the ritual of circumcision Abraham and his heirs will adopt male children into the religious family. Oddly, although the thirteen-year-old Ishmael is circumcised, he is specifically excluded in the promise: "And as for Ishmael, I have heard thee: Behold, I have blessed him, and will make him fruitful, and will multiply him exceedingly; twelve princes shall he beget, and I will make him a great nation. But my covenant will I establish with Isaac" (Gen. 17:20–21). Ishmael has been born not simply to the wrong mother but too soon. As Martin Luther explains, "The difference, Paul says, is not that one mother was a free woman and the other a slave—although this does contribute to the allegory—but that Ishmael, who was born of the slave, was born according to the flesh, that is, apart from the promise and the Word of God, while Isaac was *not only* born of the free woman *but also* in accordance with a promise" (Luther 26:434; italics mine).

Milton seems, in writing the Primal Decree, to participate in the "not only, but also" tradition begun by the writers of Genesis and expanded by the psalmist, by Paul, and by Luther. Since, according to Abdiel's testimony (5.835–41) and that of the loyal angels (3.383–92), the Son has existed prior to this moment of "begetting"—in fact, prior to everything and everyone else—then God must be using this word metaphorically rather than literally. The Son has in fact accomplished a fair bit by this time—created the universe and the angels—and is recognized for those accomplishments. God "declares" him to be special, "my onely Son," "anoints" him, and appoints him "Head" of all the angels in a way that is meant to "unite" them "as one individual Soule / For ever happy" (5.610–11). The angels are to recognize him as well: "to him shall bow / All knees in Heav'n, and shall confess him Lord" (5.607–08). Although Raphael does not at this point report what the good angels say in response to this pronouncement, he does describe the celebration, song, dance, and feasting that follow this "as other solemn dayes" (5.618). Satan may be displeased and may infect other angels with his displeasure, but the heavenly host's initial response—and that host includes the third of the angels who ultimately will follow Satan—acknowledges not only God's right to do what he pleases but, apparently, the rightness of his action as well. On the Son's return from expelling the rebel angels, the loyal angels explicitly will acknowledge the Son as "worthiest to reign" (6.888).

Like all of God's other children, the Son receives validation and encouragement. When he addresses the Son, God uses the same kind of epithets to express his love toward and delight in him that Milton has Adam use in addressing Eve: "Onely begotten Son" (3.80); "in whom my soul hath chief delight" (3.168); "in whom my glory I behold / In full resplendence, Heir of all my might" (5.718–20); "Effulgence of my Glorie, Son belov'd" (6.680). In turn, the Son expresses his recognition of and gratitude for that love, affirming repeatedly that he knows himself beloved by a father who is and will continue to be "well pleased" with him (3.256–65; 7:629; 10.70–71). He asserts that their loving mutuality constitutes

> my whole delight,
> That thou in me well pleas'd, declarst thy will
> Fulfill'd, which to fulfil is all my bliss. (6.728–30)

Whenever God presents a task he expresses his confidence that the Son can achieve it. Significantly, except for God's effusive praise upon the Son's offer of self-sacrifice during the Council in Heaven, God the Father does not respond after-the-fact to the Son's accomplishments. That task falls to the angelic host, who greet the Son with "jubilee" (6.884) upon his return from routing the rebel angels and with "acclamation" (7.558) upon his return from creating Earth. The Godhead reserves its explicit praise for Abdiel when he returns from the rebellion and for the good angels who have stood fast during the war. As I have argued in chapter 1, praise focuses on actions, describing what the individual has done rather than evaluating what kind of person the agent is. As Nell Noddings explains, "the long-range effect of encouragement is self-confidence. The long-range effect of praise is dependence on others" (Nelson 103). Having experienced constant encouragement, the Son acts with self-confidence; he does not seek out the Father's sanction for what he knows he has done well.

The first chronological actions that Milton dramatizes involving the Son show that he already possesses a highly developed moral sense. After Satan has lured his troops north, the Father draws the Son's attention to his stealthy action. It is possible that the Son, who is not foreknowing and all-seeing, *was* unaware of Satan's plot. But the Son recognizes the ironic nature of God's speech and the vanity, or futility, of the rebellion: "thou thy foes / Justly hath in derision, and, secure, / Laugh'st at thir vain designs and tumults vain" (5.735–37). How can anyone imagine that God the Father, who foresees and foreknows all, could be "surprised" and could be *worried about* being surprised? As the ensuing war will show, Satan's rebellion is as wrong-headed as it is quixotic. God here ironically adopts the Satanic misunderstanding of who and what He is. The Son responds in kind. The exchange mocks the perspective that could imagine a God invested in his monarchical prerogative and threatened by rebels who think to take him "unawares" (5.731).

Far from being "a brief study in military swagger and machismo" (Bryson 88), the Son's earliest dramatized moments contain the very rejection of conflict and the exercise of power for which Bryson will later praise him. Bryson writes, "as the War in heaven is being fought and won, when 'War wearied hath perform'd what War can do' (6.695), the Son still speaks of his own glory, but is beginning also to speak in terms of relinquishing the very power he has recently assumed" (68). In accepting the commission to rout the rebel forces, the Son declares:

> Scepter and Power, thy giving, I assume,
> And gladlier shall resign, when in the end
> Thou shalt be All in All, and I in thee
> For ever, and in mee all whom thou lov'st. (6.731–34)

The Son in these lines anticipates the future of perfect communion that the Father will foretell after his offer of self-sacrifice. He understands already that "Scepter and Power" are not values to be desired and hoarded. The Son will not "prove" himself when he routs the rebel host, although he may prove himself *to* them: the rebel angels are the only ones who want to "know whether I be dext'rous to subdue / Thy Rebels" (5.741–42). Only if physical force were a value could the Son accrue "matter of glory" from prevailing through it or be adjudged "worst" by failing.

Significantly, it is the Father who asserts that war has done "what War can do" here: the two-day stalemate has a pedagogical purpose. Through the battle the loyal angels demonstrate their perseverance, learning both that they can stand up to evil and that they cannot defeat it with their own strength. As God has explained during the Council in Heaven, the angels prove themselves through freely chosen obedience, which affirms their "true allegiance, constant Faith or Love" (3.104) and gives their obedience value. Two days of pointless fighting might have taught the rebel angels that their cause is hopeless. The experience of failing to achieve his ends through physical combat, of experiencing his contingency and createdness, might have but does not bring Satan to a sense of reality. Although "persuasion certainly is a more winning, and more manlike way to keepe men in obedience then fear" (*CPW* 1.746), there are times when it cannot "do the work of fear" (*Paradise Regained* 1.221–23). Satan has been allowed to "let loose the reins" of his "disorder'd rage" (6.696); his taunts and weaponry have provoked the loyal angels to their own "rage," plucking up mountains and throwing them at the rebel host like two-year-olds in a tantrum or adolescents in a bar room brawl. Now the Son needs to demonstrate to the angels, fallen and unfallen, that he is "worthiest to be Heir" (6.707), to teach them their limitations as contingent beings.

Milton's choice to accommodate human frailty by "lik'ning spiritual to corporal forms" (5.574) seems to encourage readers to revert to childhood. According to tradition, this is the point in the epic where schoolboys perk up, finally getting the battles that they believe make epic worth reading. I find the departure of the loyal host an intensely amusing moment:

> On they move
> Indissoluably firm; nor obvious Hill,
> Nor streit'ning Vale, nor Wood, nor Stream divides
> Thir perfet ranks. (6.68–71)

My students, on being asked to decide how to film this moment, prepare to deploy all the special effects available through digital animation and the WETA workshop. But I imagine cartoon figures pointlessly moving their legs as they "walk" on air, praised for their steady formations when the vales, woods, and streams that might divide "perfet ranks" are hundreds of feet below. For the epic battles, my students invoke *Braveheart* and *Gladiator*, but when Satan, sliced in half, heals back together, I think of Wily Coyote flattened or exploded in a Road Runner cartoon. This absurd pageantry, playing out in the impossible stalemate of the two-day conflict, ought to lead to the realization, on the part of readers, loyal angels, and rebel angels alike, that "War wearied hath achieved what war can do" because war can do nothing to any purpose. God allows the situation to continue for two days in order to help the lesson to sink in. Here persuasion might, in fact, be the one thing that war *can* do, although rather ham-fistedly.

The difficulty of dramatizing the War in a way that does not encourage readers to glamorize combat extends to dramatizing the Son's role in it, because of the tendency on the part of fallen human nature (and falling angelic nature) to misunderstand the Son's intervention, to read it as a display of strength rather than as an intervention at once compassionate and educational. As a corrective, Milton interrupts the two conversations between the Father and Son that I have just discussed with a moment that unites them in recognition of another: Abdiel. Who speaks these lines: Father or Son? The epic narrator is coy: led by rejoicing loyal angels, Abdiel is presented at the sacred hill, "from which a voice / From midst a Golden Cloud thus milde was heard" (6.27–28). Does it matter? Either way, the Son knows this message: that what Abdiel has done in standing up to the rebellion and witnessing to God's goodness is greater than what Abdiel and the loyal angels will do in the War itself and greater than what the Son will do to conclude the War—because what Abdiel has done required courage, commitment, and love expressed toward others under duress. Such a love understands that to act in a loving way is not always easy or comfortable or perceived as loving by those toward whom the love is extended.

The Son's language and behavior as he carries out his task indicates that he has internalized and can extend the pedagogy that his Father practices. Greeting the angels who have fought so hard on God's behalf he first acknowledges them and their actions as he and his actions have been acknowledged:

> Faithful hath been your warfare, and of God
> Accepted, fearless in his righteous Cause. (6:804–05)

He educates them about God's plan for the rebels, reassuring them that "the punishment to other hand belongs" (6.807) and relieving them of a responsibility that they have learned they cannot accomplish. The rage they have faced so bravely yet helplessly was not directed against them but against the Son out of jealousy,

> Because the Father, t' whom in Heav'n supream
> Kingdom and Power and Glorie appertains,
> Hath honourd me according to his will. (6.814–16)

They are asked now to "stand onely and behold / Gods indignation on these Godless pourd / By mee" (6.810–12).

This last statement may seem to give fodder to critics who read Milton's God as angry and tyrannical. But why and how is that indignation being exercised? The rebel angels started the war, they have pushed the loyal angels to rage, and their actions have begun to uproot Heaven. The Son comes forth to meet them at their level, "since by strength / They measure all, of other excellence / Not emulous" (6.820–22), to satisfy their desire "to trie with mee / In Battel which the stronger proves" (6.818–19), and to end the war. And that is all: "Nor other strife with them do I voutsafe" (6.823). When he does roll toward them in the divine chariot, he restrains himself:

> Yet half his strength he put not forth, but check'd
> His Thunder in mid Volie, for he meant
> Not to destroy, but root them out of Heav'n. (6:853–55)

In other words, the Son enacts the natural and logical consequences of the rebel angels' decision to interpret God as a tyrannical monarch rather than a loving Father. He shows them the consequences of their choice, but does not demolish them, because if he were to do that, their fates would be "fixed": how could they possibly repent?

Having demonstrated God's power in rousting the rebel angels, the Son is offered an opportunity to demonstrate that power's creative force. Again, God presents the task at hand and the pedagogical rationale behind it:

> But least his heart exalt him in the harme
> Already done, to have dispeopl'd Heav'n
> My damage fondly deem'd, I can repaire
> That detriment. (7.150–53)

In expanding on the Creation story from Genesis, Milton combines images of vibrant power with images of fertility and nurturance. "Girt with Omnipotence" (7.194), the Son calms the "furious winds / And surging waves" of the abyss; he uses huge compasses to circumscribe the location of the new creation; he speaks things that immediately take effect. But then "on the watrie calme / His brooding wings the Spirit of God outspred, / And vital vertue infus'd, and vital warmth" (7.234–36). The Son also embodies God's creative power in the intense attention to detail accorded the creation of each living thing, which in each case involves thinking through its entire lifecycle. Milton's God does not just create "oak tree," fully formed, but imagines acorn, sprout, sapling, branches leafing out, producing acorns, and the whole cycle beginning again. The descriptions of each creative act would lend themselves easily to time-lapse photography. Unlike the creativity expressed through the divine fiats of Genesis, the Son's creativity enacts a process that the human mind can comprehend.

Even at the most physical level, the Son cares for Adam and his needs. Having created the environment for this new creature "endu'd / With Sanctitie of Reason" (7.507–08), the Son then gets his hands dirty. Raphael reports:

> he formd thee, Adam, thee O Man
> Dust of the ground, and in thy nostrils breath'd
> The breath of Life. (7.524–26)

Then, in Adam's account of Eve's birth, the Son extracts Adam's rib and shapes it into Eve. Twice in two lines, Adam mentions that God forms Eve from this rib with his hands. As I will discuss in chapter 7, Milton presents here not a sanitized account of generation, but a realistically bloody birth. The Son is not squeamish about body fluids: Adam recalls seeing his rib "with cordial spirits warme, / And Life-blood streaming fresh" (7.466–67). Although he is God "substantially expressed" (3.140), "the radiant image" (3.63) of God's glory, he is also the "fullness" of "love divine" (3.225). He does not treat physical bodies as "bestial slime" (9.165) but handles both Adam and Eve literally and tenderly.

Throughout the accounts of Creation, the Son acts in ways that suggest he has chosen to take on the responsibilities of caring. According to Raphael, the Son instructs Adam about his role on Earth, leads him to "this delicious Grove, / This Garden" (7.537–38), and further sets out the terms of Adam's sovereignty. According to Adam, the divine presence is nurturing—leads him by the hand, explains, orients, responds, and apparently adapts. Like Raphael during his afternoon visit and the loyal angels who guard Eden, the Son learns about humans through intimate interaction; he responds attentively to Adam's nature and needs. As Noddings argues, "when we care, we consider the other's point of view, his objective needs, and what he expects of us. Our attention, our mental engrossment is on the cared-for, not on ourselves" (Noddings 24). Although he may not foreknow the future as the Father does, the Son does know that Adam needs a partner, and not just because Adam will need to reproduce. Having experienced first-hand a nurturing relationship "in bliss imbosom'd" (5.597), he understands its psychological, emotional, and moral importance. What pleasure must he receive in Adam's delighted, glowing response to him, what joy in Adam's demonstrated understanding of himself and his needs?

Before he is confronted with human failure, the Son has experienced gratitude as he flourishes in an environment that fosters his emotional and moral development: as psychological studies show, grateful individuals are empathic and so "more likely to attempt to render aid" to persons in distress and "more willing to forgive individuals who have committed transgressions against them" (McCullough *Affect*, 252). Having been the recipient of intimate care and encouragement, he has undertaken responsibility for others, which Fowler identifies as a signature aspect of adult moral experience; he has embraced the role of the one caring, who "desires the well-being of the cared-for and acts (or abstains from acting—makes an internal act of commitment) to promote that well-being" (Noddings 24). Perry, Fowler, and Noddings agree that emotional involvement and investment are critical components of moral experience, or, as the Dreyfuses put it, that "the highest form of ethical comportment is seen to consist in being able to stay involved and to refine one's intuitions" (Dreyfus and Dreyfus 256; see Perry *Forms*, 150ff.; Fowler 102; Noddings 47). That involvement ensures the commitment to the well-being of others that leads to the courage to act on their behalf. At the moment of crisis, the Son will model, as an alternative to the heroism of strength and cleverness of the epic tradition, a heroism based on selflessness and loving concern that he has learned from the Father and that has been reinforced through his own rich and varied experience as one caring for the world.

## II

*But with God all things are possible.*

—*Matthew 19:26*

As Irene Samuel outlined so persuasively half a century ago, Milton constructs the Council in Heaven to show "in dramatic process the Son's growth to what the Father himself calls virtual equality" (476). That growth occurs because the Father creates the occasion for it. He presents what appears to be an immutable decision that arises out of his own commitment to individual agency: he will not intervene in the human fall that he foresees because "I formd them free, and free they must remain, / Till they enthrall themselves" (3.124–25), but then concedes a mitigating circumstance — "Man falls deceiv'd" (3.130) — and a modified outcome — "Man therefore shall find grace" (3.131). God the Father presents "facts." In that sense, this conversation mirrors the one between Adam and God in Book 8. When Adam initiates that exchange with his complaint about being alone, the divine presence asks rhetorically, "what call'st thou solitude?" (8.369), points out all the creatures populating Eden, and tells Adam to "find pastime" with them (8.375). As Adam reports, the tone of that statement seems final: "So spake the Universal Lord, and seem'd / So ordering" (8.376–77). That conversation continues, and reaches the appropriate conclusion, only because Adam persists. Similarly, in the Council in Heaven, the Son answers "unbidden" (Samuel 471); he persists, and the ensuing conversation results in an outcome at which the opening speech merely hints.

That the Son's response is both "unbidden" and unscripted is crucial to the way this scene works. The Son has to be represented as a separate character from God the Father in order for his response to be authentic, the voice of "an independent being [who] speaks his own mind, not what he thinks another would like to hear" (Samuel 471). It is true, as Alan Mitchell asserts, that "the integrity and immediacy of the divine purpose is complicated but also made intelligible only by means of its setting in the 'process of speech,' the time-bound medium of narrative, where it accommodates human understandings" (75). But those complications result from human failing, not God's, and from readerly stumblings, not Milton's. Milton knew that his readers would approach this moment steeped in an awareness of Christian theology that might dilute their sense of the courage that the Son shows in standing up to the Father. That is why he presents a conversation — a drama — rather than a public service announcement. As Lieb argues, in this scene Milton purposely represents "a deity who undergoes the 'strife' of one fully aware of the demands that his own decrees have placed both upon himself and his creations" ("Dramatick" 226). He purposely presents a Son who challenges the Father, even to the point of threatening blasphemy. By dramatizing the "conflict" between Justice and Mercy, between the Father and the Son, and *within* the Father and the Son, Milton creates a scene that can engage his readers imaginatively and viscerally in the theological mystery he presents at the same time that it highlights the courage and moral heroism of the Son.

As precedent for his choice, Milton turns as always to Scripture, drawing on, among other things, Abraham's bargaining on behalf of Sodom and Gomorrah in Genesis 18 and Moses arguing for the Hebrew people in Exodus 32.[2] As Bryson warns, "if denied the emotional weight of speaking back to power *in his own voice*, the Son is denied the great dignity of Abraham" (70). But granting the Son that dignity does not require that God really intended to destroy humankind or that God lies to conceal that he had such an intention. As I have argued in chapter 1, Milton's God, like the God of the early Hebrew scripture, is passible—a feeling father who rejoices in his children's successes, grieves over their failures, and experiences righteous anger at disobedience. Milton works with this tradition, but he does so in order to transform it. In Genesis, Yahweh really does destroy Sodom and Gomorrah; in Exodus, Yahweh really means to destroy the backsliding Hebrews. Moved by Moses's plea, God forgives his people. In *Paradise Lost*, as Lieb affirms, "having already indicated that he will be merciful, Milton's God does not need to repent" ("Dramatick" 233). God never intended to destroy sinful humanity, as he will reveal in his response to the Son's impassioned speech; he always intended forgiveness. In fact, the Father will assert that the Son expresses his exact feelings: "All thou hast spok'n as my thoughts are, all / As my Eternal purpose hath decreed" (3.171–72). But the Son does not know that. For him, the information about humanity's coming failure is fresh, the danger to them extreme, and their vulnerability clear. As Abraham and Moses will do, he risks God's displeasure to be their champion.

As I will argue in chapter 6, the culture of dissent in which Milton participates desires not socialization or enculturation, but the commitment of individuals who have chosen their own values, who understand and act with courage upon their convictions. Such individuals will have reached at least what Perry would define in his schema as "Position 7." The language he uses to describe a young person who has reached this level of maturity seems particularly pertinent here:

> The drama of development now centers on responsibility. The hero makes his first definition of himself by some engagement undertaken at his own risk. Next he realizes in actual experience the implications of his initial Commitments. Then, as he expands the arc of his engagements and pushes forward in the impingements and unfoldings of experience, he discovers that he has undertaken not a finite set of decisions but a way of life. (*Forms* 171)

Milton could not represent the Son as resting in "an implicit faith" (*CPW* 2.543). Instead he represents a Son who has internalized the values of the Father and who expects the Father to live up to those values. This Son is willing to defy Authority on behalf of the values that Authority seemed to represent.

From the beginning of this scene, the Son demonstrates the autonomy that signals his moral adulthood. At the close of God's pronouncement, the Son expresses spontaneous open and explicit dissent from what appeared until the last moment to be the divine plan:

> For should Man finally be lost, should Man
> Thy creature late so lov'd, thy youngest Son
> Fall circumvented thus by fraud, though joynd
> With his own folly? that be from thee farr,
> That farr be from thee, Father, who art Judg
> Of all things made, and judgest only right. (3.150–55)

In *How Milton Works*, Fish claims that at this moment "what the Son says springs from his conviction, announced at the beginning of his speech, that what characterizes God above all is his inclination to mercy" (557); he argues that the Son is concerned about how God might be *mis*perceived because of his speech and intervenes, and I believe that Fish is right. But the Son speaks with an intensity that reveals that his *own* perception has been challenged: he *has* been thinking potentially "blasphemous" thoughts during God's speech: he *has* imagined a God who would allow his adversary to fulfill his "malice," who would "thyself / Abolish thy Creation, and unmake, / For him, what for thy glory thou has made" (3. 162–64). Although he presents these possible outcomes as rhetorical questions, they are eventualities that the Son entertains. He concludes that in such circumstances,

> So should thy goodness and thy greatness both
> Be question'd and blasphem'd without defense. (3.165–66)

He says, in effect, if you had not said what you just said at the end of your speech about being merciful to humans, you would not be a God worthy of worship and I would be the first in line to blaspheme against you.[3] His explosive language results from relief as he hears God clarify that he will be merciful, because the Son could not accept what he *thought* he was hearing.

In response to this unsolicited outburst, the Father offers praise rather than rebuke, affirming the Son as his "chief delight" (3.168). Just because God does not say during the Council in Heaven "thus far to try thee, Son, I have been pleased" does not mean this conversation is not the same kind of test as the one Adam faced at his creation. It tests both the Son's knowledge of God and his knowledge of himself. Milton's God, as he himself explains in the speech at hand, desires authentic relationships with his creatures. The Son, in articulating his ethical understanding of the situation, an understanding grounded in personal conviction, not in submission to received wisdom or authority, demonstrates the moral autonomy that God tries to foster in all his children. This test, in fact, leads to another test comparable to the one Adam will face when approached by the fallen Eve.

God the Father knows that the Son will pass these tests, but the Son does not know it. As Reichert argues, "there is simply no higher good than freedom—that condition without which such concepts as responsibility, obedience, loyalty and love, would lose all meaning" (16). And if human freedom, as Danielson explains, "requires of God a kind of self-limitation" (*Milton's Good God* 123), so does the Son's freedom. A Son who knew the future as the Father knows it would be deprived of his ability to make meaningful choices, to offer meaningful love and obedience, to receive meaningful recognition. Instead, he responds to the challenge with all the urgency and all the anxiety of any other creature. Listening to his Father pronounce the future and the fate of humankind, the Son finds himself in a conflict between his love for his Father, which includes his desire not simply to obey him but to fulfill his will, and his love for humankind. The Father's final statement, "Man therefore shall find grace" (3.131), seems to resolve the conflict and enables the Son to recover his equilibrium. He is affirmed in his belief, as Fish noted above, "that what characterizes God above all is his inclination to mercy" (*How Milton Works* [*HMW*] 557).

The Father then amplifies his will: his grace is offered freely to all, and all will be "sav'd who will" (3.173). That desire for salvation will be encouraged by grace "freely voutsaft" (3.174) that will "renew / His lapsed powers" (3.175–76). Although some individuals will receive special attention, God affirms that "the rest *shall* hear my call" (3.188; italics mine), *shall* find "within them as a guide / My umpire conscience" (3.194–95), and to their prayers "mine ear *shall not* be slow" (3.193; italics mine). The God of *Paradise Lost*, as I have pointed out elsewhere, issues an open call. He could not, I would argue, be more generous unless he were to violate his principle that he will not constrain free will, but he also understands that, in order to develop morally, individuals need to be accountable for their actions. For accountability to be effective, the consequences have to be proportionate. In this case, the natural consequence of dissociating oneself from God—alienation, which is what Satan and the fallen angels suffer—would be too much for humans to bear. God has just asserted that "Mercy first and last shall brightest shine" (3.134). He suggests as an alternative, as a logical consequence, that a volunteer might take the place of humans: some stronger being might be willing to "be mortal to redeem / Mans mortal crime, and just th'unjust to save" (3.214–15). The conflict resolved turns out to be instead the conflict intensified.

In *How Milton Works*, Fish argues that "discerning the one true obligation *is* easy; it is the obligation to do God's will" (477). In making this claim, he asserts that "there is only one value—that value of obedience—and not only is it a mistake to grant independence to values other than the value of obedience, it is a temptation" (*HMW* 53). I think Fish is correct to a point: obedience *is* the central value in *Paradise Lost*, and its God a loving and reasonable God, so that it *would* be wrong to think, "for example, that you might be asked to choose between God and your wife or between obedience and freedom or between truth and pleasure or between the clarity of moral thought and the experience of intense emotion" (*HMW* 13). But the obedience embodied in *Paradise Lost* is a way of being that flows from and expresses love—not only for God, but also for one's fellow creatures. As the Dreyfuses write, "The Christian command to love one's neighbor does not dictate how that love should be expressed" (Dreyfus and Dreyfus 254). "Loving others," which God requires of his creatures, in a way that is consonant with loving God is the difficult task that the characters in the poem face. The choices enumerated above, as Fish argues, "would be possible—would be real—only if the alternatives offered were independent of one another and could be cleanly opposed" (*HMW* 13). But the very interdependence of these values, the confluence of obedience and love, is what creates the perceived conflict between love of God and love for a fellow creature.

For humans, this conflict presents itself mainly through the experience of loss, as Adam will anticipate when faced with the fallen Eve: he feels that he must choose between life in God's favor without

Eve or death with Eve. For Adam's Puritan offspring, the choice offered by loss feels even more hopeless: having lost to untimely death someone whom they have loved—someone whom they had thought God had given them to love—they must reconcile their feelings of grief and anger with their belief that God is good and has their best interests at heart. Being unable to imagine a way in which their disloyalty to God could benefit their lost loved ones, they instead undertake the task of disciplining their grief and anger to acceptance: "but I am the Lord's and He may do with me what He will" (Shepard 229).[4] A husband grieving over his dying wife cannot "die" for her. Although he may in prayer offer his life in exchange for hers, he can't really substitute himself for her. But God has just announced that such a substitution could be effected: someone *might* choose a path that benefits both God and humans, preserving God's goodness and mercy and restoring human goodness and immortality, through sacrificing his own life for theirs.

But is this God's will? Does God, who has just asserted that "Mercy first and last shall brightest shine" (3.134) truly intend to destroy an immortal being to save humanity? As Lieb argues, the conflict the Son faces, the conflict that contingent beings experience between loving God and loving his creatures, the conflict Fish suggests is a chimera, exists not simply in created beings but in divinity itself. In Lieb's words, the Council in Heaven dramatizes "a deity who undergoes the 'strife' of one fully aware of the demands that his own decrees have placed both upon himself and his creations. As a result of that awareness, we behold a deity at pains to justify those demands and unwilling to compromise them" ("Dramatick" 226). Of course not! God cannot compromise those demands without, as I have said, compromising the freedom of his creatures; "as 'Author to Himself,' he not only accepts the responsibility of abiding by his own decrees but assumes the role of one fully conscious of what those decrees entail both for himself and for his creations" (226). Self-limiting, he cannot allow himself to resolve this situation but must ask that one of his creatures do so. His suggestion—his request—articulates that painful conflict.

The Son's spontaneous offer is a remarkable response. Around him "all the Heav'nly Quire stood mute" (3.217), but their silence is pregnant with meaning: God has closed his speech with two impossible questions: "where shall we find such love [?]" (3.213); "dwels in all Heaven charitie so dear?" (3.216). Those questions seem to the angelic host unanswerable, sound, in fact, rhetorical: after all, what being would "pay the rigid satisfaction, death for death" (3.212)? Even the fallen angels, tormented by flames, breathing in sulphurous fumes, forever exiled from Heaven, find the prospect of death appalling. Milton ventriloquizes their thoughts: not one "durst upon his own head draw / The deadly forfeiture" (3.220–21). In discussing this moment, Samuel asserts, "the Son cannot know any more than others at the council that the task named does not mean annihilation. The moment of silence includes his silence to underscore the clear enormity of the solution" (474). But the Son also cannot "know" that he will be the one to offer. By preserving the Son's separateness from the Father and his foreknowledge, Milton insures for him the ability to make genuinely free choices, the genuine choices that can earn him "merit" and prove his worth. As Lieb argues, the point of the Council in Heaven "is the proving of the Son, the establishing of his identity, an event that cannot occur before the Son has been given the opportunity to manifest his true nature" ("Dramatick" 235). That opportunity is now. Humanity is in danger of annihilation; God has just said that someone's death could benefit them; the Son volunteers.

Why does the Son do this? In making *his* "sacrifice," Satan spells out his reasons: how to do so fits with his kingly status, how undertaking this task will reinforce that position, how the rigors of the task will enhance his honor. But, of course, he knew what was coming—he proposed it (1.650–56; 2.381). Beelzebub has embellished the dangers of the journey from a fertile imagination, not from knowledge, and Satan, anticipating this suggestion, has had time to evaluate the risks independently. As Samuel argues, "when Satan then offers to go, he is the actor taking his cue in a scene he has written for himself. It is a magnificent moment designed to show his magnificent courage" (473). Although his "reasons" for volunteering may be truthful, they are self-serving and malicious: they contribute to his followers' shame by highlighting his own courage. Significantly, Milton does not write for the Son any explanation or justification of his choice. The Son does not plume himself on any special qualities he possesses or delineate the pros and cons of his decision. He says only that God's "word is past, man shall find grace / And shall not grace find means" (3.227–29). He offers himself as the substitute: "mee for him, life for life" (3.236).

Attempts to analyze ethical expertise after the fact are as wrongheaded as attempts to rationalize ethical choices ahead of time: in the Dreyfuses' words, "an ethical expert makes an immediate intuitive response to each situation" (Dreyfus and Dreyfus 243). They argue, in fact, that for these experts there may be "no intentional content" (247) in their actions: this is just what they do because it is who they are. Caring, according to Noddings, "is at bottom not rational; that is, it is fundamentally non-rational" (61). Altruism is even more nonrational. As Lewis Thomas writes, "it seems an unnatural act, a violation of nature, to give away one's life, or even one's possession to another" (101), yet, as he points out "the combat marine throws himself belly-down on the live grenade" (103) often enough that the army stocks medals for such heroism; a passer-by shoves a toddler out of the way of an oncoming car. Emergency ethical actions are not something you think through ahead of time—there *is* no time. You do what is right.

In making his offer—spontaneously, selflessly—the Son proves that he is "by Merit more then Birthright Son of God" (3.309) because in him "Love hath abounded more then Glory abounds" (3.312). Attempts to analyze why the Son does what he does lead to elaborate, and ultimately unhelpful, arguments about justification. They are the arguments of philosophy and reason, not the felt conviction of faith. The Son does not consciously set about trying to reconcile "justice" with "mercy" or to justify humanity or to "justify" the Father by interceding with humanity on his behalf. He just acts. As Noddings argues, in loving relationships, "we are not 'justified'—we are *obligated*—to do what is required to maintain and enhance caring" (95). He acts trusting in his Father's love for himself and for his Creation and out of his own love for both. Milton's poem "justifies" the ways of God by promoting gratitude that leads to worship. Milton creates in the character of the Son a being who shows, in human terms, what love incarnate might look like.

# CHAPTER 6

# RAPHAEL AND THE CHALLENGE OF EVANGELICAL EDUCATION

## I

*Though I speak with the tongues of men and of angels, and have not charity, I am become as sounding brass or a tinkling cymbal.*

—*1 Corinthians 13:1*

Raphael offers the most complex example of service and ministry among the good angels: his task is at once straightforward and paradoxical. Abdiel responds spontaneously to Satan's blasphemy; Uriel isn't aware that he's facing a test when this bright young cherub appears, but then quickly recovers; Gabriel and the angelic guard fulfill duties that are explicit and circumscribed. Each of these angels undertakes a mission that is straightforward; its successful completion, or at least the angel's faithful attempt to execute his responsibilities, can be easily defined. But God sends Raphael to earth on a mission of complexity and subtlety. He must engage Adam in conversation, "advise him of his happy state" (5.234), warn him of his danger, and remind him of his freedom. As I argue in the introduction, God sets tasks before his creatures for their benefit, not for his own: "God doth not need" ("When I consider" 9). He expects his creatures to fulfill not the letter, but the spirit of the challenges he presents them. Raphael's charge, then, should challenge his imagination and its exercise should contribute to his own spiritual development, even as he attends to the spiritual development of Adam and Eve.

Many readers have supposed that God sends Raphael to do the impossible—to prevent an event God has declared will come to pass—and that Raphael's instruction fails. In "The Dialogue in Heaven," Samuel sidesteps this objection, implying that the content of Raphael's instruction is irrelevant to Adam's choice: "whatever was to be risked demanded only Adam's faith that the benevolence he had always known would remain benevolent" (478). Nardo, on the other hand, applauds the substance of Raphael's instruction. Differentiating between the symposia at the Italian academies Milton visited and the intellectual colloquy between Raphael and Adam, she praises Raphael for providing an education that issues in political and moral action. But she qualifies her claim, because Raphael "teaches knowledge suited to life in an unfallen garden" (Nardo, "Interludes" 229), and, although she does not state it explicitly, because this education apparently fails. In these representative readings, the critics applaud Raphael's obedience and faith: despite the apparent futility of his task, Raphael earnestly and happily instructs Adam and Eve in what they need to know to prevent the fall and to continue happy in their prelapsarian state. Raphael may be seen to have acquitted himself admirably, but he also seems to have been sent on a fool's errand; this strategy acquits Raphael of incompetence by imputing to God either unreasonableness or vindictiveness.

But I believe, with Philip Gallagher, that Raphael's task is neither to prevent the Fall nor to satisfy God's sense of justice: he must "warn Adam not lest he willfully transgress, but 'Lest willfully transgressing he pretend / Surprisal' " (142). This is, of course, the way Satan responds after his initial defeat: he had no idea God was so powerful, he was provoked and led on, it was God's fault. Consequently, he is distressed but not sorry: repentance requires, first, recognition of responsibility. Discussing the action of grace in *Paradise Lost* and *Samson Agonistes*, Gallagher argues that, "through the mediation of Raphael and the Timnite, Milton's God preveniently renders these sinners inexcusable for sins they have yet to contemplate committing. He thereby lovingly hastens their regeneration by enabling them to internalize that conviction of guilt without which spiritual renovation cannot occur" (132). Raphael's instruction operates as a divine intervention of prevenient grace: "the angel's descent turns out in the event to have been a restorative work of merciful supererogation" (167). But it is unclear from Gallagher's discussion, and particularly from his linking of Raphael with the Timnite in *Samson Agonistes*, how self-conscious he considers Raphael to be in his role as enabler of divine intervention. I believe that Raphael is fully conscious of his role as enabler of prevenient divine intervention, that he exercises not simply obedience and faith, but imagination.

In describing Milton's style in *Paradise Lost*, Stanley Fish quotes from Milton's discussion of Jesus's "teaching through intangling." Milton claims that Jesus does not lay out his principles all at once, "but each thing in due place and season" (quoted in Fish, *Surprised* 21). Fish explains, " 'Due season' means when they are ready for it, and they will be ready for it when the seeds he has sown obliquely have brought them to the point where a more direct revelation of the truth will be efficacious" (21). In this sense, Fish's arguments about how learning works within the poem and how learning takes place through the poem coalesce: "Michael's strategy in Book XI is Milton's strategy in the entire poem, whereby his reader becomes his pupil, taught according to his present capacities in the hope that he can be educated, in tract of time, to enlarge them" (22). I see no reason to exclude Raphael from this illustrious company: he, too, teaches his pupils according to their present capacity; he must "repair the ruins of our first parents" before that ruin occurs by laying the groundwork that will lead to their renovation.

Raphael's situation, it seems to me, parallels the position of Puritan educators, among whom we must place Milton. Naturally enough, Milton's only explicit discussions of education come within the context of postlapsarian life: its end, "to repair the ruins of our first parents by regaining to know God aright, and out of that knowledge to love him, to imitate him, to be like him" (*CPW* 2.366–67); the teacher's responsibilities, to win his pupils to a love of virtue through "the Art, and proper eloquence to catch them with, what with mild and effectual persuasions, and what with the intimation of some fear, if need be, but chiefly by his own example" (*CPW* 2.385). *Paradise Lost* itself extends Milton's scope of influence, his teacherly and evangelical eloquence, both spatially and temporally, as it allows Milton to occupy, self-consciously, the role in which he places Raphael—that of mediator between the divine and the human, an enabler of prevenient grace. The experience of reading the poem ought to produce—beyond conviction of sin—repentance, regeneration, and, in a seasoned reader, strengthening in sanctification.

In a strictly Calvinist interpretation of salvation, grace, not human effort, effects regeneration or, to express it another way, provokes that *experimental* or deeply felt conviction that seventeenth-century protestants differentiate from *notional*, or purely intellectual, knowledge. But English Puritanism, by the Interregnum, had moved far beyond Calvin's original articulation of God's sovereignty and absolute autonomy toward a covenantal theology that provided believers

and clergy or educators with a more workable model.[1] In this modified Calvinist system, clergymen identified stages of conversion—
conviction of sin produces repentance, regeneration, and, finally,
sanctification—and worked to produce the first in order to prepare
for the later stages.[2] As N. Ray Hiner points out, "conversion, the
Puritan's overriding educational objective, was essentially affective in
nature, but Puritan pedagogy, or preparation for conversion, was
largely cognitive" (17). The Puritan curriculum and pedagogical
project moves toward what he aptly characterizes as the "rigorous
'final examination' " (5) of conversion, a moment that tests the quality
of the instruction as much as it does the student. This educational
practice recognizes instruction as an "efficient cause," even if "the
final cause" is God (P. Miller, "Marrow" 93). An educator attempting
"to repair the ruins of our first parents" could not simply wait for God
to raise the building.

One might extrapolate from this discussion that the end of prelapsarian education would be to kindle further an already inherent desire
to know and love God. As a teacher, Raphael must, as Regina
Schwartz argues, confirm Adam in an approach toward knowing that
will issue in praise (52). As a creature, Raphael must trust in God's
benevolence, and he must remember his experience of God's flexibility, as when, having announced that man must die, God apparently
backed off, allowing the Son to offer himself instead. Gallagher asserts
that "faithful angel that he is, Raphael will execute these orders to the
last jot and tittle" (138). But I argue that if Raphael were to leave it at
that, to teach toward the examination, he would have failed God even
as he fulfilled the letter of the task.

What God expects of his creatures is not exact obedience, but
active, imaginative, energetic waiting. Dayton Haskin develops the
model for this creative service in his reading of the sonnet, "When
I Consider." There, "the voice of patience does not offer full assurance
but only invites an active waiting upon the Lord's bidding" (108). Like
the speaker in that sonnet, like every contingent being, Raphael "is
not yet certain of the future, but is poised at a moment in a dynamic
process that he cannot hurry towards closure, even as he knows that
he is responsible for the way in which it will develop" (109). Raphael
must both trust God to know what He's doing and throw himself into
his task. Since he can't instruct Adam and Eve in such a way as to
secure their obedience (God has foretold their fall), he goes about
teaching them things that may be "useful" in a postlapsarian world,
not simply things that might be useful in preventing the fall, but

information that they will need to know to recover, to regain their spiritual balance. Raphael's instruction, far from failing in its overt intent, fulfills its even greater goal—to prepare Adam and Eve to explore the possibility of repentance—because, in discharging his task, Raphael exercises not simply obedience and faith, but imagination.

In his instruction of Adam and Eve, Raphael is "foreknowing," but in the way that we human parents and teachers are "foreknowing," rather than in the way that God is. He knows what his responsibility is, as well as the impossibility of "fulfilling" it. In this way, Raphael's example may be more useful to us, more clear, than God's—who seems to be in complete control, or at least to be capable of complete control, in a relationship (parenting) in which control is truly neither possible nor desirable. Like Raphael, we are only too aware of our students' and our own failings; as parents and educators, we frequently assume that our responsibility is to prevent transgressions, and we blame ourselves—either our instruction or our supervision—when the young adults in our charge fail to act responsibly. We must, as Gallagher cautions, beware "the fallacy that to be adequately fore-warned is ipso facto to be insuperably forearmed" (141); we also must assign responsibility where responsibility lies, both in our analysis of Raphael's instruction and in our evaluation of our own. His response to the task God presents him offers a model for imaginative, committed teaching. He is not simply a teacher who inspires learners, but a teacher who inspires teachers.

## II

*Well done, thou good and faithful servant.*

*—Matthew 25:21*

Raphael imaginatively shapes his instruction so that it prepares Adam and Eve to cooperate in the "repair" of their ruin. Understanding his responsibility not simply to transmit information, but to foster Adam's, and by extension Eve's—she is Adam's student—spiritual and intellectual growth, Raphael chooses to dramatize in detail parts of the rebellion story that will have particular resonance for Adam's and Eve's situation. He chooses these moments not simply because of their causal connection to the young couple's present spiritual danger—Satan's rebellion and decision to seek revenge for his fall—but because of their appropriateness as models to which Adam and Eve can respond imaginatively: the mystery of angelic joy in Heaven, Abdiel's courage in the face of peer pressure, the horrible suffering to which evil exposes the bad angels, and the glorious and nurturant process of Creation. As Milton urges educators to do, Raphael exercises that "art and proper eloquence" that should "season and win them early to the love of virtue and true labor"; he offers "such lectures and explanations upon every opportunity, as may lead and draw them in willing obedience," and balances "mild and effectual persuasions" with "the intimation of some fear" (*CPW* 2.384, 385). In this sense, Raphael's method is not simply Socratic or humanist, but evangelical.

Milton has modeled his own, and Raphael's, educational method on Paul's and the tradition of evangelical instruction that Paul inaugurated. In the most famous chapter of 1 Corinthians, Paul admonishes that contentious community:

> Though I speak with the tongues of men and of angels, and have not charity, I am become as sounding brass or a tinkling cymbal.
> And though I have the gift of prophecy, and understand all mysteries, and all knowledge; and though I have faith, so that I could remove mountains, and have not charity, I am nothing. (1 Cor. 13:1–2)

Milton articulates this same principle, in highly allusive language, at the opening of the pamphlet *Of Education*:

> And though a linguist should pride himselfe to have all the tongues that *Babel* cleft the world into, yet, if he have not studied the solid things in them as well as the words and lexicons, he were nothing so much to be esteemed a learned man, as any yeoman or tradesman competently wise in his mother dialect only. (*CPW* 2.369–70)

For Milton, the purpose of language study—of all education—is a knowledge that embraces and fosters greater appreciation of God and the Creation. Although the tone of the pronouncements may modulate in light of the audience and context of their utterances, his position doesn't change much from his exhortation in the seventh *Prolusion* to Raphael's advice in *Paradise Lost* Book 8. In the prolusion, a young Milton asserts that "the more deeply we delve into the wondrous wisdom, the marvellous skill, and the astounding variety of its creation . . . the greater grows the wonder and awe we feel for its Creator" (*CPW* 1.292); in the poem, Raphael, while encouraging Adam to "be lowly wise" (8.173), praises him for his interest in the world around him, "for Heav'n / Is as the Book of God before thee set, / Wherein to read his wond'rous Works" (8.66–68). Both *Of Education* and *Areopagitica* articulate Pauline precepts through Pauline rhetorical stances. In *Of Education*, Milton, like Paul, admonishes a community preening itself over its gifts. In *Areopagitica*, he speaks out, like Paul before the Areopagus in Acts, accusing the government of being superstitious.[3] With Paul, he argues that Parliament should "prove all things, hold fast that which is good" (Thes. 5:21).

Unlike his more pedagogically conservative colleagues, Milton designs an educational method that is at once evangelical and Socratic, religious and humanist. As John Morgan explains, in the tradition of humane learning, students worked with their own books, moving at their own pace and engaging with information, potentially, independent of their supervisors. But the general pattern for religious instruction required that a parent or master read aloud to an assembled group, making it "exclusively an aural/oral programme" (J. Morgan 189); students might read along with the instructor, but they were primarily listeners. Morgan argues that "such a programme of delivering information to a passive audience would also help to maintain the hierarchy of learning by repressing, at least temporarily, the spirit of inquiry by a swaddling of the mind" (189). But in Milton's hands this aural and oral program, while insuring greater supervision by the instructor, also encourages interaction between teacher and student. In this sense, Raphael's teaching strategy is both ancient, modeled on Socratic symposia and on Christian catechetical tradition, and modern, drawing from the instructional practice of Milton's Puritan contemporaries and anticipating discussion sessions and the interactive classrooms of liberal arts colleges. Far from "swaddling" Adam's mind, Raphael's method of teaching encourages its exercise.

Puritan parents and educators desired their children's and students' engagement and personal commitment. As N. Ray Hiner argues, "the Puritans viewed enculturation, the process by which the central values of a culture are internalized by the child, as more critical than socialization, the process by which a child learns the ways of a society so that he can function within it" (7).[4] But I would qualify this assertion: if the end of socialization is individuals who behave well in public out of self-interest—even such subtle self-interest as the desire for praise, the fear of shame—and the end of enculturation is individuals who internalize and conform to the values of their society, then the culture of dissent or nonconformity must be seeking a next step: individuals who define their own values and act upon them out of personal conviction of their worthiness. The whole point of withdrawing from mixed multitudes, of emphasizing spiritual testimonies as a prerequisite to church membership, of shifting from infant to adult baptism is to move beyond conformity (the thing they despised) to mature commitment.

Raphael works hard to provoke such commitment. He does not deliver an education, but instead interacts with a student who claims one (Rich 231–35). His class plan is, consequently, flexible, interruptable, and interrupted. His instruction begins with a creative response to Adam's offer of refreshment. In the course of this initial conversation, he asserts the relationship between all created beings in their "need[ ] / To be sustained and fed" (5.414–15), highlights the variety of creation, both as evidence of God's beneficence and as source of pleasure to creatures, and models gratitude in both his words and his "keen dispatch" (5.436) of the proffered meal. Then, intuiting Adam's convoluted questions about food to be questions about the relationship between humans and angels, between earth and heaven, Raphael further develops the interrelationship between created beings in their shared "first matter" (5.473) and source, introduces the idea of a prelapsarian progress from earth to heaven, and raises the central concern of his instruction—obedience and free will—in such a way as to provoke Adam's interest so that Adam pursues, rather than endures, the lesson.

Although Adam and Eve spend only an afternoon in his company, Raphael teaches by his own example, declaring his own political convictions—"freely we serve, / Because we freely love, as in our will / To love or not" (5.539–40)—and constantly interjecting his own response. To encourage interpretive sophistication, he emphasizes, before describing the War in Heaven, that he will not be telling literally what happened, but rather "lik'ning spiritual to corporal forms, / As may express them best" (5.573); before embarking on the story of Creation, he again qualifies his tale: "Immediate are the Acts of God, more swift / Than time or motion, but to human ears / Cannot without process of speech be told" (7.176–78). His narratorial interjections, however, highlight more than the epistemological difficulties of his project: they make explicit his own relationship to the story he will tell.

Just as the teacher of *Paradise Lost* needs to encourage interpretive distance, to keep reminding students that Raphael, not the narrator and not "Milton," relates this part of the story, Raphael reminds

Adam that he is offering a version of what happened and that Adam must ponder it and determine how to interpret it himself. He articulates narrative choices, for example, as he explains why he will not enumerate the exploits of the war: not simply because the good angels "seek not the praise of men" (6.376) but because the fallen deserve to remain "nameless in dark oblivion" (6.380). He asks aloud not simply "how shall I relate / To human sense th' invisible exploits / Of warring spirits" (5.564–66), but "how without remorse / The ruin of so many glorious once / And perfect while they stood" (5.566–68). He acknowledges and shares his emotional response both to the events and to the act of narrating them; he offers his own evaluation. But Raphael also insists that his version, although it may be partial in both senses of the word, is one in which he passionately invests himself. The question he poses for Adam is not simply how Adam should interpret this story, but how that interpretation should influence his life. He encourages *experimental*, rather than *notional*, knowledge.

Naturally, then, Raphael chooses to emphasize in his instruction aspects of the War in Heaven and the Creation that will contribute toward perseverance, worship, gratitude, and, as he foreknows Adam's and Eve's fate, renovation. His account highlights Abdiel's story, rather than Michael's or his own, as a model for moral action because Abdiel's success clearly derives from his loyalty and love, rather than from any unusual physical or intellectual abilities. Tricked into joining a conspiracy because he cannot correctly interpret "the suggested cause" and "ambiguous words" (5.702–03), astonished at Satan's "bold discourse" (5.803), unable to persuade a single rebellious angel to return with him to God's camp, clueless enough not to expect to find "Already known what he for news had thought / To have reported" (6.20–21), the Abdiel whom Raphael presents is an eminently emulable role model. He may be "alone / Encompass'd round with foes" (5.875–76), "Among innumerable false" (5.898), and subject to "hostile scorn" (5.904), but he is physically safe and intellectually single-minded: to imitate Abdiel, one must just say "no." On the other hand, Satan, for all his verbal quickness, never figures out how the world works. Paired together, their stories provide reassuring and accessible models for how to and how not to conduct oneself in the world.

Even before introducing Abdiel as an avatar of loyalty, Raphael introduces the theme of right worship, describing at length the celebratory dance and feast that follows the Primal Decree. He augments his personal witness to God's power, glory, and love with the antiphon of angelic praise throughout his narration. As Thomas Copeland argues, Raphael "encourage[s] virtue by showing love to be part of a universal cycle of creation and adoration" (117). He explains how the good angels celebrate the Son's elevation, how they rejoice at Abdiel's return, how they assert their love and loyalty verbally in the midst of battle. He reports their joy as they witness the Son's routing of the rebel forces and then welcome him home in triumph. Then, as Regina Schwartz points out, even as observers of Creation the angels are not silent: "each act of creation is rehearsed and remembered upon its completion" (72). As Adam has noticed earlier, the good angels "with ceaseless praise his works behold" (4.679); they model in their continuous praise a right interaction with the world, a receptive frame of mind that recognizes interrelatedness and interdependence as sources of joy and strength rather than as evidence of self-diminution. If, as the philosopher Nell Noddings argues, the human capacity for "affective response," for empathizing with another being, is "the very wellspring of ethical behavior" (3), then Raphael's repeated presentation of angelic rejoicing reinforces that quality in Adam and Eve most likely to enable their godly choices.

Above all, Raphael works creatively with "teachable" moments—Adam's question about the heavens (8.13–37), his suggestion that he tell Raphael his own experience of creation, and his later expression of confusion about his passionate physical response to Eve's beauty. Because Raphael responds to God's command imaginatively and flexibly, he is able to meet Adam at his level of intellectual development: he is able to teach the student, rather than simply the material. Faced with Adam's criticism of celestial economy, Raphael neither ridicules the question, nor supplies a simple answer, but instead praises the act of questioning even as he corrects the misassumptions implicit in the question as asked. As Nardo points out, Raphael "draws Adam's attention to his premises," continuing a pattern in which "he redirects Adam's attention away from factual knowledge toward an approach to knowledge more suited to human life" ("Interludes" 230), and, I would add, that approach includes asking the right questions, framing questions that will direct him toward useful answers. As Copeland points out, Raphael "gently correct[s] Adam's excessive modesty" (123). When Adam deprecates his own ability to contribute to their conversation, suggesting that his story-telling were "Fond, were it not in hope of thy reply" (8.209), Raphael again corrects his misassumption, pointing out that Adam is eloquent, graced with God's gifts, and, like the angels, a "fellow servant"

(8.225). Far from finding Adam's story childish or redundant, Raphael would "inquire / Gladly into the ways of God with Man" (8.224–26). He engages with Adam not as an inferior being whom he must fill with information, but as a fellow creature with whom he can explore the ways of God.[5]

By responding sensitively to Adam's initiative, Raphael encourages him to assume the role of teacher, for although Raphael has heard about the creation of man, he has not heard about it from Adam's perspective. Raphael's openness suggests that he understands that there is not one "true" or authoritative account of this event, but many true and authoritative accounts that combine to create a more complete picture, for, as Fowler puts it, "truth is more multidimensional and organically interdependent than most theories or accounts of truth can grasp" (186). Milton has been exposing his readers to this central moment, the Creation itself, from the first lines of the poem, when the narrator calls upon the Holy Spirit who "from the first / Wast present, and with mighty wings outspread / Dove-like satst brooding on the vast Abyss / And mad'st it pregnant" (1.19–22). The subsequent retellings, by Uriel, then Raphael, and finally Adam, do not bring us closer to what "really" happened but expand our understanding of it; unlike the multiple presentations of the event in *Rashomon*, these retellings do not complicate and confuse what happened, but lead toward clarity. If, as Regina Schwartz argues, these accounts of creation are both "mediated" and "internally entangled with difficulty, marked, as they are, by oscillation between epistemological confidence and uncertainty" (49), they are entangled in order to push readers toward interpretive commitment. We must be "still searching what we know by what we know not, still closing up truth to truth as we find it" (*CPW* 2.551). By encouraging Adam to explain himself and his experience, Raphael facilitates just such commitment: he requires Adam to claim his faith.

The conversation about his birth day reinforces Adam's sense of God's fairness and approachability by allowing him to rehearse his first intimate experience of God. As Raphael most likely anticipates, this conversation also brings into Adam's present consciousness God's gift to Adam of the garden and the attendant prohibition against eating from the Tree of Knowledge. Finally, it allows Adam to articulate both his initial and his developing understanding of his relationship to and responsibility for Eve and for himself, and I believe that this conversation is one that Raphael also anticipates and for which he skillfully creates the occasion. Adam reports that he requested a companion who has turned out to be both his "wish exactly to [his] heart's desire" (8.451) and to provoke something he did not quite expect: "here passion first I felt, / Commotion strange, in all enjoyments else / Superiour and unmov'd, here onely weake" (8.530–32). Eve's physical presence incites in Adam a physical passion that he *would like to allow* to overwhelm him.

Critics disagree about both Raphael's preparation for and success in addressing Adam's concerns about passion. In his discussion of this moment, Michael Allen argues that Raphael loses control of his classroom (115), responding sharply and unhelpfully, in fact disastrously, to Adam's expression of "his *feelings*: how Eve 'seems' to him and what 'seems' wisest, not how she is in reality or how he has decided to behave" (116). But Adam is not innocently expressing his "feelings" for Eve, here; he is trying to deflect onto Eve's physical attractiveness, and onto the Creator of that attractive body, his own desire to yield to sensation and passion, to relinquish the responsibility to decide how to behave. He offers three possible factors that might excuse this evasion of responsibility:

> Or Nature faild in mee, and left some part
> Not proof enough such Object to sustain,
> Or from my side subducting, took perhaps
> More then enough; at least on her bestow'd
> Too much of Ornament. (8.535–39)

In each scenario, "Nature" or God is accused of making it impossible for Adam to exercise his own wisdom, authority, and reason. By responding directly and firmly to Adam's excuses, Raphael is able to assert the expectation that "a person has a moral responsibility to remain in control of his or her will" (Lickona 393). During the separation colloquy, Adam will provide the same instruction, reinforcement, and encouragement to Eve, with the same potential results: that, confronted by temptation shortly after a serious conversation about personal agency and privilege, the tempted will not only remember what is right, but choose to do right.

Copeland has argued that Raphael's own experience of intense intimacy qualifies him to speak about passion: "if Raphael who knows ultimate sexual pleasure loves 'first of all / Him whom to love is to obey' (8.633–34) Adam surely can do the same" (126). Ronald Levao disagrees, arguing that humans, unlike angels, "cannot transcend their 'unity defective' " (99) except through intimacy. Nardo suggests that because Raphael has had no direct experience of Eve and has never experienced the intense loneliness Adam felt upon his creation, he cannot offer Adam any useful advice about his relationship. But, as I have argued in my earlier discussions of the angels and the Son, each created being in *Paradise Lost* must, as Levao claims of humans, "complete itself simultaneously in two directions, vertically and horizontally" (81). Raphael, too, is a created being who must love the Lord with all his heart even as he rejoices in and completes himself through relationships with other created beings. His lack of direct experience with Eve or with loneliness does not disqualify him as a mentor: intensity of feeling is intensity of feeling; right response to temptation is right response to temptation, be the stimuli passion, loneliness, or desire for self-aggrandizement. The God of *Paradise Lost* expects of his creatures to maintain control of the will in the face of temptation, whatever form that temptation takes.

If angels learn about humans discursively, as Nardo suggests ("Education" 195, 200), then Raphael has learned about the particularities of Adam's loneliness and need from Adam's own lips, and he responds to those particulars. He has heard Adam report what he desired in a mate: "fellowship . . . fit to participate / All rational delight" (8.389–91). He provokes Adam to articulate again his understanding of Eve's true value—her "graceful acts, / Those thousand decencies" (8.600–01)—and to reassert his freedom to "approve the best, and follow what I approve" (8.611). In enjoining Adam to love "what higher in her society thou find'st / Attractive, human, rational" (8.586–87), Raphael reminds him of what he already knows and of his responsibility to act on that knowledge. Far from being unable to "give Adam the advice Adam most needs" (Nardo, "Education" 204) or from losing control with disastrous consequences (Allen 116), Raphael engages Adam in a conversation that ought to keep the matter, and Adam's priorities, clearly in focus at the moment of trial. It is also a conversation that ought to reverberate in Adam's mind after his disastrous attempt to avoid loneliness by sinning with Eve proves only to intensify his misery and sense of isolation.

It remains to sketch out briefly what might have happened differently, and, most importantly, what does happen to Adam and Eve as a result of Raphael's care. Adam might have responded with more sensitivity to Eve's suggestion that they garden separately, listening to her actual words and addressing her suggestion dispassionately, rather than allowing emotion to escalate the situation to an actual separation. Eve might have remembered the example of Abdiel when she stands before the Tree and so refuse to discuss further the pros and cons of eating the fruit. Confronted with the transgressing Eve, Adam might have remembered his responsibility to love "first of all / Him whom to love is to obey" (8.634) or his own assertion that he "Approve[s] the best, and follow what I approve" (8.610–11). He also might enlist his recently articulated awareness of God's approachability and flexibility in figuring out how to handle Eve's transgression in a way that truly considers her welfare. The speech in which he rationalizes his choice contains several alternative narratives that he chooses not to pursue, narratives that, if he did pursue them, might lead to a reconciliation of Eve with God, rather than to further estrangement. None of these events transpires as I have outlined. But prepared by Raphael's prevenient ministry, Adam and Eve can, as Haskin suggests Patience urges, "risk a creative response to what has been given" (106). Unlike Satan, they recognize their sinfulness, accept responsibility for their disobedience, and actively reach out for God's free gift.

Raphael conducts himself throughout his mission to Eden as a dedicated servant of God, responding imaginatively and creatively to God's charge that he engage Adam in conversation that will increase Adam's self-awareness and reinforce his faith. Raphael has advised Adam of his happy state, his free will and responsibility in the exercise of it, his danger and the nature of his adversary, and rendered him incapable of claiming that his willful transgression results from "surprisal" or lack of warning. But Raphael has done more than that. He has trusted in God's benevolence and summoned all in order to enable Adam to participate actively in his own renovation, to pass the initial test of repentance and the final examination of conversion. He has responded actively and whole-heartedly to his Lord's bidding, in loving obedience to his Creator and loving concern for his fellow creatures, even though his errand is daunting and he knows that his charges face calamity "which [his] sincerest care could not prevent" (10.37). In fulfilling this demanding and complex task, he too earns the praise, "Servant of God, well done" (6.29).

# CHAPTER 7

# ADAM AS PARENT

## I

*God setteth the solitary in families.*

—Psalm 68:6

As with the good angels, God gives Adam and Eve responsibilities and freedoms appropriate to their intellectual and social development. Observing the fatherly or parental qualities of his interaction with Adam and Eve may be easier than teasing out his parental relationship with angels; Adam and Eve seem, in the schema of the poem, younger than the angels, and their conversations with God, mediated through his embodiment as the Son, more intimate than the heavenly colloquies and directives. God places them in an environment conducive to their physical and emotional comfort and gives them reasonable tasks that confer responsibility and dignity. He provides for them companionship with one another, fellowship in the form of Raphael, and encouragement and support in the example of the guardian angels populating the night landscape of Eden. He also sets a limit upon their freedom—the prohibition to eat from the Tree of Knowledge—which highlights that freedom and increases its value. This prohibition, this limit, also communicates to Adam and Eve their own value, as Adam points out in discussing the command to work, which "declares [our] Dignity, / And the regard of Heav'n on all [our] ways" (4.619–20). By presenting Adam and Eve with responsibilities and limits, as well as with privileges, God provides them with a secure environment in which to test their abilities.

Milton's God expresses his affection and nurturance for Adam and Eve through the physical details of the Garden in which he has placed them. He states explicitly that the Garden is a gift and a gift intended to provide security:

> This Paradise I give thee, count it thine
> To Till and keep, and of the Fruit to eat:
> Of every Tree that in the Garden grows
> Eat freely with glad heart; fear here no dearth. (8.319–22)

It is a fertile and abundant landscape that provides for every human need and stimulates every human sense: not simply a temperate environment dotted with "Nectarine Fruits which the compliant boughes / Yielded them" (4.332–33), but also groves, "Lawns or level Downs" (Book 4.252), "Grots and Caves / Of cool recess" (4.257–58), murmuring streams and choirs of birds. In his birth narrative, Adam reports viewing this new home from above: "a Circuit wide, enclos'd, with goodliest Trees / Planted" (8.304–05). God has described it as "thy Mansion" (8.296). Milton has moved far beyond the simple Garden of Genesis to create the country estate of a landed gentleman. It is "a happy rural seat of various view" (4.247), designed for human happiness, signaling human value, and providing a supportive environment in which to flourish.

God first parents Adam and Eve by establishing rules. In his biblical source, Milton finds three commandments that God delivers to his new creatures: the first—to be fruitful and to have dominion over the earth—in Genesis 1:28; the second—to tend the Garden—in Genesis 2:15; the third—not to eat from the Tree of Knowledge—in Genesis 2:17. Within *Paradise Lost*, however, he presents these commands in inverse order, beginning with the prohibition, reported by Adam himself during his first speech in the poem, "not to taste that only Tree / Of Knowledge" (4.423–24). Georgia Christopher has written of this moment that "Adam has accepted as axiomatic the divine right of God's voice to command. He judges the arbitrary and irrational prohibition of the Tree of Life [*sic*], not on its merit, but on its authorship" (149). But the arbitrariness of the prohibition does not make the rule "irrational"; it is the very arbitrariness of the choice that provides its meaning and insures its reasonableness. As Adam's explanation highlights, this Tree is a "sign,"

> The only sign of our obedience left
> Among so many signs of power and rule. (4.428–29)

God might have chosen to deny them access to any of the trees in the Garden. Adam later reports to Raphael that God set off the tree as "the Pledge of [our] Obedience and [our] Faith" (8.325), not because of any special attributes within it.[1]

Adam's explanation prepares readers to understand the logical fallacy in Satan's subsequent "reading" of the Tree: it is not some magical fruit that "contains" knowledge. That would be as absurd as the little wafers the projectors in the third book of *Gulliver's Travels* attempt to inoculate with mathematical propositions (Swift 159). The prohibition only "works" if the tree chosen is arbitrary: *which* tree doesn't matter; *a* "tree" does. As Regina Schwartz argues, "like the later injunctions in Leviticus, the force of that first law is not simply to forbid, to exact obedience, but to commemorate and sanctify the creation" (15). Adam recognizes the symbolic significance of the Tree, its arbitrary nature, as the contractual basis for their relationship with God; the prohibition defines the relationship. Adam presents it in the context of his awareness of another commandment: it is a trivial but not insignificant reminder of their dependence on God "among so many signs of power and rule / Conferr'd upon us, and Dominion giv'n / Over all other creatures that possess / Earth, Air, and Sea" (4.429–32), and the honor these signs impart. His speech immediately follows the narrator's own lush and lengthy description of this lavish Eden in which God has placed them. From Adam's perspective, the freedom and dignity conveyed through the other commandments far outweighs the restrictions of "this one, this easy charge" (4.421). This prohibition limits their dominion and their responsibility in a manner that is appropriate to their needs, as Eve's later anxiety about fulfilling the injunction to keep the garden demonstrates. Boundaries are necessary to both security and growth.

So is responsibility. Adam and Eve must not only refrain from eating of the Tree of Knowledge, but they must also care for the Garden in which they are placed. As Adam explains,

> Man hath his daily work of body or mind
> Appointed, which declares his Dignity,
> And the regard of Heav'n on all his ways. (4.618–20)

His assertion inversely articulates the point of God's statement during the Council in Heaven:

> Not free, what proof could they have givn sincere
> Of true allegiance, constant Faith or Love,
> Where only what they needs must do, appeard,
> Not what they would? what praise could they receive? (3.103–06)

The God of *Paradise Lost* does not attempt to "confer" feelings of dignity and self-worth upon his creatures, but instead creates situations in which their dignity can flourish. Humans, like angels, have both responsibilities and the freedom to undertake them. God observes their actions and acknowledges their successes. From this recognition, they derive "dignity": it does not descend upon them like a hereditary title, but develops through their choices.

This responsibility—their "labor"—is what distinguishes humans and angels from animals, of whose "doings God takes no account" (4.622): it is what makes them moral creatures. As Lickona asserts, "the capacity to work is a central moral competence. That competence requires developing other traits—such as self-discipline, persistence, self-evaluation, and at least a minimal sense of duty" (*Educating* 212). Through work, individuals learn about themselves. Significantly, Adam recognizes the representative nature of the work; he and Eve cannot "performe / Aught whereof [God] hath need" (4.418–19). The Garden is self-sustaining, right down to its automatic sprinklers and irrigation system; and the Garden is their dwelling place, not God's "plantation" in any conventional sense. Raphael explains the situation in this way: God created humans as the link between earth and heaven, as creatures "self-knowing, and from thence / Magnanimous to correspond with Heaven, / But grateful to acknowledge whence [their] good / Descends" (7.510–13). The command to tend the Garden enables Adam and Eve to enact this self-knowledge daily.

Tending the Garden enables Adam and Eve to develop a genuine sense of self-worth as they exercise their sense of responsibility for the Garden and to God. By undertaking and accomplishing tasks, by making choices about how and where to garden, Adam and Eve come to understand their own abilities and to discover their own resourcefulness. As Matthew Jordan argues, "much like praise, work in Eden is for the most part an activity of self-fulfilment in keeping with and completing the rest of creation" (135). The work, self-discovery, and praise go hand in hand: in his research, William Perry discovered that "the satisfaction the students expressed when they felt they had gained was less one of self-'approval' than of measured gladness" (*Forms*, 51). In their prelapsarian life, Adam and Eve respond joyfully to their accomplishments and gifts: they thank God for the day,

> Which we in our appointed work imploy'd
> Have finisht happy in our mutual help
> And mutual love. (4.726–28)

and "extol [his] goodness infinite" (4.734). Their satisfaction in a day's work well done issues not in self-congratulation but in gratitude and praise.

Adam and Eve must not only care for the Garden, but also for each other. As Lickona writes, "to develop responsibility, young people need to have responsibility. To learn to care, they need to perform caring actions" (*Educating* 312). Nell Noddings argues, in the tradition of David Hume, "that morality is founded upon and rooted in feeling" (79) not in duty or in reason: "it is our longing for caring—to be in that special relation—that provides the motivation for us to be moral" (5). As I have outlined in the introduction, each individual in the poem bears the responsibility for nurturing and educating another, who is, at present, less fully developed, less well-informed, but not lesser in value than himself. In considering Adam's moral development in this poem, I would like to return to the statement by James Fowler: that emotional and ethical maturity comes only after "the experience of sustained responsibility for the welfare of others and the experience of making and living with irreversible moral choices" (82). In order to help further Adam's emotional and ethical development, God provides him with a family. It is this experience of parenting—the sustained responsibility for the well-being of another—that gives Adam the courage to recover from his sin, to repent and move forward.

In Milton's version of the Creation story, Adam is a far more active figure than the Adam in Genesis. His God has orchestrated this day as a means of educating Adam about who he is and how he fits into Creation. Certainly, like the God of Genesis, Milton's God pronounces to Adam some of that information, but a good part of this process requires independent self-discovery, as Adam peruses his limbs, tests his voice, and reasons to the conclusion that he is a creature "Not of my self; by some great Maker" (8.278) made. Then, instructed by the divine voice, he learns that he is called Adam, "First Man of Men innumerable ordain'd, / First Father" (8.297–98), and that the Garden, the Earth, and everything on it are gifts he now possesses. He enacts that dominion by naming the animals. But throughout this scene, Milton balances language of dominion with the language of gift: the Garden is "thy Mansion" (8.296), "thy seat prepar'd" (8.299); he should "count it thine" (8.319). He is to "eate freely" (8.322) and "possess it" (8.340). The Garden comes to him with instructions about how he should exercise his authority and a restriction—a very slight one— that marks the boundary of his dominion.

Adam's conversation with God about needing a companion arises out of their discussion of his relation to the Garden, its status as both his possession and a divine gift. Milton has rewritten the action of Genesis so that Adam must ask for a partner. In this slightly teasing, Socratic colloquy, God forces Adam to think self-consciously about what exactly he needs, a need that God already fully understands. By doing so, he creates a situation in which Adam is more likely to appreciate the gift of Eve and more likely to appreciate her for the truly valuable qualities she possesses—her intelligence and companionability—than for her stunning beauty. The Eve God provides is so perfect, so attractive, so "exactly to [Adam's] heart's desire" (8:450) that this conversation is a necessary inoculation: Adam must appreciate Eve for the right reasons and as a gift that is his but that, like the Garden, is his to nurture. As William Flesch explains, to avoid idolizing a gift, the recipient must understand that "its ultimate value does not reside in itself but in the relations that it makes possible and that it stands for" (Flesch 224). This conversation with God insures that Adam will not take God's great gift for granted and that he will not misunderstand it.

Nowhere in his request for a partner does Adam discuss sexual passion. Milton saves that topic for Adam's afternoon with Raphael. This conversation is about something entirely different—that "rational delight wherein the brute / Cannot be human consort" (8.391–92). Although he stumbles in his attempts to articulate his desire, Adam consistently insists that what he wants is a companionship that will enhance his appreciation of Creation: looking at the glorious paradise, he first comments, "with mee, / I see not who partakes" (8.363–64). Pressed, Adam clarifies that he seeks "fellowship . . . fit to participate / All rational delight" (8.389–91). It is only in his third attempt to explain to God what he wants that Adam touches on the problem of procreation: because man, unlike God, is imperfect, he desires "by conversation with his like to help / Or solace his defects" and, ultimately, to "beget / Like of his like" (8.423–24). But even after making that statement, Adam reverts to his earlier objection to animals as a solution to his solitude: Adam desires "social communication" (8.429), and, unlike God, he cannot endue animals with human intelligence "by conversing" (8.432). He does not object that he cannot reproduce with animals.

Adam's desire for intimacy is not desire for sensual pleasure. He has been created "grateful to acknowledge whence his good / Descends, thither with heart and eyes / Directed in Devotion, to adore / And worship God supream" (7.512–15). He expresses the conviction that right worship requires fellowship, the participation of more than one person in appreciating God's creation: "In solitude / What happiness, who can enjoy alone, / Or all enjoying what contentment find?" (8.364–66). Joyful activity in the world requires others: he cannot imagine either the activity of "enjoying" or the feeling of "contentment" without it. In fact, his preferred verb for pleasurable activity is *to partake, to participate*. Positive feelings, such as "happiness" and "contentment" or, later, "harmonie" and "delight," require "fellowship" and "societie." He is, as Milton explains in *The Doctrine and Discipline of Divorce*, by nature a "wanting soul" (*CPW* 2.252).

In his discussion of masculinity in *Paradise Lost*, Jordan writes that "Adam, created as a desiring being, separate from something that is essential to him, confesses to both God and Raphael the internal motion inevitable in such a being" (105). But that internal motion should not be interpreted as a failing in Adam or a flaw in God's conception of human nature. As Thomas Luxon explains, the satisfaction of this longing is spiritual, rather than physical, and conducive to worship: prelapsarian desire "is vertical toward God, never horizontal between Adam and Eve. They perform the spontaneous ritual of evening prayer unanimously, and they also perform the mysterious rites of connubial love unanimously; that is to say, their desire is unanimously directed toward God" ("Wedded Love" 53). Adam knows he cannot "enjoy" Eden or worship God in a self-centered way, cannot express his appreciation singly. For fallen humans, marriage may allow partners to offer each other a "mutuall help to piety" (*CPW* 2.599); for Adam, an intimate relationship is as necessary and natural to appreciating God's universe as breathing. He looks for a help that is meet for him.

In this conversation with God, Adam proves that he is "self-knowing," understanding both his place in the universe and his own nature. But equally important for Adam's moral development, he chooses to enter into a relationship. Although God did always plan to provide Eve and to provide her as a "good," in Adam's experience, she is something that he chooses, and he must argue for her. He describes his behavior in this conversation as "presumptuous" and reports his persistence in explaining exactly what he needs even in the face of God's apparent thick-headedness. As Mary Ann Radzinowicz argues, in *Paradise Lost* both predestination and God's foreknowledge are "adjusted to liberty so that from the human point of view it will always appear that God improvises after the event" (*Toward Samson* 47). In asking for

Eve, Adam accepts the responsibility for her, for his relationship to her, and for the consequences, both physical and spiritual, of that relationship. At this moment, Adam exercises the two capacities that Fowler identifies as the signs of moral adulthood: he makes an irreversible moral choice and by that choice he undertakes the sustained responsibility for the welfare of another.

In prelapsarian life, the essential act of procreation is not the physical engendering of children but the spiritual desire to glorify God by expanding the community of worshippers. God has told Adam that he is the "First Man, of Men innumerable ordain'd / First Father" (8.297–98), but waits for Adam to figure out how that fatherhood will come about. By requesting a companion, Adam both secures that future and becomes a father. In a spiritual sense, being a father and being a spouse were synonymous in Milton's time. Theologically, a man was the head of his wife as well as of his household; he stood in relation to his wife as Christ does to the Church and as a minister to his congregation, in other words, as a father to a dependent. As Luxon points out, "Eve often calls Adam her 'Author' (*PL* 4.635, 5.397), in a sense virtually synonymous with parent" ("Wedded Love" 52). But in Adam's case, the parental relationship to Eve is not simply spiritual: he is her biological parent, and Milton writes the story of her birth to emphasize that fact.

When God praises Adam's articulation of what he needs, he promises to provide "Thy likeness, thy fit help, thy other self, / Thy wish exactly to thy heart's desire" (8:450). Then, as the story requires, he creates Eve from Adam's side. But Genesis can only be partly responsible for the birth imagery Milton uses. Milton need not have given Adam such a graphic vision of what happens. The language of Genesis is fairly clinical, and the Adam of Genesis has been cast into "a deep sleep" (Gen. 2:21). Milton's Adam, by contrast, narrates a very physical, realistically bloody birth: in his dream he sees one "Who stooping op'nd my left side, and took / From thence a Rib, with cordial spirits warme, and Life-blood streaming fresh" (8:465–67). Then Adam reports watching groggily as God fashions this rib into a lovely person whose presence "infus'd / Sweetness into my heart, unfelt before" (8:474–75). Milton's Adam has given birth to a daughter and experienced that profound jolt of identification that contemporary psychologists refer to as "bonding."[2] She may become his bride, but she is first his offspring and one for whom he longed and pleaded. The doubleness of his relationship to her intensifies his attachment and ought to heighten his sense of responsibility.

# II

*Whomsoever shall save his life shall lose it.*

—*Matthew 16:25*

How does Adam's prelapsarian responsibility for Eve affect his development as a moral creature? First, it enhances his self-knowledge. As McColley writes, "his instruction of her will exercise his intellect as well as hers" (89). In helping Eve to learn not only about her biological relationship to him but about the love and caring that brought her into the world, Adam must articulate his own understanding of her creation and its meaning:

> to give thee being I lent
> Out of my side to thee, neerest my heart,
> Substantial life, to have thee by my side
> Henceforth an individual solace dear. (4:483–86)

Read as the utterance of man to wife, this statement might sound possessive and proprietary. But Adam has only done what any mother does, and, as I have shown, he has done so for the same reason as many ordinary parents: he desires a companion who will be "part of my Soul" (4:487) and expects satisfaction and comfort from the new relationship. Milton has composed this reported scene so that Adam must call out to Eve to persuade her to stay with him, so that Adam's first encounter with her enacts the reality that Eve's love for him cannot be coerced. Although Adam "brought her into the world" through his desire for companionship, if he wants her love, he must earn it—through his explanation of their relationship and his loving interactions with her. It is here first and foremost—in relationships— that force upon free will hath no place and constrained obedience provides no pleasure.

Caring for Eve broadens and enriches Adam's own understanding about being in relationship. Adam provides Eve with information about the physical world, even if he must occasionally speak with more assurance than he feels. At every opportunity, he connects information about the world around them to instruction about that world's Creator. He explains in our hearing, but not for the first time, not only the prohibition against eating from the Tree of Knowledge, but also its moral significance in defining their relationship to the

Garden and to God. He discusses both the fact of their responsibility to tend the Garden and the role of that work in helping them establish their moral worth. He answers Eve's question about the stars in such a way as to encourage her interest in the world around her while at the same time correcting her misassumption about their place in the universe, and he further uses his answer as an occasion to foster her devotion to God. In each instance, he encourages her moral and spiritual growth, as well as her understanding of her location within a fabric of loving relationships; in encouraging Eve's understanding of human responsibilities and her appreciation for God's goodness, Adam strengthens his own.

But to genuinely care for another requires risk: in order to care for Eve, Adam has to empathize with her, to imagine himself into her situation, to think outside his own responses—and perhaps against them—as he endeavors to act in her best interests. This effort can be extremely discomfiting—it is precisely this discomfort, as Fowler has argued, that contributes to moral growth—and Adam experiences three occasions before the Fall that challenge his empathy: Eve's dream, her perspective on her creation, and her suggestion that they garden separately.

Adam's response to Eve's dream is surely a missed opportunity to flush out their enemy and to learn more about the challenge that enemy presents. The couple misses it precisely because Adam does not take the dream seriously enough. Like any parent faced with a distressed child, Adam wants to soothe, to comfort, to make everything all right. The Eve he knows is innocent and devout. He reassures her that her dream means nothing about her (and he is right, of course, that it doesn't). But, as Margo Swiss argues, "Adam's limited response to her anxiety, though appropriate to the procedures of edenic life to date, has now, by Satan's intrusion, become insufficient" (272). Eve confides to him, in McColley's words, "a dream so unnatural that she wonders whether it was indeed a dream" (98). In response, Adam develops an ad hoc theory of the origin of dreams; he offers a comforting maxim—"Evil into the mind of God or Man / May come and go, so unapproved, and leave / No spot or blame behind" (5:117–19); he expresses his confidence in her goodness. But he doesn't follow up on what has happened by mentioning the event to Raphael. In this case, his physiological theory is plausible and his moral theory sound, but his assumption about the dream's origin sadly inaccurate. Instead of responding carefully to the depth of Eve's distress and determining to discover its source, he constructs a narrative that explains away an upsetting event that does not fit comfortably into his understanding of the world.

Eve's dream is not the only prelapsarian event that Adam finds unsettling. In recounting her birth experience to Adam, Eve does not conceal her initial distaste for Adam's appearance, but later, when Adam recounts this story to Raphael, he leaves out this uncomfortable fact. As Levao comments, Adam's retelling "overrides the complex, emotional contingencies of Eve's" (93). Levao emphasizes here Adam's "stunned disbelief" (94) as the being for whom he has argued must be persuaded to play her part in the relationship he anticipates. Adam reinterprets, or perhaps did initially interpret, Eve's turning away from him as "modesty." He blocks out the memory of what he subsequently has learned about that moment because it challenges his belief that she is *his* individual solace dear, part of *his* soul, *his* other self, *his* wish exactly to *his* heart's desire. She is also, of course, his *other* self—her *own* self.

The recognition that those we love love us freely is at once joyous and scary: if they love by choice, then they could leave by choice. Just as when confronted with Eve's dream, Adam tries to create a narrative of its origins that will comfort Eve, in retelling his first meeting with Eve, Adam constructs a narrative that reassures himself. This desire to see the world in his own way is a natural stage of human development and one that Adam could not work past without a parental as well as a romantic attachment to Eve. Interactions with Eve push Adam to enlarge his perspective so that it accommodates that of another individual, an individual who is at once dependent on him and independent of him.

Adam's most intense prelapsarian confrontation with differing perspectives occurs when Eve suggests that they garden separately. Adam's sense of responsibility for Eve, his desire to keep her safe and to keep her with him, is natural and understandable. This conversation becomes a debate about Eve's "maturity," her independence, a debate with which every parent is familiar, and, in many ways, Adam handles his part well. His task as he sees it is to ensure that Eve understands the potential danger she faces and what is expected of her and, more importantly, what she should expect of herself should she encounter it. I do not think that Adam's decision to let Eve go is wrong, but I also don't believe that Eve truly wanted to garden separately. She has only suggested a possible solution to what she perceives to be their inefficiency—these are her "first thoughts"; Adam seems to understand this fact. But Adam also struggles to balance his own emotional resistance to her suggestion with his responsibility to listen receptively to Eve.

What explains this failure of responsiveness? First, Eve's suggestion has thrown Adam off-balance. In a discussion of solitude in *Paradise Lost*, Mary Beth Long suggests that Adam, because of his initial experience in the Garden, perceives solitude as a source of loneliness and isolation, whereas Eve, because of her different experience, perceives solitude as a source of reflection and pleasure. She argues that in Adam's initial response to Eve's suggestion he reveals that he has been trying to listen to others: in his conversations with God in Book 8 and with Eve in Book 4, Adam has learned *notionally* that "solitude sometimes is best society" (9.249). As she writes, "he is dependent on God and Eve, rather than his own experience, for his knowledge of such a sentiment. Adam himself has never mentioned solitude as positive, much less 'best society' " (Long 107). For Adam, the association of solitude with loneliness and his own anxiety about being left again to relive such an unpleasant experience interferes with his ability to respond effectively to Eve's suggestion: for at least a moment, he is thinking more about his own feelings and needs than about Eve's. In that moment, he escalates the stakes of her departure and does so in a way that incites her desire to prove herself.

Throughout this conversation, Adam misinterprets Eve's motives and intentions through mis-imagined empathy. Each moment of mis-reading begins with "But." In the first instance, Adam has addressed Eve's suggestion, corrected her mistaken assumption about the reason for their labor, and reassured her that their efforts are appreci-ated. This first "but"—"But if much converse perhaps / Thee satiate, to short absence I could yield" (9:247–48)—may represent, as Long suggests, an attempt to understand Eve's perspective, but it also, unfortunately, prevents the logical conclusion of Adam's initial response: that the couple need not separate to tend the Garden because God is not evaluating them on the number of weeds pulled. By reading into Eve's initial suggestion a desire for private time, Adam introduces both a plausible reason for temporary separation and an unsettling new possibility: that Eve does not desire his com-pany as much as he desires hers. This discomfort leads to a second "but" designed to impress upon Eve how much she needs him: "But other doubt possesses me, least harm / Befall *thee* sever'd from me" (9:251–52). Like any young person confronted with such a challenge, Eve bristles, and the debate about the limits of her independence begins.

This debate is both necessary and useful. I disagree with Fish here when he asserts that "the relationship of this episode to the Fall is entirely oblique; nothing follows from it in one direction or the other" (*HMW* 550). Certainly both Adam and Eve are strengthened in their understanding of individual responsibility by their conversation. In language that suggests his effort to exercise both parental responsibility and flexibility, Adam offers Eve permission to depart: "But if thou think, trial unsought may finde / Us both securer then thus warnd thou seemst, / Go" (9:370–72). *She* hadn't really wanted to go; she certainly did not initiate this conversation because she wished to seek a trial of her virtue. *He* doesn't want her to go, but he fears being overbearing or coercive. Although his empathy misreads her motives, his understanding that "force upon free will hath here no place" leads him to that final "but," and once he has said she may go, it appears to both of them that she must. As Levao argues, "it is Adam's moral intelligence, his developing grasp of his own mixed motives that leads him to comply" (101) with what he thinks is her request for independence.

Although in the event, Eve will succumb to the serpent's lies and Adam will fall with Eve rather than risk saving her, this conversation could strengthen the determination each has to do what is right. I will discuss how Eve might have applied the lessons of the Separation Colloquy in chapter 8. For Adam, it is the experience rather than the information exchanged here that could reinforce his understanding of his responsibilities toward God and toward Eve and prepare him to intervene for her rather than sin with her. As Fish argues, in this scene "Adam has lost sight of what he should be caring about: not the management of his domestic life, but the larger context (of God's charge and their attendant obligations) in relation to which domestic concerns acquire their significance" (*HMW* 545). This losing sight occurs long before the narrator accuses Adam of being "domestick in his care" (9.318): almost as quickly as Adam assumes that Eve is tired of his company, he wonders whether Satan's "first design be to withdraw / Our fealtie from God, or to disturb / Conjugal love, then which perhaps no bliss / Enjoyed by us excites his envie more" (9.261–64). These seem to be nearly simultaneous gut responses, and it is important to notice the blasphemy of imagining these two "designs" as morally equivalent. Adam may as well ask whether Satan intends to stain their honor or their new brocade. When confronted with the fallen Eve, Adam will act from just this gut response. But in this scene, Adam recovers his right understanding of his role and responsibilities and a right distinction between essential and contingent values.

Adam's conduct in this scene confirms his belief that "Evil into the mind of God or Man / May come and go so unapprov'd, and leave / No spot or blame behind" (5.117–19). Like the Son who, during the Council in Heaven, entertains and rejects the idea of an unmerciful Father, Adam here entertains and rejects the idea that his relationship with Eve might be more important than his relationship with God. As Fish argues, "rather than an instance of an exchange going out of control, the conversation is an illustration of how easy it is to come under the control of imperatives proffered not by any tempter but by the legitimate needs and desires of all human beings" (*HMW* 543). But the conversation also shows Adam recovering "control" of himself, regaining his balance, in a moment of intense emotion: it is this "gripping, holistic" (Dreyfus 242) experience, the experience of almost giving way to emotion and feeling in his relationship with Eve, that should prepare him for their next encounter. By considering and rejecting the idea that their relationship is self-sustaining rather than rooted in their love for God, Adam reinforces for himself what he will most need to remember.

In the Separation Colloquy, I think it's six of one, half dozen of the other, whether you approach your interpretation thinking about Adam as Eve's parent or as her husband. In the seventeenth century, after all, husbands were perceived as having parental responsibilities for their wives.[3] But I would argue that Adam's Fall "reads" very differently if you take seriously the fact that he *is* Eve's parent. When Adam faces Eve, who is flushed with disobedience and now "to death devote," he cries out, "loss of thee would never from my heart!" (9:912–13). I had always read that line as provoked by sexual passion and possessiveness—I am not alone in this—and considered it romantic piffle, evidence of Adam's selfish uxoriousness. But that was before I had faced a child of my own, distraught, voicing doubts about the value of his own life, or considered as a parent the fate of other parents who had lost a child. Eve is literally flesh of his flesh; from his body Adam gave her "Substantial Life" (4.485). His assertion here is not melodramatic; it is absolutely, ruthlessly true: "to loose thee were to loose my self" (9:959). If he were to lose Eve, he would never get over it.

Like any young person, Adam faces, in this moment, the challenge of trying to control himself in the face of intense emotional stress. As I argue in chapter 6, Adam reports that Eve's presence incites in him a physical passion that he *would like to allow* to overwhelm him so that he could forget that "a person has a moral responsibility to remain in control of his or her will" (Lickona 393), but that he has been able to control. At this moment of crisis, it is not sexual passion but a more intense sensation—the fear of loneliness and loss—that provokes in Adam the same desire to absolve himself of responsibility for his choice. In the future that Adam allows himself to imagine at this moment—"to live again in these wilde Woods forlorn" (9.910)—the loneliness is physical but it is focused on his parental relationship to Eve: she is "Flesh of Flesh, / Bone of my bone" (9.914–15); he cannot "Another Rib afford" (9.912). The loneliness and longing that Adam felt before receiving Eve, that he felt upon her disappearance after witnessing her birth, and that he felt when she suggested in the morning that they garden separately has now returned with greater intensity and threatens to engulf him. In the morning, he was able to regain control of his feelings and to engage with Eve as a loving and caring parent and partner. In this moment of crisis, however, Adam relinquishes control. He chooses to allow feeling to overwhelm reason.

In *"Paradise Lost* and the Forms of Intimacy," Levao argues that "Adam's choice is no unholy parody" (103) of the Son's offer and that readers of this scene face the same painful awareness of their own inadequacy that the angelic host feels when faced with God's request for a volunteer: "our admission that Adam's choice is one we might not have made" (102). He suggests that we, like the good angels, might not have been brave enough to sacrifice our lives for another. But Adam's sacrifice does not appear, in this moment, to be a sacrifice: he talks about his choice, instead, as a way to avoid unspeakable loneliness. Adam's original loneliness developed out of his desire to find someone with whom to enjoy God's gift of Creation and with whom to express gratitude for that gift; rooted in love for the Creator and a desire to become creative and caring himself, Adam's longing led to intimacy and joy. Now, rather than risk losing Eve, Adam decides to betray the God who has provided this wondrous gift.

Adam's choice to eat the fruit with Eve is a wrong choice not simply because it goes against God's express command. His choice is sinful because it is rooted in selfishness: it violates the larger responsibility that God placed on Adam in giving him Eve. Just as Adam's double role as Eve's parent and husband intensifies his anxiety about losing her, his double responsibility ought to intensify his desire to do what is best for her. As Noddings argues, in the ethic of caring, a choice "is right or wrong according to how faithfully it was rooted in caring—that is, in a genuine response to the perceived needs of the others" (53). Or as Lickona states, "*Love is wanting what's best for the other person, now and in the future*" (*Educating* 368). At this point, Fish explains, "what is best for Eve is the preservation of her relationship to God and if Adam would prove his love for her ('O glorious trial') he should attempt to maintain her in that relationship or if the worst happens intercede for its restoration" (*Surprised* 336). Fish's statement implies, correctly, that Eve's sin is not irremediable. Adam is, unfortunately, unwilling to risk the possibility of losing her companionship in order to help her.

Instead, he thinks about what is best for him or, more accurately, what will best enhance his comfort: he thinks about himself. As he "explains" his decision—"Certain my resolution is to Die" (9.907)— Adam lays out the scenarios that reinforce his gut response to the possibility of losing Eve: he cannot live without her; he cannot forego her "sweet Converse" (9.909); he cannot afford to lose another rib; he would not like another Eve as much. Nowhere among these scenarios does Adam anticipate Eve, fallen, distraught, in need of his comfort; nowhere does Adam envision himself guarding her or with her enduring the worst (9.268). Instead, he imagines a world in which he is alone, bereft, in need of comforting. He does not, in this moment, choose Eve over God. He chooses having Eve for himself over caring for Eve for herself.

My favorite science fiction character, Cordelia Vorkosigan, argues, "tests are a gift. And great tests are a great gift" (Bujold 235). The test that God has allowed Adam challenges him to the full measure of his humanity. But he is too busy thinking about his own feelings and future to remember that as Eve's parent and husband he is responsible for insuring her welfare. He eats the fruit, sinning against God and violating his responsibilities to Eve, and in that moment he makes the second of those irreversible choices that Fowler argues constitute one of the twin requirements for true adulthood: the first was, of course, asking for Eve.

If Adam's decision to sin against God is motivated in part by his parental love for and connection with Eve, that very loving connection rightly tempered enables his repentance. Because he is already a parent, Adam is able to imagine God's possible responses to Adam and Eve as children, and because he has had sustained responsibility for Eve's welfare, Adam cannot remain immune to her suffering. His soliloquy in Book 10 opens with an expression of anguish about future offspring who will suffer for his sin and feel "the evil on him brought by me" (10.734). This realization provokes a childish retort about how he never asked to be born, but Adam rejects his own petulance by imagining a dialogue with a potential son in which he plays both roles.[4] His relationship with Eve has enlarged his ability to think outside himself. His subsequent reasoning about death and a possible afterlife circles back to regret for the patrimony he will leave his as-yet-nonexistent sons.

It is the renewal of his relationship with Eve that provides Adam with the courage to continue living. Her utter desolation in the encounter that follows this soliloquy "in Adam wrought / Commiseration" (10.939–40). Her suggestion that life is no longer worth living provokes in Adam the sudden discovery that life is absolutely necessary to be lived. Fewer than 200 lines beyond Adam's lament "why comes not Death?" (10.854), he is reassuring Eve that God must have a plan and suggesting that they "seek / Some safer resolution" (10.1028–29). His suggested resolution, to cast themselves on the ground before the judgment place and water it with tears, reproduces the gesture with which Eve has besought his own forgiveness: if he as a parent responded with pity and forgiveness to the suffering of his child, then perhaps God will respond in the same way to his repentant offspring. This whole encounter, culminating in Eve's cry that "miserable it is / To be to others cause of misery, / Our own begotten" (10.981–82), provokes Adam from the stasis of self-pity into accepting responsibility for what has happened and taking action on behalf of others. Because he is a parent, Adam has learned to think beyond himself and his own needs, to empathize with others, to consider their perspectives, and to value relationship at the expense of pride. He has become fully human, fully adult. Unlike Satan, he discovers the courage to care, the courage to say he's sorry, and, by being willing to risk suffering, he opens himself to the future experience of great joy.

# CHAPTER 8

# EVE, IDENTITY, AND GROWING IN RELATIONSHIP

## I

*When I was a child, I spake as a child, I understood as a child, I thought as a child; but when I became a man, I put away childish things.*

— *1 Corinthians 13:11*

In *Paradise Lost*, individuals exist in a temporary hierarchy of relationship in which each person—angel or human—is responsible for nurturing and educating another, who is less fully developed, less well-informed, but not lesser in value than himself, so that the two may grow into a relationship of full social equality. That Eve has no one to educate may be partly responsible for critics' tendency to read her as inferior to Adam in a qualitative rather than social sense and to misread their conversations as reinforcing her subordination rather than increasing her autonomy and responsibility. In *Milton's Eve*, Diane McColley argues persuasively for Eve's spiritual agency and responsibility independent of Adam: as she points out, Milton's Eve is "distinguished from all other Eves by the fact that she takes her work seriously" (110). That work includes serving God through tending the Garden with Adam and serving God through caring for Adam. In addition, the poem insists upon Eve's future parental status, from the divine voice's first mention of her title "Mother of human race" (4.475) to the narrator's final naming of "our Mother Eve" (12.624), which culminates the poem's sustained consideration in Books 10 through 12 of the *protoevangelum*. As we have seen, Adam has parental as well as spousal responsibilities toward Eve—to nurture and educate her in order to prepare her for parenting; as part of her apprenticeship, Eve cares for and nurtures Adam. This chapter will look first at Eve's developing sense of identity through her interactions with God and with Adam and her growing ability correctly to interpret the world and her role in it. It then will address Eve's more mature efforts to respond to her multiple callings, to learn from her experiences, and to fulfill her responsibilities despite disastrous mistakes.

Chronologically, Eve is the "youngest" character in *Paradise Lost*, being born several hours after Adam. As with Adam, Milton presents Eve's entire developmental history, from when she "first awak't, and found [her] self repos'd / Under a shade of flours" (4.450–51) to her decision to ask Adam's forgiveness after their sin. More significantly, she is the only character in the poem to have an *infancy*: Milton introduces the angelic host only after their adult roles are established; although Adam tells the story of his "birth," he awakes to life blessed with the ability to understand accurately what he sees, to command language, and to reason, so in one sense intellectually fully grown. Eve, on the other hand, awakes "much wondring where / And what I was, whence thither brought, and how" (Book 4.451–52), and explores her environment "with unexperienc't thought" (4.457). The story that she tells addresses her process of self-discovery: as Kristin Pruitt writes, "how she, like Adam, first discovers an independent identity and achieves a measure of self-knowledge" (McColgan 29). The story also reveals what she thinks, upon reflection, about these earliest experiences and how they help her to understand her relationship to Adam, the intended audience for her tale. As McColley points out, "Eve narrates the episode (4.440–91) with far greater depth and perspicacity than she was capable of when it occurred" (80). Any reading of this episode must attend to the double layer of interpretation it contains: Eve's initial interpretation of the world around her and her more experienced interpretation of that earliest response.

In order to address and dismiss the inherited "problem" of female vanity, Milton boldly has Eve relate her encounter with a "mirror" in her very first speech in the poem. He has crafted her response to this "mirror," however, in a manner that is highly resistant to tradition. Both Milton and Eve make it clear that her story opens before she reaches the stage of intellectual development at which a child becomes aware that the reflection she sees is "herself." Eve reports that, lying before a lake that she could not yet even identify as water, let alone as a reflective surface, she saw a shape responding to her "with answering looks / Of sympathie and love" (4.464–65) and was delighted. Any parent will remember this moment, when the baby sees the baby in the mirror and reaches for it. Any person can also repeat this famous experiment: put rouge on a child's nose; a toddler before a certain developmental moment will try to touch the nose of the toddler in the mirror; a child who has reached the point where he understands reflection will touch his own nose (Lewis and Brooks-Gunn 198–221). Although Milton did not have access to modern psychological research, he did live in a world with infants and reflective surfaces. Far from signaling incipient narcissism or self-love, this episode makes clear that Eve hadn't yet any idea that this pleasing shape, which she refers to as "it," was herself. The episode signals instead her innate responsiveness.

To address this issue in more theoretical terms, Eve has been created *to love*; she has been created to love *Adam*, in whose image she has been made. In her unfocussed exploration, she seeks and appears to have found someone responsive to her responsiveness. Luxon rightly points out that Milton identifies Adam as a desiring subject, "the wanting soul" of *the Doctrine and Discipline of Divorce* (*CPW* 2.252), with Eve to be the object of his desire ("Wedded Love" 55). But she is also a desiring subject, looking to love and be loved. Human infants instinctively recognize and prefer human faces or images organized to resemble human faces to other arrangements. According to a summary of the psychological research, newborns also respond more to human speech than to sounds generally; infants quickly develop "signs of intersubjectivity and social attunement" and "develop expectations about communicative interactions with people" (Markova 132). A newborn even prefers its mother's face and voice to those of other humans (Markova 132). Although Milton did not have access to this research, he had fathered three children before he went completely blind and would have had the opportunity to interact with them and to watch his wife do so. Like other human infants, Eve identifies accurately the qualities of the right object of her attention. As John Reichert remarks, "in one sense she truly sees an image or reflection of one who was made in God's image—one in whose 'looks divine / The image of [her] glorious maker shone' (4.291–92). The beauty of the image inspires appropriate feelings of sympathy, love, and desire" (Reichert 29). When the divine voice intervenes, it does not rebuke Eve for her error. Although Eve in her retelling labels its words a warning, what she quotes is simply gentle instruction:

> What there thou sees't fair Creature is thy self,
> With thee it came and goes: but follow me,

> And I will bring thee where no shadow staies
> Thy coming, or thy soft imbraces, hee
> Whose image thou art. (4.468–72)

The divine voice explains to her the nature of the image and directs her toward a more satisfactory object.

As many readers have noticed, Milton has constructed the birth stories of Adam and Eve to reveal their complementary relationship, their differing roles and gifts. Despite the difference in their innate understanding of their surroundings, however, Adam and Eve report remarkably parallel experiences. Like Adam upon his creation, who "stray'd I knew not whither" (8.283) searching for someone to worship, Eve upon hers wanders about seeking someone to love. Like Adam, who falls asleep after fruitless searching, Eve reports that her initial search was unsuccessful. Like Adam's, Eve's stasis is interrupted by a divine voice that explains to her who she is and how she fits into the world: Adam will be "First Man, of Men innumerable ordain'd / First Father" (8.297–98); Eve will be "Mother of human Race" (4.475). In each case, the Voice is disembodied: Adam experiences "a dream" (8.292) or "inward apparition" (8.293) who seems to stand at his head or to come to him in a "shape Divine" (8.295); Eve simply reports a voice. In each case, the voice gently commands the auditor—Adam should "rise," Eve should "follow"—and provides gentle guidance: as Adam reports, "by the hand he took me rais'd" (8.300). At this point in their narratives, God leads the new humans to an encounter with the person "for whom" he or she was formed: Adam with God, Eve with Adam.

Eve has been made from Adam to be his "fit help" (8.450) and the mother of humankind, but she *is* given a choice about whether to accept that role and relationship. Seeing Adam in the flesh, she hesitates, turns back, pauses at his words, and yields to his persuasion and grasp. Her physical movements enact her choice of Adam over her image and of companionship over isolation. As McColley explains, "it is important to Milton's concept of domestic liberty that Eve should respond spontaneously yet preparedly to Adam, and not only to his appearance but to his speech and the clasp of his hand, in full knowledge of who she is" (82). In telling Adam the story of that initial experience— a story that he surely already knows—Eve reaffirms her decision and expresses her continued satisfaction with her relationship to him.

Although Eve may appear to make a choice that has no fruitful alternative, her choice is no less real and meaningful than Adam's choice to accept his role in Creation.[1] Interestingly, in this part of her birth story Milton gives Eve more agency than he gives Adam in his. The still dreaming Adam floats through the air to Eden, "led" passively by the dream vision to his encounter with his Maker. God then raises Adam, identifies himself as the one "whom thou soughtst" (8.316) and "Author of all this thou seest" (8.317). He gives Adam the gift of the Garden, warns him to refrain from eating from the Tree of Knowledge on pain of death, and then turns to the business of naming animals. Adam does not speak at this time, nor is he offered the opportunity to decline the gift of the Garden or the terms of the gift. Although the divine voice offers to lead Eve to Adam and Eve asks rhetorically, "what could I doe, / But follow strait, invisibly thus led?" (4.475–76), she does walk to meet Adam of her own volition on her own feet.

Some of our difficulty as twentieth-century interpreters of this relationship rests in its poetic formality. The length and instructive nature of Adam's speeches do not conform to our expectations for expressions either of emotional engagement or of "conversation." The epithets Adam uses to describe Eve are complimentary but studied: "Sole partner and sole part of all these joyes, / Dearer thy self then all" (4.411–12), "Fair Consort" (4.610) and "accomplisht Eve" (4.660). To modern ears, Adam may seem at times to be composing those delicate compliments that Austen's Mr. Collins believes ladies find so gratifying, as when he concludes, "But let us ever praise him, and extoll / His bountie, following our delightful task / To prune these growing Plants, and tend these Flours, / Which were it toilsom, yet with thee were sweet" (4.436–39). Eve's full-blown love poem, "With thee conversing I forget all time" (4.639), communicates the depth of her attachment to Adam, but her epithets for him—"O thou for whom / And from whom I was formed" (4.440–41), "My Author and Disposer" (4.635)—are harder to integrate into our expectations about healthy relationships, especially because of the elaborations of gender hierarchy that follow: my students groan when they read Eve assert that "what thou bidst / Unargu'd I obey; so God ordains, / God is thy law, thou mine: to know no more / Is womans happiest knowledge and her praise" (4.635–38); they recoil from her claim that without Adam she is "to no end, my Guide and Head" (4.442–43). A reasonable reader might suppose, as Luxon suggests, that Eve seems "destined never to outgrow the role of student and beloved" ("Wedded Love" 50), or extract from these statements the belief that Eve's subordination to Adam includes surrendering to him her independent responsibility for her actions and decisions.

But the story that Eve tells about her birth dramatizes her independent moral and intellectual development. Having learned from the divine voice about the difference between image and reality, she now expresses gratitude for its intervention, lest "there [she] had fixt / [her] eyes till now, and pin'd with vain desire" (4.465–66). Explaining how she learned from Adam about her origin both in his desire for companionship and his physical gift of "substantial Life" (4.485), Eve reaffirms her discovery at the pool that internal qualities, such as grace and wisdom, matter more than external ones. Her continued experience of relationship with Adam has reinforced that belief, for "from that time" (4.489) she sees "how beauty is excelld by manly grace / And wisdom, which alone is truly fair" (4.490–91). She does not, in this statement, say that she is "beauty" to Adam's "grace and wisdom";[2] the thoughtfulness of her discussion here should belie any reader's assumption that Eve possesses only superficial qualities. In her own words, she explains the series of readings and interpretations of experience that have led her to her present understanding of herself, her relationship to Adam, and her gratitude to the Creator who has made it all possible.

Milton's Eve clearly appreciates Adam not simply for himself but as a gift from God. Her retelling of her birth story opens with an affirmation of his worship, for "wee to him *indeed* all praises owe, / And daily thanks, I chiefly who enjoy / So far the happier lot, enjoying thee" (4.444–46, italics mine). As McColley has argued, by including this statement, Eve signals her independent assent to his assertion that they should be grateful to God. By placing her dependence on Adam, her guide and head, in the context of her debt to God, Eve expresses her recognition of their marriage as a means to the end of worship. She also qualifies the nature of her devotion to Adam, recognizing that she is "for *God* in him" (see McColley 42, italics mine). The prelapsarian "Eve is neither 'absolute' nor made 'occasionally,' but part of an intended pair" (88), the end of which is not Adam's satisfaction, but their mutual spiritual growth as responsible, grateful children of God.

Eve's rehearsing of her birth story responds to Adam's expression of his own gratitude to God for the gift of the Garden and of Eve. This exchange initiates a pattern of prelapsarian interactions between the couple that Milton uses to reinforce his understanding of how a successful marriage works: Adam makes a statement about their blessedness, to which Eve responds with affirmation. They have been created to serve as the link between Earth and Heaven through their gratitude and praise (7.505–16); their relationship has been ordained as "a mutuall help to piety" (*CPW* 2.599). In their loving conversations, Adam and Eve, like the angelic guard in Eden, are "responsive each to others note / Singing thir great Creator" (4.683–84). As Matthew Jordan writes, "Adam and Eve's vocal worship is as much a part of their being as perfume is part of the flowers', while the implication of the creatures 'wanting voice' is that the human couple is essential to creation" (133). Their interactions embody "that meet and happy conversation" that Milton argues "is the chiefest and noblest end of mariage [*sic*]" (*CPW* 2.246).

## II

*Prove all things; hold fast that which is good.*

*— 1 Thessalonians 5:21*

Just as asking for and receiving Eve contributes to Adam's moral development, requiring him to become self-conscious about his place in Creation and to examine the web of relationships that make up the animate world, entering into relationship with Adam creates the framework for Eve's own moral development. In her pleasure at her discovery of identity and relationship, in her enumeration of the natural beauties described in her love poem, in her question about the audience for gorgeous star-light "when sleep hath shut all eyes" (4.658), Eve delights not only in her life and surroundings, but in the relationship that anchors her. In Adam, she has someone to answer her questions who cares for her, who rejoices in her successes and reinforces her accomplishments. As Noddings argues, "when the attitude of one-caring bespeaks caring, the cared-for glows, grows stronger, and feels not so much that he has been given something as that something has been added to him" (20). As the one who claims that Adam is "praeminent by so much odds" so that he "like consort to [him]self canst no where find" (4.447–48), Eve needs as much as Adam to develop "self esteem, grounded on just and right" (8.572); Adam's loving responsiveness and articulate appreciation of Eve's gifts encourages that growth in self-knowledge and self-esteem.

Adam engages Eve as a moral equal and takes her education seriously. It is from Adam that she learns the role of the Tree in signifying their responsibility to God as stewards of Creation and from Adam that she learns of the dignity that responsibility bestows upon them. When she asks "for whom / This glorious sight, when sleep hath shut all eyes" (4.657–58), Adam not only explains for whom—the "millions of spiritual creatures" (4.677)—but also offers a complex discussion of his understanding of how light staves off moral darkness, of how "stellar vertue" (4.671) sustains Creation as a life force, and of how their future offspring will spread out across the Earth to populate "Nations yet unborn" (4.663). Even when he wishes to correct a misunderstanding, Adam first acknowledges Eve's intellectual effort, as, in response to her suggestion that they garden separately, he asserts "well hast thou motioned, well thy thoughts employed" (9.229). In this context, it is not surprising that Eve prefers to learn from Adam rather than from Raphael. In the presence of the angel, she is an auditor only, but with Adam she can participate in the process as active learner.

Eve's response to her Satanically imposed dream demonstrates her growing ability to interpret the world, as well as her trust in Adam's concern for her. Where Satan clearly hopes that the dream will encourage her transgression, either by enhancing the Tree's attractiveness or by familiarizing the idea of disobedience, the dream he feeds her appears unintentionally to increase her aversion to violating the command. She expresses her distress by telling Adam fully and freely about the nightmare, prefacing her account by stressing her extreme discomfort: "such night till this I never pass'd" (5.31) filled with "offence and trouble" (5.34). Significantly, although Eve relates that she behaved with credulous docility at the beginning of the dream and that she thought she "could not but taste" (5.86) when offered the fruit, in her retelling she now corrects her initial impressions: she heard "a gentle voice, I *thought* it thine" (5.37, italics mine); she "rose *as at thy call*" (5.48, italics mine). She expresses doubt about whether it was an angel that she saw, describing the creature as "one shap'd and wing'd *like one of those from Heav'n*" (5.55, italics mine). Although she admits reacting with horror when the angel ate, she does not conceal from Adam either what appears to be her complicity in the action or how much the experience has unnerved her. She is upset: she feels guilty, and she does not understand how the nightmare has happened, but she has not been taken in. She concludes her tale by exclaiming, "O how glad I wak'd / To find this but a dream!" (5.92–93).

As I argued in chapter 7, Eve's dream merits a more serious and active response than Adam's cursory reassurance provides, for it is a serious event, the first intrusion of Satanic agency into their paradise. In addition, as Margo Swiss asserts, "Eve's grief is unquestionably worthy of Adam's full attention and participation" (277); a more sustained discussion of her emotions might have reinforced more powerfully the lesson of this event. But even without further assistance from Adam, Eve can learn from this dream. She has encountered temptation and remorse *experimentally* rather than simply *notionally*. As McColley contends, "Eve's unwilled dream is an opportunity to confirm and strengthen her freely willed obedience by means of a fully formed imagination" (103). By mimicking lived experience, the dream "provides opportunity for imaginative and emotional grasp as well" (91). As the Dreyfuses explain, "the ability to remember with involvement the original situation while emotionally experiencing one's success or failure is required if one is to learn to be an ethical expert" (10). Through this dream, Eve has experienced virtually both the process of temptation and the swift deflation of disobedience. Her powerfully felt distress about the experience lends support to Adam's claim that "what in sleep thou didst abhor to dream, / Waking thou never wilt consent to do" (4.120–21). Awake and faced with the real Tree, Eve should "remember with involvement" her nightmare and leave it be.

As Adam cares for the Garden and for Eve, Eve has a responsibility to care for the Garden and for Adam. It is her developing sense of those responsibilities that initiates the separation colloquy and creates the occasion for her actual temptation. Both Reichert (134) and Jordan point out that Eve's understanding of her role in caring for the Garden develops out of Adam's own concern about stewardship. Jordan notes "parallels between Eve's speech [in Book 9] and Adam's [in Book 4]. It repeats, or nearly repeats, phrases and ideas—for instance, the need for 'more hands' to help them" (145). But Eve does not simply parrot Adam's earlier statement. In Book 4, Jordan argues, "Eve's inclinations towards the timeless bonds of love are expressed, but kept in their proper place by Adam's attention to their duties and his recognition of the need for disciplined and regular habits" (144); in the Separation Colloquy, it is Eve who encourages disciplined attention, while Adam "speaks up for pleasure" (145). In their exchanges, Adam and Eve are working toward a mutual understanding of how to express their gratitude to God through their care for his Creation, how to balance their responsibilities to love and nurture both the Garden and each other. By making her suggestion, Eve is, as McColley argues, contributing to the process of forming "a holy community," the community of their marriage and family (166).

Initially, Adam addresses Eve's suggestion by reproducing the expected pattern of conversations in *Paradise Lost*: a teacher praises a subordinate creature for having asked a question or made a suggestion, as happens in Book 4 when Eve asks Adam about the stars and again in Book 8 when Adam poses his own question about stars to Raphael. The teacher then corrects the assumption behind the question or suggestion: don't imagine that we are the only sentient creatures on the earth; don't imagine that you can design a universe more efficiently than God. Here, Adam praises Eve's interest in domestic economy: "Well hast thou motion'd, well thy thoughts imploy'd / How we might best fulfill the work which here / God hath assign'd us" (9.229–31). He then assures her that God is no taskmaster, that love is "not the lowest end of human life" (9.241), and gestures toward the desirable future in which their love will have created younger hands to help with the gardening. If Adam had stopped here, this scene would simply reproduce the interactions of other prelapsarian scenes and issue in resumed mutual gardening, coupled with a clearer understanding by both parties of the meaning and end of their labor.

But Adam does not stop. Chapter 7 addressed this scene from the perspective of Adam's parenting. Elsewhere I have considered it in relation to Eve's wifely responsibilities.[3] Here I will focus, instead, on what this conversation reveals about Eve's developing intellectual and moral autonomy as she argues for her independent agency. The amount of scholarly ink spilled over the Separation Colloquy confirms that it marks a transition in the interactions that Milton represents between Adam and Eve. That transition is triggered not so much by Eve's suggestion as by Adam's response to it. Jordan argues that this conversation is not about "the pros and cons of separation *per se*, but whether it is wise to separate at this time: a matter of domestic authority" (148). But Jordan is only partly right: the question of Adam's domestic authority is necessarily bound up with the question of separation *per se*. It is true that Eve has gardened independently of Adam before: she left Adam and Raphael deep in conversation, nothing untoward occurred, and Adam did not panic on discovering her absence or lecture her upon her return. Her absence at that time appears to have been "unremarkable." But it is not true that only *now* are they aware that Satan is in the Garden. Raphael had already told them that, at the conclusion to his narrative of the War in Heaven, well before the moment of Eve's earlier departure. In point of fact, nothing has changed. From Eve's perspective, Adam's objection to her suggestion and his assertions that she is particularly vulnerable to their "malicious Foe" (9.253) are surprising and unaccountable. His speech threatens her sense of self and of their relationship. Fish goes so far as to say that "what is at stake here is the conception each has of the other" (*HMW* 541).

Although I have argued in chapter 7 that Adam's response to Eve's suggestion is colored by his own emotional response and by his misattribution to her of motives she has not expressed, Adam does say things that are hurtful and incorrect in their implications about her moral sufficiency: he is worried "least harm / Befall *thee* sever'd from *me*" (9.251–52, italics mine) and asserts the principle that "the Wife, where danger and dishonour lurks, / Safest and seemliest by her Husband staies" (9.267–68). Such an assertion of principle and precedent amuses me, considering that he's the *only* husband and she's the *only* wife, but does not amuse Eve. As Eve points out, she cannot be harmed physically, so Adam must fear "that my firm Faith and Love / Can by his fraud be shak'n or seduc't" (9.286–87). Adam renews his argument for caution, but his way of making that argument again implies concerns about Eve's sufficiency. It is necessary for her moral development, and for the health of their relationship, that Eve defend herself by articulating her sense of her own responsibility, balanced with her own liberty.

As William Perry discovered in his interviews with college students, "perhaps the most critical point in most of the records comes at the moment where the student has indeed discovered how to think further, how to think relatively and contingently, and how to think about thinking. For here it is up to him in what crucial spirit he is to employ this discovery" (*Forms* 41). Eve demonstrates in this conversation that she can "think further." In formulating her original suggestion, she has been anticipating their future, imagining the days to come, their responsibilities, and how best they might fulfill them: she has chosen to put her mind to good use. She is not, however, committed to her position; it is simply one of her "first thoughts" (9.213). She is willing to listen to Adam's ideas. In responding to his anxiety, she entertains a hypothetical point of view—"if this be our condition, thus to dwell / In narrow circuit straitened by a foe" (9.322–33). As Reichert points out, this is not her position but the position that she believes Adam's last speech would require him to hold (137). She engages Adam's position, recognizing "the requirement that an answer or opinion be reasonable," which brings with it the recognition of contingency, "that some questions may have *some* legitimate answers" (Perry, *Forms* 113). She wants to know his reasons; she offers him hers.

McColley and Keith Stavely put the Separation Colloquy in the context of Puritan deliberations about church governance, "the question of what an individual, a community, or a congregation must do to preserve both the integrity of faith and goodness and the liberty to exercise and develop them" (McColley 166; see Stavely, *Legacies* 37ff.). Adam articulates what Milton's contemporaries would call "Christian responsibility": Eve speaks for "Christian liberty." Their exchange, however, is not a "debate," in the sense that there would be "sides" and "winners" and "losers." It is, as Marilyn Farwell explains, a conversation in which "two growing individuals attempt to discover and work out the most viable answer to their immediate problem" (15), how to fulfill their responsibilities without limiting their freedom. Eve takes issue with the implications of Adam's first statement; Adam elaborates on that statement in a way that he hopes will be "healing" (9.290) rather than authoritative. Eve spells out further the implications of his position. Adam accedes to the justice of her criticism by affirming that God's "creating hand / Nothing imperfet or deficient left / Of all that he Created, much less Man" (9.344–46), reminds her of her responsibility, and consents to her departure. As I have argued before, neither one "wins," but neither side loses either. In fact, to return to Jordan's earlier statement, Eve in her responses presses not her suggestion that she garden independently *on this particular occasion*, but rather the abstract principle of separation *per se*. She does not raise the prospect of imminent departure again, until Adam challenges her to "Go" (9.372).

Dennis Danielson blames Adam for his "failure to be 'firm and fixed' in his dissent" (*Good God* 128): "because it is constraint, not command, that negates freedom, he *can* forbid it" (127). To claim that Adam is wrong to let Eve go implies that Eve is insufficient on her own, which absolves her of responsibility for her sin even as it convicts not only Adam, but also God, of failing to do his part. Although it is true that "mutual minding" (145) might have strengthened Eve and Adam in their resistance to temptation, their resistance does not require it: they are both also responsible for "minding" themselves. Remaining together might have been a safer choice, especially in hindsight, but that does not make separation necessarily a bad choice. It does not even make staying together a better one. A "safer" choice, as this discussion reveals, comes at a cost: the cost of Eve's independence, the cost of that "Faith, Love, Vertue" (9.335) that she might develop and demonstrate, the cost of God's satisfaction in her growth, the cost of that freedom "for the sake of which the possibility of falling exists" (McColley 167). If I forbid my teenage son to learn to drive, I insure that he won't crash the car, but at a cost both to his actual independence and to his sense of it. If I forbid my handicapped child to go to school or to seek employment, as my grandmother did, I insure that he won't be ridiculed by others, but at a crippling cost to his psychological and emotional development.

In this scene, Eve's developing sense of her responsibilities toward God and toward Adam initiates a conversation that issues, without premeditation, in her departure to garden independently. They have canvassed questions of liberty and responsibility, of Eve's sufficiency and Satan's duplicity, that ought to have prepared Eve to resist temptation, just as Adam's conversation with Raphael about passion ought to have strengthened Adam in his determination to keep the proper hierarchy in his affections. And their conversation has issued in Adam's own statement on the necessity of Reason controlling Will, a principle that ought not only to instruct Eve but also to prevent him from joining Eve in disobedience. Milton has constructed this scene so that Eve departs, in McColley's words, "as the result of a responsible and considered choice whose outcome might have been, though it was not, the greater good of the human race" (141).

## III

*Wherefore let him that thinketh he standeth take heed lest he fall.*

*— 1 Corinthians 10:12*

Part of the difficulty of mastering skills, be it for chess or driving or ethical choices, is that not all situations perfectly repeat previously encountered situations: an opponent moves a different piece, the road conditions change, the person offering the joint is not the scruffy drug dealer from Health class enactments, but your clean-cut first-year roommate. For Eve, the differences between the dreamed and lived temptation scenes will mute the emotional memory that ought to assist her in making a right choice. Satan tries to catch her off-guard by modifying his approach: he shifts from overt assault to oblique deception, adopting the disguise of a lowly serpent and fabricating a story about how it came to speak. He hopes the story that he constructs will offer Eve strong incentive to taste the forbidden fruit. As McColley argues, "a desire for any good thing, such as Eve's desire for wisdom, is not wrong in itself, but an ingredient of virtue to be rightly tempered" (193). The fruit may be fair, but she knows she should not eat it. She ought to remember her earlier experience, even though the situation may not exactly duplicate the one in her dream and a week may have elapsed since that disturbing night. As Fish explains, "the distance between [Eve] and sin [is] measured, as always, by the strength of her will, which is, as always, sufficient" (*Surprised* 236). Milton would agree with Lickona that "a person has a moral responsibility to remain in control of his or her will" (*Educating* 393). All Eve needs to do, as Nancy Reagan would advise her, is "just say 'no.' "

That assertion may be a bit flip. Eve is new at resisting temptation. She has had only one personal experience—the Satanically imposed dream, which did not allow much scope for choice but which did create a strong emotional experience of revulsion. But, as her birth story demonstrates, she has experience evaluating options and making choices; she has heard with Adam about the fall of Satan and the rebel angels. Raphael's storytelling, by exciting her moral imagination, has allowed her to experience "from the outside what a situation is like on the inside" (Lickona, "Preparing" 124). Finally, she has just discussed at length with Adam the competing claims of liberty and responsibility. In her encounter with the serpent, Eve will face more such interpretive challenges and more such choices. Eve is not proficient at resisting temptation, but neither is she a novice. In fact, she and Adam have considerably more experience making choices and recognizing evil than did either the rebel or the loyal angels. She is "competent," in other words, "sufficient." As the Dreyfuses write of mastering chess, "choosing a plan, goal or perspective is no simple matter for the competent performer" (241). But if she were to resist the serpent's suggestions, her success and elation, "the gripping, holistic experience[ ]" (Dreyfus and Dreyfus 242), would strengthen her resolve to remain loyal and so become "an ingredient of virtue."

During her encounter with Satan disguised as serpent, Eve makes some decisions that prove in retrospect not to have been the best possible choices, but, as I argued about Satan's followers, poor decision-making is not necessarily sinful decision-making. As he did with those angels and with the angel Uriel, Satan takes advantage of Eve's innocence and trustingness: he tells her a plausible lie. As he did with Uriel, he adopts a disguise: in this case, he pretends to be a serpent who acquired speech and wisdom by eating fruit. Imagining that he understands her desires, Satan attempts to flatter Eve rather than appeal to her piety. What attracts her attention, though, is "the really interesting question of how the Serpent acquired the consummate gift of speech" (McColley 196): "what may this mean? Language of Man pronounc't / By tongue of Brute, and human sense exprest?" (9.553–54). Eve is intrigued by the narrative of transformation and curious about the location of the tree the serpent claims has effected it: it is, after all, her charge to tend the Garden, so she rightly desires to learn more about its contents. It might have been better for her to have consulted Adam about this unusual turn of events, but we can only say that in hindsight. She is, as the narrator asserts after Eve has met, spoken with, and followed the serpent to the Tree of Knowledge, "yet sinless" (9.659).

Eve herself demonstrates that conversing with the serpent and following it to the Tree does not mean that she has surrendered her independent judgment. As Fish has asserted, "listening is not sinning" (*Surprised* 254): Abdiel listened to Satan and responded with outrage. Once at the Tree of Knowledge, Eve states twice her recognition that this is the forbidden tree and articulates clearly its role as the one sign of their obedience. In stating her understanding, she demonstrates that she is "sufficient" to withstand temptation on her own. She may be "unwarie" (9.614)—unsuspicious, as Uriel had been—but she is neither deceived about the identify of the Tree nor ignorant of its significance. She is not outraged, as Abdiel was, because the serpent has not uttered any blasphemy yet. It is not until the serpent's next speech that Satan encourages Eve to disobedience. Yes, he has told "a persuasive story about the efficacy of the fruit" but Eve is not "thus deprived of meaningful agency" or "right judgment" (Mitchell 77). To make such a claim belittles Eve's intelligence and responsibility in a way that Milton certainly does not. More importantly, it misses the point: a person's "first moral responsibility is *to use [her] intelligence to see when a situation requires moral judgment*—and then to think carefully about what the right course of action is" (Lickona, *Educating* 54). Eve still thinks she's talking with a serpent and she still believes that the serpent ate from the Tree of Knowledge, but she certainly knows what God has asked her to do. When he suggests that she also eat the fruit, Eve should not follow the serpent's advice; she should not eat it.

At this moment, Eve should see that "the situation requires moral judgment" and exercise hers. To return to Fish, "listening is not sinning, but it does signify a tacit acceptance of the situation and of the relevance of logical or experimental inquiry to a commandment of God's" (*Surprised* 254). He continues, "Eve need not be won by reasons, merely won to reason" (254). I believe that Milton places a greater faith in Right Reason than Fish acknowledges. As I have argued, the command to refrain from the Tree is not "unreasonable" or "irrational" (*pace* Fish *Surprised* 242; Christopher 149), even if it is "arbitrary" in the sense that God could have chosen any tree. Eve understands both the reason and the reasonableness of this prohibition; she also understands that the prohibition is peculiar to Adam and to her. The "fact" that the serpent has eaten the fruit is, logically, irrelevant; for her to eat as well would not be a "petty Trespass" (9.693). Disobedience is not heroism.

As he did in his address to the rebel angels, Satan invites Eve to accept his alternative interpretion of a divine decree: the Tree is not "the only sign of our obedience left / Among so many signes of power and rule" (4.428–29), but a source of wisdom and power; God forbids them to touch it out of fear and greed. Regina Schwartz has pointed out that, in his soliloquy on Mount Niphates, Satan "interprets" rather than "expresses" gratitude (67). Here, he encourages Eve to practice the wrong kind of interpretation: to interpret analytically rather than to respond affectively. In Raphael's terms, he urges her to "admire," to question and second-guess, where she ought rather "admire," or worship. As Fowler argues, "the model of disinterestedness represented by scientific inquiry does not fit with the kind of knowing involved in moral reasoning or in faith's composition" (102) because in matters of faith and love, "the knowing self is continually being confirmed and modified in the knowing" (102). To return to the Dreyfuses, "the highest form of ethical comportment is seen to consist in being able to stay involved" (256). Emotionally invested reasoning is still reason, is, perhaps, the best definition of Right Reason.

Reading Eve's encounter with the serpent as a trial that may issue in her greater glory is itself a test: it requires that the reader read as if she did not know the outcome and it requires that the reader read against all her own experience of rationalization. In choosing sin, Eve adopts Satan's pattern of "reasoning" through linked questions, a hermeneutics of suspicion, which ought to be directed against the serpent's claims, that she directs instead against God's. Satan's speech is long and complex, filled with claims and rhetorical questions and redefinitions; it ends with the dizzying assertion that, although God is probably not the Creator, if God is the Creator then disobeying him is not disobedience because the Tree of Knowledge is one of his creations. But its final point, and its overall import, is that God denies them the Tree because God envies them wisdom, wisdom that is an end in itself, rather than a means to an end. How is it that she accepts such a claim? The short answer is that she chooses to believe it: the words and the idea "into her heart too easie entrance won" (9.734). The fruit looks good, its fragrance "wak'd / An eager appetite" (9.739–41). She wants to eat it.

Oddly this capitulation to appetite occurs as Eve adopts Satan's analytical response to the world, because "analytical," in Satanic terms, means figuring out "what's in it for me?" Eve has allowed Satan's monologue to re-orient her from thinking about her relationships and responsibilities to thinking about her "self," from affiliation to self-enhancement.[4] As will happen with Adam, Eve makes up her mind to eat and then rationalizes that decision. Her rationalizations are based on substantial false data—that the serpent ate and has not died, but benefited; that the serpent having eaten has brought her to the Tree out of generosity—but so are Adam's, for his rationalizations depend on the fruit having been "profan'd first by the Serpent. . . . / Nor yet on him found deadly" (9.930–32). The rhetorical questions allow her to deflect the answers she knows to the questions she asks: that God does not forbid them to be wise, that the fruit is, in fact, denied to humans alone, that she knows the true reason. But she has decided that God's prohibition "inferrs [not only] the good / By thee communicated, [but also] our want" (9.753–55). Her speech ends in a cruelly ironic rhetorical question: "what hinders then [?]" (9.778). Apparently nothing, except all her lived experience of God's goodness and of Adam's loving concern for her welfare, all her trust and love and loyalty. That is all we expect of our children: that their experience of our loving care for them will sustain them when they face moral choices.

Having committed herself to eating the fruit, Eve focuses completely on self-gratification, what she might call, if asked, her "own well-being": "greedily she ingorg'd without restraint" (9.791). She worships the Tree and promises to tend it "till dieted by thee I grow mature / In knowledge" (9.803–04) because she believes it will benefit her. She begins to express alienation from God, "Our great Forbidder," the good angels, his "Spies" (9.815), and even Adam, because she wishes to avoid consequences, including their disappointment in her, which would disturb her self-satisfaction. In determining whether to tell Adam she entertains the idea of concealing knowledge, both the information that she has eaten the fruit and the wisdom that she anticipates the fruit will communicate. This strategy, she imagines, would "keep the odds of Knowledge in my power" (9.820) and render her "more equal, and perhaps, / A thing not undesireable, somtime / Superior"

(9.823–35). The selfishness of her decision to share the fruit with Adam, lest she die and be replaced by "another Eve" (9.828), needs no elaboration. That selfishness then manifests itself in her attempt to manipulate Adam through a series of lies: that she missed him, that she had never been away from him before (!), that she ate the fruit for his sake, that she fears, if he doesn't eat, she will be above him, unable to "renounce / Deitie for thee" (9.884–85). She even claims that she would happily "die / deserted" if she "thought Death menac'd would ensue" (9.977), even as she presses the fruit into his hands.

I have already discussed the selfishness of Adam's decision to eat. Their mutual willingness to exploit the other to enhance the self culminates in their using each other sexually. Their mutual mortification upon awaking is perhaps the easiest part of the text to teach, as students resonate powerfully with their experience: they are "oppress'd" and "wearied" (9.1045), unsatisfied by a "grosser sleep / Bred of unkindly fumes" (9.1049–50), and embarrassed to look each other in the eye, although direct and provocative glances played a large part in getting them to that shady bank. On our campus, students talk about "the walk of shame": the mythic parade of students leaving the dorms of partners they picked up at last night's drunken party to return to their own dorms, wearing paper bags over their heads and hoping to avoid the Dean of Students, who walks her dog on the main quadrangle around six o'clock each morning. They have no difficulty understanding Adam's and Eve's embarrassment, or the finger-pointing that follows. The self-serving nature of those recriminations, with "neither self-condemning" (9.1188), is also clear.

It may be unfair to young people to label such behavior "adolescent": many adolescents never demonstrate such egregious self-centeredness; many "adults" never outgrow it. As I have argued in discussing Adam's recovery from sin, his recognition of responsibility for Eve, his willingness to resume caring for her, enables him to repent and move forward. Adam resumes caring for Eve because she persists in seeking his forgiveness and his love, a persistence that demonstrates on her part recognition of responsibility for what she has done and for Adam's situation. That recognition on each of their parts signals moral adulthood: the willingness to accept responsibility for one's choices and the consequences of those choices, and the willingness to invest in the sustained responsibility for the welfare of another.

Although as daughter Eve depends on Adam for guidance, in her role as wife, Eve experiences "sustained responsibility for the welfare of another" (Fowler 82) as she cares for and responds to him. In prelapsarian Eden, Eve enacts her wifely ministry unself-consciously through her innate responsiveness. She becomes the occasion for Adam's gratitude through her simple presence, through her responsiveness to his expressions of gratitude, and through "those graceful acts, those thousand decencies that daily flow / From all her words and actions mixt with Love" (8.600–02), including her participation in spontaneous prayer. She also initiates worship and praise in her appreciation of the natural world. Suggesting that they garden separately may in fact be her first conscious attempt at fulfilling her wifely role, as she tactfully broaches the question of the couple's success in balancing their responsibilities to tend the Garden with their interest in one another, to control those "looks" and "smiles" that create mutual distraction (9.222–24).⁵ She is trying to exercise her responsibility to serve God through caring for the Garden and through creating an environment conducive to Adam's spiritual equilibrium.

After the Fall, Eve's wifely ministry becomes necessarily more self-conscious, more explicitly a chosen activity. Although she has been betrayed by Adam's attempt to shift all the blame to her during their conversation with the Son, she still perceives Adam's misery and responds with compassion. In response to Adam's vicious denunciation, Eve persists in her efforts to resume their relationship. She accepts responsibility for what she has done, and she asks for forgiveness. She is the first character in the poem to do so. Her actions provide Adam with a model for his own behavior and provoke his realization that God, who is also a Father, may respond to his repentant children with something other than stern judgment. Although Eve does not become a parent during *Paradise Lost*, she demonstrates in her loving concern for Adam her full moral adulthood.

# CONCLUSION

As part of his justification for eating the fruit with Eve, Adam asks rhetorically, "but past who can recall, or don undoe?" (9.926). One of the hard truths of life is that actions have consequences and that those consequences remain, despite a person's penitence. At some point "but I said I was sorry" no longer resolves our responsibility. Raphael's retelling of the War in Heaven introduces Adam and Eve to this fact conceptually. In the final books of the poem, they confront it *experimentally*: they begin to live with the consequences of an irreversible moral choice.

Milton is more constrained by the Genesis story in his conclusion of *Paradise Lost* than he is in his representation of the Fall itself. Genesis provides only the bare outlines of the temptation scene: Eve must eat the fruit and offer it to Adam, who must also eat. Milton has complete freedom in developing how these actions occur. But Genesis is explicit about the punishments for that sin: they are expelled from the Garden; Adam will earn his bread by the sweat of his brow; he will "rule over" Eve, who will suffer pain in child-bearing; the serpent will crawl on its belly and eat dust. Milton chooses not to join his more radical contemporaries, such as Rachel Speght and Margaret Fell, in arguing that sexual subordination is itself a consequence of sin, a perversion of God's creation rather than an exaggerated expression of divine decree. But he does shift attention from these physical consequences—toil and hierarchy, pain and death—to spiritual ones.

Genesis itself suggests the foundation for Milton's reinterpretation of the punishments: although God says of the Tree of Knowledge, "Ye shall not eat of it, neither shall ye touch it, lest ye die" (Gen. 3:3), the Adam and Eve of Genesis eat, but live long lives. Milton interprets this delayed death sentence as a pedagogical strategy as much as a gift: a time of "Grace, wherein thou may'st repent, / And one bad act with many deeds well don / Mayst cover" (11.255–57). As God explains his plans for Adam's and Eve's postlapsarian future, their suffering on earth becomes a purgative process, a Keatsian vale of soul-making: "after Life / Tri'd in sharp tribulation, and refin'd / By Faith and faithful works" they will find themselves "wak'd in the renovation of the just" (11.62–65). Their physical banishment becomes not the defensive gesture of a selfish god, but the spiritual expression and continuing reminder of their alienating trespass.

The experience of sin, although traumatic and emotionally exhausting, has provoked repentance in Adam and Eve, but not that conviction of sin necessary to salvation. The morning following their penitent prayers at the place of judgment, Adam initiates a conversation about consolation through prayer that reproduces their earlier pious exchanges—"easily may Faith admit, that all / The good which we enjoy, from Heav'n descends" (11.141–42). Prayer, he says, has brought spiritual relief and the recollection of the protoevangelum, which "assures me that the bitterness of death / Is past, and we shall live" (11.157–58). Eve demonstrates her renewed loyalty to God and assistance to Adam by reminding him that they should resume their labor. But she also assumes that they can return to "before"—"while here we dwell, / What can be toilsom [?]" (11.178–79). They think that they can just pick up where they left off.

Despite Eve's and Adam's repentance, and God's forgiveness, their transgression cannot be undone or treated as if it never happened, "For still they knew, and ought to have still remember'd / The high Injunction not to taste that Fruit / Whoever tempted" (10.12–14). Adam and Eve are adult human beings, "sufficient to have stood" (3.99), with responsibility for their actions and for the consequences of those actions. Michael's charge in Books 11 and 12 is to carry out their banishment, but in such a way as to leave them "not disconsolate" (11.113); as he interprets this task, he needs to educate Adam (and through Adam Eve) about the new plan for human salvation that their sin has occasioned. Fortunately for Michael, and for Adam and Eve, God and Raphael have laid the groundwork. In discussing the moral education of young people, Lickona writes, "if they consented in advance to the consequences, it's easier to get them to look at what they did and take responsibility for their behavior" (*Educating* 118). God set before Adam the terms for life in the Garden; Raphael reinforced the system of privilege and obligation within which they lived there. Adam and Eve cannot sidestep their responsibility, cannot claim "surprisal, unadmonisht, unforewarnd" (5.245). The expulsion from Eden becomes, as I have explained in my discussion of God's parenting, the natural and logical consequence of their disobedience.

But truly learning life's lessons requires living a life. An epic poem, although it attempts to contain and explain the universe, cannot follow Adam and Eve on into old age in real-time. Instead Michael presents to Adam a story about the consequences of his sin. Like the story that Raphael told about Satan's rebellion, this narrative allows Adam to experience vicariously a lifetime of postlapsarian human experience. As I outlined in the introduction, engagement with stories enhances the moral imagination by encouraging empathy: it lets students see "from the outside what a situation is like on the inside" (Lickona, "Preparing" 125). Michael's instruction begins with dramatized vignettes of the central moments in Genesis. These three-dimensional theatrical events are disorienting for Adam in the way that Rabinowitz argues is fundamental to first-readings of texts (*Authorizing* 100).

Not until the narrative portion of his instruction, in Book 12, does Michael provide the "organized reading" Rabinowitz identifies with formalist reading for coherence (*Authorizing* 98). Instead, he provides Adam with "the gripping, holistic experiences" that Dreyfus argues promote proficiency of moral response (242). He presents first the story of Cain and Abel, to which Adam responds with distress and horror, then a vision of physical sufferings so graphic as to reduce Adam to tears. These visions encourage Adam to identify with other human beings, to respond to their suffering, and, through Michael's commentary, to recognize his complicity in their sinfulness and grief.

It is essential to the success of Milton's poem that Adam's story conclude with his salvation. Michael's instruction provokes in Adam what Puritans would call "a True Sight of Sin," "th'effects which [his] original crime hath wrought" (11.424): sin, old age, death, murder, sickness, treachery.[1] One does not have to believe in hereditary original sin in order to recognize the consonance between the behaviors depicted in these two final books and actual human behavior. The narrative portion of Michael's story, leading Adam through biblical history, prepares him to understand the Crucifixion intellectually, but also to experience viscerally the connection between his own sin and that terrible sacrifice. This "conviction of sin" leads to a deeper repentance than that penitence Adam felt earlier. Once Adam accepts that the Son will become incarnate and die for *his* sins, once he can "acknowledge *my* Redeemer ever blest" (12.573), he becomes a Christian and his story, the essential part of his story, ends. The other consolation that Michael offers—the repeated example of God's protection of the just, however solitary, the evidence of God's continued willingness to covenant with humans, the extension of that convenant to all humans—pales beside this essential comfort. As Michael notes, this moment completes Adam's education: "thou hast attaind the summe / Of wisdome" (12.575–76). Building on the inward turn Jesus establishes in the Sermon on the Mount, Milton antici- pates for Adam and Eve and the regenerate reader a paradise within that is an inversion of the hell that Satan finds within himself.

But what of our students? They will not, for the most part, com- plete their first reading of *Paradise Lost* by undergoing a conversion experience, nor would I suggest such an outcome as an appropriate pedagogical goal. For students, unlike for Adam, Michael's instruc- tion is all "narrative" and pretty cursory at that. As my creative writ- ing colleagues would argue, there is not enough showing, too much telling. For this reason I tend to move quickly through the final books of the poem: they are not as compelling to contemporary undergrad- uates as the well-developed story of Adam's, Eve's, and Satan's choices. In terms of the moral education of undergraduate readers, the real teaching in *Paradise Lost* ends before Adam's vision. Our students cannot live an entire life, however vicariously, through one reading of a poem. They can, however, come to think more self-consciously about moral responsibility as they read about characters making choices, listen in on the rationalizing behind those choices, and watch the unfolding of consequences. With just the slightest nudging, they can begin to draw connections between the events in the poem and events in their own lives: the temptation to cheat on a Calculus test, to help a friend with a take-home exam in Economics, to have another drink even though you are the one with the car keys. In our students' world, as in *Paradise Lost*, the consequences for choices are both physical—a wrecked car, a dead friend—and more ephemeral, but equally long-lasting—guilt over the fudged data on a Biology lab report, broken trust in a relationship, the sense of having failed one's parents, or of having failed oneself.

Beyond inviting students into the vicarious experience of poor choices and failures, *Paradise Lost* offers hope. Satan, it is true, never accepts responsibility for anything that he has done, for the personal consequences of his alienation—his own psychological torment and physical suffering—or for the sufferings that he causes to others, even to others with whom he has relationships—his dear companion Beelzebub, his fallen troops, his daughter Sin. The final vision of Satan within the poem, "punisht in the shape he sin'd" (10.516), embodies his psychological stasis in physical form. But Uriel and Gabriel correct their mistakes; Abdiel makes the right choice despite intense peer pressure and his initial naiveté. Adam and Eve finally come up with the courage to say they are sorry—first to each other and then to God. They knew the rule and had accepted life in Eden on those terms; they accept their banishment from Eden as the natural and logical consequence of their disobedience. They step out into the world to begin the rest of their lives.

As a student recently pointed out, the final lines of the poem resonate strongly with young people facing graduation, "leaving their last moments of parent-sponsored security," the comfort of the communal dining hall, the predictable expectations of academic life:

> The world was all before them, where to choose
> Thir place of rest, and Providence thir guide,
> They hand in hand with wandering steps and slow,
> Through Eden took thir solitarie way. (12.646–49)

The prospect is at once hopeful and daunting. Like Raphael, we teach students for whom we have great hopes, but whose futures are unclear to us, who will encounter challenges that we cannot anticipate. We do know, however, that successfully navigating these challenges will require understanding that "their first moral responsibility is *to use their intelligence to see when a situation requires moral judgment*—and then to think carefully about what the right course of action is" (Lickona, *Educating* 54). Reading *Paradise Lost* ought not to be an end in itself; Milton would not have expected it to be. Instead, like the gardening that Adam and Eve undertake—a process that develops in them a sense of both their dignity and their responsibility—reading *Paradise Lost* can become a means to a greater end. Engaging seriously with this challenging text not only leads to a sense of accomplishment and satisfaction, but also provides that experience with examining choices that will help them move from competence to proficiency, from adolescence to adulthood, as they become their own choosers.

Reading *Paradise Lost* also ought not to be a dessert reserved for only the most ambitious English majors; it offers too much solid nourishment. Teaching *Paradise Lost* by attending to the moral development of its main characters will open the poem to most undergraduate readers. Expanding the readership of *Paradise Lost*, even if it is not an end in itself, seems to me to be a worthy goal, for, especially in this case, "books are not absolutely dead things" (*CPW* 2.492).

# Notes

## Introduction

1. All references to *Paradise Lost* will be from *The Riverside Milton*, ed. Flannagan.
2. See Danielson, *Milton's Good God*; Reichert, *Milton's Wisdom*; and Stavely, "Satan and Arminianism."
3. For further discussion see Perry Miller, "The Marrow of Puritan Divinity."

## 2 Satan, Interpretive Choices, and the Danger of Fixed Stories

1. See also Carey, "Milton's Satan"; and Patrides, "The Salvation of Satan."
2. For a discussion of Satan's response to Eden see Stavely, "Satan" 133–35.
3. For a thorough discussion of varieties of allegorical characters, see Van Dyke, *The Fiction of Truth*.
4. To supplement Louis Schwartz's discussion of the specifics of child-bed trauma in the Early Modern era, see Scholton, *Childbearing in American Society: 1650–1850*.
5. In the context of the biblical and literary sources of the allegory of Satan, Sin, and Death, Milton's emphasis on the familial qualities of the relationship is quite startling. He may draw Sin's physical appearance from Ovid and Spenser, but in *The Metamorphoses* Scylla is not the object of her father's attentions and in *The Faerie Queene* Errour has neither an identifiable parent nor any human qualities. He may be influenced by Bacon's treatment of the stories of Scylla and of Dionysus and Persephone, but neither Scylla nor Persephone is impregnated by her father (Martin 4–5). An incestuous relationship is latent but completely undeveloped in the Epistle of St. James: "when lust hath conceived, it brings forth sin, and sin, when it is finished, brings forth death." The allegory in this passage is so abstract as to be hardly pictorial. He may have considered the representation of female vice figures in other Renaissance epics treating the War in Heaven, but these poems, like the original myth of Athena springing fully armed

from Zeus's head, establish familial relationship without including incest (Revard 159, 162). Essentially, Satan's complex and physical parenthood is something that Milton has made up.

# 3  Abdiel, Peer Pressure, and the Rebel Angels

1. See Elledge, *Milton's God* 394; and Campbell, "Paradisal Appetite" 244.
2. See also *De Doctrina Christiana, CPW* 6.343ff.
3. Empson wrongly assumes that the birth of Sin must have taken place before the action of the poem because Raphael does not mention it in recounting the beginning of the War in Heaven, although he concedes that Abdiel, and therefore Raphael's narrative attention, may have departed before this event. He also assumes an earlier gathering because Raphael's narrative does not leave enough time between the conspiracy at the end of Book 5 and the War in Book 6 for Sin's seduction and pregnancy to take place, as if events in Heaven, Eternity, and allegory occur over time in the same way that events on Earth do. Following his way of reading, one might ask whether Satan also needed to gestate Sin over time in his brain, and, if so, why no one commented on his steadily swelling head?

# 5  The Education of the Son

1. For further discussion of this point, see Bryson, *The Tyranny of Heaven*; Lieb, "Dramatick"; and Samuel, "The Dialogue in Heaven."
2. See, among others, Lieb, "Dramatick" 231–33; Bryson, *The Tyranny of Heaven* 117.
3. For a complementary discussion, see Lieb "Dramatick" 229.
4. For further discussion of this tension, the problem of "weaned affections," see Thickstun, "Milton among Puritan Women."

# 6  Raphael and the Challenge of Evangelical Education

1. See Perry Miller, "Marrow" 60–63, and Cohen, *God's Caress*. See also the section of *De Doctrina Christiana* titled "Of Renovation and also of Vocation," which, in distinguishing penitence from faith, and temporary and historical faith from saving faith (*CPW* 6.458–60), implies human activity in responding to God's call, and "Of the Visible Church," which addresses the role of ministers, who act as God's agents, although their activity "is not able to confer grace by itself" (*CPW* 6.569).

2. For a full discussion of the Puritan morphology of conversion, see Edmund Morgan, *Visible Saints*.
3. For amplification of the Pauline presence in Areopagitica, see LeComte, "Areopagitica as Scenario"; and Burt, " 'To the Unknown God.' "
4. For an argument that Puritans in Colonial Massachusetts regressed to socialization through public shaming, see Demos, "Shame and Guilt in Early New England."
5. For an analysis of Milton's departure from his biblical sources in presenting Raphael's sociability, see Farris, "Angelic Visitations."

## 7   Adam as Parent

1. For supporting discussion, see Lieb, *The Poetics of the Holy* 95; and Anderson, "Unfallen Marriage" 132.
2. Anderson discusses the realism of this birth scene, to different purposes, in "Unfallen Marriage" 137.
3. See, for example, William Gouge, *Of Domesticall Duties* (London 1622), 79; and William Perkins, *Works* (Cambridge, 1618), 3:670. Consider also the legal doctrine of coverture, in which a woman had no independent legal status, being "covered" by her husband's authority.
4. For an alternative attribution of sinfulness, rather than parenting, as the source of Adam's ability to imagine a public self, see Robertson 69.

## 8   Eve, Identity, and Growing in Relationship

1. For a discussion of this scene as enacting compulsory heterosexuality, see Halley, "Female Autonomy."
2. For a useful discussion of Milton's dissociation of "manliness" from gender, see Hausknecht, "The Gender of Civic Virtue."
3. See Thickstun, "Milton among Puritan Women."
4. For discussion of these terms, see Jean Miller, *toward a new psychology of women* 23.
5. For full development of Eve's prelapsarian ministry, see McColley's *Milton's Eve*.

## Conclusion

1. See Thomas Hooker, "A True Sight of Sin," in Perry Miller, *The American Puritans*.

# WORKS CITED

Allen, Michael. "Divine Instruction: Of Education and the Pedagogy of Raphael, Michael, and the Father." *Milton Quarterly* 26 (1992). 113–21.

Anderson, Douglas. "Unfallen Marriage and the Fallen Imagination in *Paradise Lost.*" *SEL* 26 (1986). 125–44.

Aronson, Elliot. *The Social Animal.* 8th ed. New York: Worth Publishers, 1999.

Barton, Carol. " 'They also Perform the Duties of a Servant Who Only Remain Erect on Their Feet in a Specified Place in Readiness to Receive Orders': The Dynamics of Stasis in Sonnet XIX ('When I Consider How My Light Is Spent.' " *Milton Quarterly* 32 (1998). 109–21.

Bloom, Harold. *Ruin the Sacred Truths: The Charles Eliot Norton Lectures 1987–88.* Boston: Harvard U P, 1989.

Booth, Wayne C. "The Ethics of Teaching Literature." *College English* 61 (1988). 41–55.

Bryson, Michael. *The Tyranny of Heaven: Milton's Rejection of God as King.* Newark: U Delaware P, 2004.

Bujold, Lois McMaster. *Shards of Honor*, copyright 1986. *Cordelia's Honor.* Riverdale, NY: Baen Books, 1999.

Bunyan, John. *The Pilgrim's Progress.* London, 1678.

Burt, Stephen. " 'To the Unknown God': St. Paul and Athens in Milton's *Areopagitica.*" *Milton Quarterly* 32 (1998). 23–31.

Callahan, Daniel and Sissela Bok, eds. *Ethics Teaching in Higher Education.* London: Plenum Press, 1980.

Campbell, W. Gardner. "Paradisal Appetite and Cusan Food in Paradise Lost." McColgan and Durham. 239–50.

Carey, John. "Milton's Satan." Danielson, *Cambridge Companion.* 131–45.

Christopher, Georgia. *Milton and the Science of the Saints.* Princeton: Princeton UP, 1982.

Cleaver, Robert. *A Brief Explanation of the Whole Book of Proverbs of Salomon.* London, 1615.

Cohen, Charles Lloyd. *God's Caress: The Psychology of Puritan Religious Experience.* Oxford: Oxford UP, 1986.

Copeland, Thomas A. "Raphael, the Angelic Virtue." *Milton Quarterly* 24 (1990). 117–28.

Crump, Galbraith, ed. *Approaches to Teaching Paradise Lost.* New York: MLA, 1986.

Danielson, Dennis Richard. *Milton's Good God: A Study in Literary Theodicy.* Cambridge: Cambridge UP, 1982.

———, ed. *The Cambridge Companion to Milton.* Cambridge: Cambridge UP, 1989.

Davies, Stevie. *Images of Kingship in Paradise Lost: Milton's Politics and Christian Liberty.* Columbia: U of Missouri P, 1983.

Demos, John. "Shame and Guilt in Early New England." *Emotion and Social Change: Toward a New Psychohistory.* Ed. Carol Z. Stearns and Peter N. Stearns. New York: Holmes & Meier, 1988. 69–85.

Dod, John and Robert Cleaver. *A Godlye Form of Household Government.* London, 1621, 1st ed. 1614.

Dreyfus, Hubert L. and Stuart E. Dreyfus. "What Is Morality? A Phenomenological Account of the Development of Ethical Expertise." *Universalism vs. Communitarianism.* Ed. David Rasmussen. Boston: MIT Press, 1990. 237–66.

Durham, Charles. " 'To Stand Approv'd in Sight of God': Abdiel, Obedience, and Hierarchy in Paradise Lost." *Milton Quarterly* 26 (1992). 15–20.

Emmons, R. A. and McCullough, M. E. "Counting Blessings versus Burdens: Experimental Studies of Gratitude and Subjective Well-Being in Daily Life." *Journal of Personality and Social Psychology* 84 (2003). 277–89.

Empson, William. *Milton's God.* Westport: Greenwood Press, 1961.

Farris, Janna Thatcher. "Angelic Visitations: Raphael's Roles in the Book of Tobit and *Paradise Lost*." McColgan and Durham. 183–92.

Farwell, Marilyn R. "Eve, the Separation Scene, and the Renaissance Idea of Androgyny." *Milton Studies* 16. Ed. James D. Simmonds. Pittsburgh: U of Pittsburgh P, 1982. 3–20.

Fell, Margaret. *Womens Speaking Justified.* 2nd ed. London, 1667.

Fischer, David Hackett. *Albion's Seed: Four British Folkways in America.* Oxford: Oxford UP, 1989.

Fish, Stanley. *Surprised by Sin: The Reader in Paradise Lost.* Berkeley: U of California P, 1967.

———. *How Milton Works.* Cambridge: The Belknap Press, 2001.

Flesch, William. *Generosity and the Limits of Authority: Shakespeare, Herbert, and Milton.* Ithaca: Cornell UP, 1992.

Fong, Bobby. "Called to Teach." *Finding God at Harvard.* Ed. Kelly Monroe. Grand Rapids: Zondervan, 1996. 304–06.

Fowler, James. *Stages of Faith: The Psychology of Human Development and the Quest for Meaning.* San Francisco: Harper and Row, 1981.

Frost, Robert. "The Most of It." *Selected Poems of Robert Frost.* New York: Holt, Rinehart and Winston, Inc., 1963. 224.

Gallagher, Philip. *Milton, the Bible, and Misogyny.* Columbia: U of Missouri P, 1990.

Gouge, William. *Of Domesticall Duties* (London 1622), reproduced from the Bodleian Library copy. Amsterdam: Theatrum Orbis Terrarum, 1976.

Griffin, Dustin. "Milton's Hell: Perspectives on the Fallen." *Milton Studies* 13. Ed. James D. Simmonds. Pittsburgh: U of Pittsburgh P, 1979. 237–54.

Halley, Janet. "Female Autonomy in Milton's Sexual Poetics." *Milton and the Idea of Woman*. Ed. Julia Walker. Urbana: U of Illinois P, 1988. 230–45.

Haskin, Dayton. *Milton's Burden of Interpretation*. Philadelphia: U of Pennsylvania P, 1994.

Hausknecht, Gina. "The Gender of Civic Virtue." *Milton and Gender*. Ed. Catherine Gimelli Martin. Cambridge: Cambridge UP, 2004. 19–33.

Hiner, N. Ray. "The Cry of Sodom Enquired Into: Educational Analysis in Seventeenth-Century New England." *History of Education Quarterly* (1973). 3–22.

Hooker, Thomas. "A True Sight of Sin." *The American Puritans: Their Prose and Poetry*. Ed. Perry Miller. Garden City: Anchor-Doubleday, 1956. 153–64.

Janis, Irving. *Groupthink: A Psychological Study of Policy Decisions and Fiascoes*. Boston: Houghton Mifflin, 1982.

Jordan, Matthew. *Milton and Modernity: Politics, Masculinity, and Paradise Lost*. London: Palgrave, 2001.

Kahn, Victoria. "Allegory and the Sublime in *Paradise Lost*." Patterson. 185–201.

Katz, Daniel and Richard L. Schanck. *Social Psychology*. New York: J. Wiley & Sons, 1948.

LeComte, Edward S. "Areopagitica as Scenario for Paradise Lost." *Achievements of the Left Hand*. Ed. Michael Lieb and John T. Shawcross. Amherst: U Massachusetts P, 1974. 121–41.

LeMay, Eric. " 'To the Highth of This Great Argument': The Plummet of Postmodern Undergraduates from Milton's Early Modern Epic and Its Prevention." *Milton Quarterly* 37 (2003). 92–99.

Levao, Ronald. " 'Among Unequals What Society': *Paradise Lost* and the Forms of Intimacy." *Modern Language Quarterly* 61 (2000). 79–107.

Levernz, David. *The Language of Puritan Feeling: An Exploration in Literature, Psychology, and Social History*. New Brunswick: Rutgers UP, 1990.

Lewis, C. S. *A Preface to Paradise Lost*. Oxford: Oxford UP, 1942. Reprinted, 1974.

Lewis, Michael and Jeanne Brooks-Gunn. *Social Cognition and the Acquisition of Self*. New York: Plenum Press, 1979.

Lickona, Thomas. *Educating for Character: How Our Schools Can Teach Respect and Responsibility*. New York: Bantam, 1991.

——. "Preparing Teachers to Be Moral Educators: A Neglected Duty." McBee. 51–64.

——. "What Does Moral Psychology Have to Say to the Teacher of Ethics?" Callahan and Bok. 103–32.

Lieb, Michael. *The Poetics of the Holy: A Reading of Paradise Lost*. Chapel Hill: U North Carolina P, 1981.

——. "Milton's 'Dramatick Constitution': The Celestial Dialogue in *Paradise Lost*," Book III. *Milton Studies* 23. Ed. James D. Simmonds. Pittsburgh: U of Pittsburgh P, 1987. 215–40.

Lieb, Michael. "Reading God: Milton and the Anthropopathetic Tradition." *Milton Studies* 25. Ed. James D. Simmonds. Pittsburgh: U of Pittsburgh P, 1989. 213–43.

Long, Mary Beth. "Contextualizing Eve's and Milton's Solitudes in Book 9 of *Paradise Lost.*" *Milton Quarterly* 37 (2003). 100–15.

Low, Anthony. "Milton's God: Authority in *Paradise Lost.*" *Milton Studies* 4 (1972). Ed. James D. Simmonds. Pittsburgh: U of Pittsburgh P, 1972. 19–38.

Luther, Martin. *Luther's Works.* Ed. Jaroslav Pelikan. St. Louis: Concordia. 1963.

Luxon, Thomas. *Literal Figures: Puritan Allegory and the Reformation Crisis in Representation.* Chicago: U Chicago P, 1995.

———. "Milton's Wedded Love: Not about Sex (as We Know It)." *Milton Studies* 40. Ed. Albert C. Labriola. Pittsburgh: U of Pittsburgh P, 2001. 38–60.

Mankoff, Ellen. "Approaching *Paradise Lost* through a Reading of Milton's Sonnets." Crump. 74–81.

Markova, Gabriela, and Maria Legerstee. "Contingency, Imitation, and Affect Sharing: Foundations of Infants' Social Awareness." *Developmental Psychology* 42.1 (2006). 132–41.

Martin, Catherine Gimelli. "The Sources of Milton's Sin Reconsidered." *Milton Quarterly* 35 (2001). 1–8.

McBee, Mary Louise, ed. *Rethinking College Responsibilities for Values. New Directions in Higher Education* 31. San Francisco: Jossey-Bass, 1980.

McColgan, Kristin Pruitt. " 'The Master Work': Creation and Education in *Paradise Lost.*" *Milton Quarterly* 26 (1992). 29–36.

McColgan, Kristin Pruitt and Charles W. Durham, eds. *Arenas of Conflict: Milton and the Unfettered Mind.* Selinsgrove: Susquehanna UP, 1997.

McColley, Diane. *Milton's Eve.* Chicago: U of Illinois P, 1983.

McCullough, M. E., Emmons, R. A., and Tsang, J. "The Grateful Disposition: A Conceptual and Empirical Topography." *Journal of Personality and Social Psychology* 82 (2001). 112–27.

McCullough, M. E., Kirkpatrick, S., Emmons, R. A., and Larson, D. "Is Gratitude a Moral Affect?" *Psychological Bulletin* 127 (2002). 249–66.

Melchior, Bonnie. "Teaching *Paradise Lost*: The Unfortunate Fall." *College Literature* 14.1 (1987). 76–84.

Miller, Jean Baker. *Toward a new psychology of women.* Boston: Beacon Press, 1976.

Miller, Perry, ed. *The American Puritans: Their Prose and Poetry.* Garden City, NJ: Anchor Books, 1956.

———. "The Marrow of Puritan Divinity." Reprinted in Perry Miller, *Errand Into The Wilderness.* Cambridge: The Belknap Press, 1956. 48–98.

Milton, John. *The Complete Poems and Major Prose.* Ed. Merritt Hughes. New York: The Odyssey Press, 1957.

———. *The Complete Prose Works of John Milton.* Gen. ed. Don M. Wolfe. New Haven: Yale UP, 1953–82.

——. *John Milton: Paradise Lost*. Critical Edition. Ed. Scott Elledge. New York: W. W. Norton, 1975.

——. *The Riverside Milton*. Ed. Roy Flannagan. New York: Houghton Mifflin, 1998.

Mitchell, J. Allan. "Reading God Reading 'Man': Hereditary Sin and the Narrativization of Deity in *Paradise Lost*, Book 3." *Milton Quarterly* 35 (2001). 72–86.

Morgan, Edmund. *Visible Saints: The History of a Puritan Idea*. Ithaca: Cornell UP, 1963.

Morgan, John. *Godly Learning: Puritan Attitude toward Reason, Learning, and Education*. Cambridge: Cambridge UP, 1986.

Nardo, Anna K. "Academic Interludes in Paradise Lost." *Milton Studies* 27. Ed. James D. Simmonds. Pittsburgh: U of Pittsburgh P, 1991. 209–42.

——. "The Education of Milton's Good Angels." McColgan and Durham. 193–211.

Nelson, Jane. *Positive Discipline*. New York: Ballantine Books, 1981, 1987.

Noddings, Nell. *Caring: A Feminine Approach to Ethics and Moral Education*. Berkeley: U of California P, 1984.

Nussbaum, Martha. *Cultivating Humanity: A Classical Defense of Reform in Liberal Education*. Cambridge: Harvard UP, 1997.

O'Brien, Dennis. *All the Essential Half-Truths about Higher Education*. Chicago: U of Chicago P, 1998.

Oh, Seiwoong. "The Bad Angels before Their Fall in *Paradise Lost*: Millions of Morons or Corrupt Intelligences." *Conference of College Teachers of English* 56 (1991). 55–61.

Parr, Susan Resneck. "The Teaching of Ethics in Undergraduate Nonethics Courses." Callahan and Bok. 191–203.

Patterson, Anabel, ed. *John Milton*. London: Longman, 1992.

Patrides, C. A. "The Salvation of Satan." *Journal of the History of Ideas* 28 (1967). 467–78.

Perkins, William. *The Works of that famous and worthy minister of Christ in the Universitie of Cambridge, M. W. Perkins*, 3 vols. Cambridge, 1618.

Perry, Jr., William G. "Examsmanship and the Liberal Arts: A Study in Educational Epistemology." Reprinted in *The Norton Reader*. 9th ed. Ed. Linda Peterson et al. New York: W. W. Norton, 1996. 543–53.

——. *Forms of Intellectual and Ethical Development in the College Years: A Scheme*. Holt, Rinehart, and Winston, 1968. San Francisco: Jossey-Bass. Reprinted, 1999.

Rabinowitz, Peter. *Before Reading: Narrative Conventions and the Politics of Interpretation*. Ithaca: Cornell UP, 1987.

Rabinowitz, Peter and Michael W. Smith. *Authorizing Readers: Resistance and Respect in the Teaching of Literature*. New York: Teachers' College Press and NCTE, 1998.

Radzinowicz, Mary Ann. "The Politics of *Paradise Lost*." Patterson. 120–41.

Radzinowicz, Mary Ann. *Toward Samson Agonistes: The Growth of Milton's Mind*. Princeton: Princeton UP, 1978.

Reichert, John. *Milton's Wisdom: Nature and Scripture in Paradise Lost*. Ann Arbor: U Michigan P, 1992.

Revard, Stella. *The War in Heaven: Paradise Lost and the Tradition of Satan's Rebellion*. Ithaca: Cornell UP, 1980.

Rich, Adrienne. *On Lies, Secrets, and Silence: Selected Prose, 1966–1978*. New York: W. W. Norton, 1979.

Robertson, David. "Soliloquy and Self in Milton's Major Poems." *Of Poetry and Politics: New Essays on Milton and His World*. Ed. P. G. Stanwood. Second Printing. Tempe, AZ: Medieval and Renaissance Text Society, 1997. 59–78.

Samuel, Irene. "The Dialogue in Heaven: A Reconsideration of *Paradise Lost*, III, 1–417." PMLA 72 (1967). 601–11. Reprinted in Elledge. 468–78.

Scholes, Robert. *The Crafty Reader*. New Haven,: Yale, 2001.

Scholton, Catherine. *Childbearing in American Society: 1650–1850*. New York UP, 1985.

Schwartz, Louis. " 'Conscious Terrours' and 'The Promised Seed' ": Seventeenth-Century Obstetrics and the Allegory of Sin and Death." *Milton Studies* (32). Ed. Albert C. Labriola. Pittsburgh: U of Pittsburgh P, 1995. 63–89.

Schwartz, Regina. *Remembering and Repeating: On Milton's Theology and Poetry*. Chicago: U of Chicago P, 1988.

Shepard, Thomas. *God's Plot: Puritan Spirituality in Thomas Shepard's Cambridge*. 1972. Revised and Expanded. Ed. Michael McGiffert. Amherst: U Massachusetts P, 1994.

Speght, Rachel. *A Mouzell for Melastomus*. London, 1617. *The Polemics and Poems of Rachel Speght*. Ed. Barbara Kiefer Lewalski. Women Writers in English 1350–1850. Oxford: Oxford UP, 1996. 1–27.

Stavely, Keith W. F. *Puritan Legacies: Paradise Lost and the New England Tradition, 1630–1890*. Ithaca: Cornell UP, 1987.

———. "Satan and Arminianism in *Paradise Lost*." *Milton Studies* 25. Ed. James D. Simmonds. Pittsburgh: U of Pittsburgh P, 1989. 125–39.

Swift, Jonathan. *Gulliver's Travels*. London, 1726.

Swiss, Margo. "Repairing Androgyny: Eve's Tears in *Paradise Lost*." *Speaking Grief in English Literary Culture: Shakespeare to Milton*. Ed. Margo Swiss and David A. Kent. Pittsburgh: Duquesne UP, 2002. 261–93.

Thickstun, Margaret Olofson. *Fictions of the Feminine: Puritan Doctrine and the Representation of Women*. Ithaca: Cornell UP, 1988.

———. "Milton among Puritan Women: Affiliative Spirituality and the Conclusion of *Paradise Lost*." *Religion and Literature* 36.2 (Summer 2004). 1–23.

Thomas, Lewis. *Late Night Thoughts on Listening to Mahler's Ninth Symphony*. Toronto: Bantam, 1983.

Van Dyke, Carolynn. *The Fiction of Truth: Structures of Meaning in Narrative and Dramatic Allegory*. Ithaca: Cornell UP, 1985.

Webber, Joan. "Milton's God." *ELH* 40 (1973). 514–31.

West, Robert. *Milton and The Angels*. Athens: U of Georgia P, 1955.

Wooten, John. "Teaching *Paradise Lost* at the United States Naval Academy." Crump. 60–66.

# INDEX

moral adulthood—*continued*
  Son's, 99
  students and, 161
moral growth
  *see also* commitment as moral
    maturity; sustained
    responsibility for the welfare
    of others
  accepting responsibility and, 154
  angelic, 72
  emotional involvement as crucial
    to, 5, 81, 96, 145
  of children, 26–27
  dissent from authority and, 98–99,
    111–112
  ethical expertise and, 5, 81, 103–104,
    145
  failure and, 80–81
  vs. glory and shame, 70
  gratitude and, 76
  loneliness of, 64
  narrative imagination and, 4–5, 7, 13
  unconscious proficiency and, 5, 150
moral imagination, 5, 159
  *see also* moral growth, narrative
    imagination and; vicarious
    knowledge
morality
  emotional basis of, 123
  importance of one's intentions to,
    19, 37, 48
Morgan, John, 111
motherhood *see* parenthood
Multiplicity, 2, 39

Nardo, Anna, 33, 54, 72, 73, 74, 77, 81,
  84, 106, 114, 116–117
narrative imagination *see* moral
  growth, narrative imagination
  and; vicarious knowledge
natural law, 30, 31
Nelson, Jane (psychologist), 31
New Criticism, 6
Niebuhr, Reinhold (theologian), 3

Noddings, Nell (feminist
  philosopher), 24, 33, 47, 48, 75, 80,
  90, 95, 104, 114, 123, 133, 143
notional vs. experimental knowledge,
  44, 46, 69, 72, 107, 113, 130, 145,
  157, 159
  *see also* affective engagement in
    *Paradise Lost*; analytical
    thought, limits of; Right
    Reason
Nussbaum, Martha (philosopher), 4, 7

obedience
  imaginativeness required by, 19
  as necessary to growth, 121
  as a theme in Raphael's instruction,
    112
  primacy of, 101
*Of Education*, 111
Oh, Seiwoong, 53
Origen, 42

Parable of the Talents, 38, 44
*Paradise Regained*, 92
parental love
  Adam's, 123, 126, 129, 131–134, 137
  God's, 41, 119, 120
  as enabling repentance, 134, 135, 154,
    155
  nature of, 26, 30
  Puritan fathers and, 27–28
parenthood, 21, 24–25, 26, 47, 48,
  95–96, 126, 137
  *see also* sustained responsibility for
    the welfare of others
parenting modeled in *Paradise Lost*, 18,
  19, 20, 137
Patrides, C. A., 42
Paul
  evangelical education and, 110–111
  moral development and, 22
  sons and, 88–89
  moral responsibility according to, 7
  will to sin and, 55